The Economy of the Roman World

The Economy of the Roman World

Jean Andreau

translated by Corina Kesler

with Ellen Bauerle and David Potter

Michigan Classical Press
Ann Arbor

Published by Michigan Classical Press
PO Box 130194
Ann Arbor, MI 48113

www.michiganclassicalpress.com

Translated from the French by Corina Kesler
With Ellen Bauerle and David Potter

ISBN 13 (cloth, alk. paper) 978-0-9799713-5-8
ISBN 10 (cloth, alk. paper) 0-9799713-5-7

Printed on acid-free paper by Edwards Brothers Malloy Inc., Ann Arbor, MI 48103

Manufactured in the United States of America
18 17 16 15 1 2 3

First published in French as *L'économie du monde romain*
ISBN 978-2-7298-5331-0

32, rue Bargue 75740 Paris cedex 15 France

Library of Congress Cataloging-in-Publication Data

Andreau, Jean.
[Économie du monde romain. English]
The economy of the Roman world / by Jean Andreau ; translated by Corina Kesler with Ellen Bauerle and David Potter.
pages cm
Originally published in French as *L'économie du monde romain,* by Editions Ellipses, 2010.
Summary: "This volume examines the economic history of Rome in the Republican and Imperial periods. It considers evidence from archaeological and literary sources, and it offers an updated modern economic analysis after examining popular economic theories of previous years, including but not limited to those of M.I. Finley and M.I. Rostovzeff. Jean Andreau offers translations of relevant ancient economic and literary texts, and considers what these passages show us about farming and agriculture, manufacturing, shipping, and particularly the role of slaves in the Roman economy"--Provided by publisher.
Includes bibliographical references and index.
ISBN 978-0-9799713-5-8 (hardcover : alkaline paper) -- ISBN 0-9799713-5-7 (hardcover : alkaline paper)
1. Rome--Economic conditions. 2. Rome--Economic policy. 3. Economics--Rome. 4. Rome--Antiquities. 5. Rome--Economic conditions--Sources. I. Title.
DG85.A5313 2015
330.937--dc23

2015017631

To my friends in Ann Arbor, with whom I passed four very stimulating, pleasant, and collegial months, in 1995 and in 2010.

Table of Contents

Publisher's Note to the English Edition

We have endeavored to represent the French original of this volume accurately, occasionally taking liberties for better sense. In a few cases it seemed desirable to include a French term in square brackets after the English translation. Page numbers in the original edition of *L'Économie du Monde Romain* have been indicated as [p. 15].

Works in the bibliography have occasionally been adjusted to cite the more familiar Anglophone edition of a volume rather than a French translation of that volume, e.g., M.I. Finley's *The Ancient Economy* rather than *L'Économie antique*.

Introduction

Rome's history begins like that of a very small town. The small town in turn became a city, and little by little the city conquered first the Mediterranean basin and then vast interior territories, to form an enormous empire—the Roman Empire. It took Rome three centuries, almost four, to achieve the bulk of these conquests. Central and southern Italy were subjugated at the end of the fourth century B.C.E. and, at the risk of some oversimplification, it could be said that the geographic boundaries of Roman domination were basically fixed at the moment of Augustus' death, in 14 C.E. After that, the new conquests (Britain and the two provinces of Mauretania under Claudius, Dacia, Arabia, and other ephemeral acquisitions in the Near East under Trajan) were much more limited. In general and despite various vicissitudes, the Empire maintained the same dimensions for about four centuries, until the end of the fourth century C.E.

In the third century B.C.E., 272 to be precise, the Italian peninsula fell to Rome. Northern Italy, and the regions outside its borders, had economies either linked with political and social organization very close to that of the territories already controlled by Rome, or with structures that were radically different. Additionally, certain regions still independent of Rome cultivated exchange relations with the Italian peninsula. At the end of the second century B.C.E., at the time when Gaul Narbonensis (southern France) had just been conquered and the rest of Gaul was still independent, countless "Dressel 1" amphorae containing Italian wine were transported via the Rhone and Saône, in places north of Lyon (later, the location of the Roman colony of Lugdunum), as for example at Chalon-sur-Saône. To study the economic history of Rome and that of its empire, thus, it would be necessary [p. 6] to examine the economic life of the independent territories with which Rome had contact. Such an approach is conceivable when it is applied to a precise region or to a clearly delimited period of time: in these cases, it seems even indispensable. It is, however, impossible to do so in such a short book as this one, which studies the whole of the Roman economic history. In this volume I must limit myself to what is relevant to Rome. At the most, I can risk making some allusions to outside regions or to suggest some relevant bibliography.

In the second and first centuries B.C.E., Rome progressively subjected to its domination regions where Greek was spoken, which were partially or entirely organized into cities. Most of these cities were not fully independent at the moment of the Roman conquest. Some were dependent on the sovereigns of Hellenistic kingdoms and some had regrouped within the framework of leagues or confederations. These cities preserved their own unique political and administrative organizations—organizations that were perpetuated, in one form or another, until the Roman period. To a certain degree, the economic history of the Roman Empire is, likewise, that of the Greek cities that found themselves included within its boundaries. The present book therefore partially overlaps with that of Léopold Migeotte, *L'Économie des Cités Grecques*: the volumes overlap for cities of Greek tradition, and for the period between the conquest and the end of the Principate (that is, the first decades of the third century C.E. or the middle of the same century), but a big part of the Roman Empire was not of Greek tradition. In this volume I will refer to Migeotte's book on several occasions, indicating in parentheses only Migeotte's name and the page numbers of the second French edition (2007).

In all time periods, economic life is composed of the production, circulation, and consumption of material goods and services. [p. 7] This definition of economic life explains the structure of this book, which contains seven chapters in addition to the introduction, the conclusion, and the bibliographical references. Two of these chapters, the second and the third, are dedicated to production: one to agriculture and livestock (chapter 2), the other to handicrafts and manufacturing (chapter 3). Chapter 4 focuses on financial and banking activities, and chapter 5 on commerce. I have chosen to give particular importance to the two chapters dealing with production. Although a chapter has been devoted to commerce, I have decided to introduce in chapters 2 and 3 certain observations on the commercialization of the goods described therein. In fact, the logic of economic organization and its complexity seemed to me best understood by following specific goods from production through consumption. The same approach is applied in chapters 2 through 5, which also include occasional references to consumption. So, the discussion of commerce will not be limited to chapter 5. That chapter addresses a small number of large questions related to commercialization and commercial relationships. It also contains some observations on the commercial and manufacturing agents that are brought together in that chapter, because these observations fully apply to the artisans and the manufacturers of goods.

Economic life depends on very diverse factors: the study of climates and soils (pedology); the evolution of techniques; mineral resources; the knowledge of plant and animal species and their uses; law, and especially private law (referring here to the organization of property and of contracts, for instance contracts of leasing and of loans); social factors (the existence, spread, and methods of enslavement; the existence of other forms of statutory dependence), etc. So, it is [p. 8] inconceivable to speak of "economy" without addressing political or social problems, or the cultural domain. On the other hand, economic life is strongly dependent on the attitudes that in this respect point toward the authorities, that is, the city of Rome, and thereafter the Roman Empire. It is for this reason that chapter 6 examines the hypothetical economic policy of the Roman authorities.

For a century, or perhaps even two, the economic history of Greco-Roman antiquity has been the subject of great theoretical and methodological debates. Without exception, all the works that discuss this history mention these debates in greater or lesser detail. During the second half of the twentieth century, the work that had the greatest influence on this issue and incited the most vehement opposition was M.I. Finley's *The Ancient Economy*, published in 1973 and translated into several languages. For the Greek domain, M. Austin and P. Vidal-Naquet, A. Bresson, R. Descat, L. Migeotte, and many others have dealt extensively with these debates in their publications. For the Roman domain, pertinent information could be found in the books and articles of J.H. D'Arms, P. Garnsey, K. Hopkins, Y. Roman, and C.R. Whittaker. I myself devoted several articles to this debate, one of which was written in collaboration with Roland Étienne. Chapter 1, one of the longest of this book, explains the debate's ins and outs and emphasizes several of its important characteristics.

One of the themes of these debates deals with the unity of Greco-Roman antiquity, particularly from its archaic period to the last centuries of the Empire in the west. M.I. Finley insisted on this unity, and he explained his view by the cultural continuity which, according to him, determined economic life and made it very different both from that of the present, and likewise from that of the Middle Ages, in Western Europe. The unity of the ancient world was, for Finley, connected to its economic archaism. On the other hand, others, [p. 9] most notably M.I. Rostovtzeff, have tried to show that in the Hellenistic period and in the Roman world there were very primitive periods as well as periods in which the economy was very advanced. Such scholars have therefore insisted on discontinuities within the ancient world. For my part, I think that the archaic periods, in Greece as in Rome, were very specific. For this reason, chapters 1 through 5 do not focus on the earliest period (from the foundation of Rome in the eighth century to the fourth century B.C.E.). Material pertinent to this topic is found in chapter 7, dedicated to economic evolutions in the history of Rome. As this book is very short and synthetic, it was necessary to discuss seven other centuries of Roman history in a global way, as certain structures as well as certain overarching anthropological, social, and political aspects persisted for a long time.

The last period of the western Empire, from the third century to the beginning of the fifth C.E., has also been the subject of great debates: some perceived it as a period of decline, while others vigorously opposed such an interpretation; some insisted on the similarities connecting it to the preceding centuries, while others insisted on the differences that distinguished it from them. Chapters 1 through 5 of this book address this particular period as well as the centuries that precede it; chapter 7, dealing with developments, contains both a section on the archaic period and one on the problems posed by the third and fourth centuries C.E. Such an approach does not imply that I consider the Roman economy "archaic," nor does it mean that I minimize the magnitude of the developments that took place between the Hannibalic War (the end of the third century B.C.E.) and the reign of Augustus (31 B.C.E.–14 C.E.), or between the reign of the latter and that of Constantine (the first half of the fourth century C.E.).

Greco-Roman antiquity is characterized in particular by certain central institutions through which the Greek cities were close to the Roman [p. 10] world. The most important of these institutions, politically and administratively, as well as culturally and ideologically, is the city itself. Greek and Italic city-states were integrated in the grand plan of the Roman Empire: they were no longer independent, but by no means did they vanish as civic entities. The Roman genius was that of knowing how to facilitate the inclusion of these city-states in the imperial structure without ending their particular form (see L. Migeotte, who extensively treats the role of the city, especially in his introduction and chapter 1). In this sense, the Roman Empire does not resemble any other empire. Some have even said that it was a federation of cities. This conclusion is exaggerated and even wrong, but it clearly attests the originality of such an institutional structure. Besides, the existence of the cities is not simply an institutional reality; it influences social and economic matters, too.

Another foundational institution of the Greco-Roman world is slavery. All chapters touch on this topic (chapter 2 in particular, in reference to the "slave villa"), but I did not find it necessary to dedicate an entire chapter to the subject because, according to the economic sectors, according to time periods and regions, its manifestations and forms evolved, even if its substance remained the same, at least from the fourth century B.C.E. to the end of the western Empire.

I will finish this introduction with two or three remarks on the bibliography at the end of the book. Apart from several titles of general works on the ancient economy or on the Roman period, it consists of a single list, arranged in alphabetical order. It is necessarily brief. It favors the most recent titles (in which the reader can find older bibliography), and French titles (the most accessible), as well as those providing the most abundant and useful bibliographical information. Finally, books have been prioritized over articles. This preference, however, was flexible: when a work in a foreign language (those in English [p. 11] in particular), or an article, seemed more important, I did not hesitate to include them. I have left aside, or ignored, many important titles, and I ask the forgiveness of their authors for doing so. I had to take into account the limited space and the reality that, in the publications I included in the bibliography, prior bibliographical information is almost always included. On the other hand, every time the name of an historian or archaeologist is mentioned in the text, that person's book or article is with very few exceptions mentioned in the bibliography. [pp. 12, 13]

Chapter 1
The Historiography and Structures of the Roman Economy

The history of the ancient economy, Greek as well as Roman, was and continues to be the object of vigorous debate. It is very important to accumulate detailed knowledge, for example about livestock, wine commerce, or monetary exchange. However, this amassed knowledge, indispensable because it facilitates the systematic reconstruction of a more precise and exact model of the economic life of antiquity, only makes sense in connection with a series of global questions that have sparked lengthy debates. This chapter is dedicated to exploring these debates and the enduring questions that continue to preoccupy scholars.

I. The "Bücher-Meyer" Controversy

The most important of these debates is longstanding; indeed it is now some two centuries old, having started in the second part of the eighteenth century, at the moment when economic science gained momentum and when the industrial revolution made it clear to historians that material life—the production and circulation of goods—has changed since antiquity or the Middle Ages. Exactly how were they transformed and how could we explain these transformations? Since then, historians of antiquity, as well as some economists, sociologists, and anthropologists, have been divided into two camps. Above all else, one [p. 14] group has insisted on the enormous importance of these economic and social alterations and changes, and on the disparities between antiquity and the modern era. On the other hand, the second group has tended to minimize these changes and emphasize a certain continuity instead. Debates quite similar to these existed in medieval and modern history, but they have tended to be less significant in both areas.

This debate is referred to as that between the "primitivists" and the "modernists," or the "minimalists" and the "maximalists," appellations obviously both pejorative and inexact. Even more often, we hear this debate being referred to as "the Bücher-Meyer Controversy," after the names of two German scholars from the end of the nineteenth century and the beginning of the twentieth, or that between the "Finleyites" and the "anti-Finleyites," named after Moses I. Finley, its main protagonist in the 1970s and 1980s. The "Finleyites" are the "primitivists" (like Karl Bücher, a century ago) and the "anti-Finleyites" are the "modernists" (like Eduard Meyer, a century ago).

The debate focuses on the capacities of ancient economies, and on what differentiates them from the industrial world. The proponents of the second of these two tendencies, the "modernists" or the "anti-Finleyites," even though they know that the ancient economies are different from those of the eighteenth, nineteenth, and twentieth centuries, are inclined to reduce these differences. According to them, such differences are quantitative rather than structural. They are convinced that modernization and industrial revolution could also occur in antiquity. These events did not, of course, happen in the ancient world but, according to these scholars, their failure to do so had nothing to do with the logic and the specific organization of the ancient economy itself. This economy was comparable, *grosso modo*, to those of the seventeenth and eighteenth centuries in Western [p. 15] Europe. The failure to develop was provoked by non-economic factors, which destroyed the assets and qualities of the economic system. For some, external pressures and territorial invasions were the most important factors. For others, like M.I. Rostovtzeff, it was the internal social crisis of the Empire that undermined its prosperity and growth.

It could be said that the "modernists" are guilty of casting antiquity into a modern form (so that its structures resemble our epoch and the two or three centuries preceding it), and thus of not accepting its "otherness," of too closely conceiving the overall aspect of history as a reflection of the modern world. From an economic point of view this means that they accepted economic science without questioning any of its presuppositions.

"Primitivists" like M.I. Finley believe that the ancient economy had inherent limitations that prevented it from taking part in whatever industrial revolution was possible. Not only do they insist on the gap separating antiquity from our era, but they argue that the period could not have achieved better results than those it produced. When antiquity later declined, it was not due to sabotage, but because it had reached the end of its evolution. In some respects, ancient culture displayed more brio and liveliness than the last centuries of the Middle Ages. However, if the end of the Middle Ages reinforced some of the elements that went on to spawn the Industrial Revolution, did it not reveal more modernity than Athens and Rome, despite the prestige that both cities for various reasons enjoyed as a result of their architecture, sculpture, literature, Greek philosophy, Roman law, and so on?

Quite often, the "primitivists" point to the logic of present-day economic science, since they are convinced that this train of thought does not apply to other periods of [p. 16] history. On the other hand, they have been accused of idealizing the ancient world that, their adversaries say, they are using as a foil for the problems of the modern world: its materialism, excessive obsession with money, and harsh social struggles. We can see that this debate is not confined to antiquity and that it has enduring relevance to our times. It is not possible to study the economic life of Greek or Roman antiquity without being familiar with the basics of this controversy. Also, when working on Greek or Roman history it is necessary to study both fields because, even if they evolved separately, they remained, at all times, linked to each other.

The better to understand this debate, it is necessary to return to the point of origin in the last years of the nineteenth century. We can identify four main phases that have elapsed since, the first two introduced by German historians, economists, and sociologists; the last two more international and primarily involving English-speaking historians.

The first of the four phases pitted the economist Karl Bücher against several historians of antiquity, principally Eduard Meyer and Julius Beloch. According to Bücher, the history of Europe had gone through three stages. These stages were not founded on the means of production, as Marx would have it, but on the distribution of goods and the range of trade. The first stage was that of household (or domestic) economy (*Hauswirtschaft* or *Oikenwirtschaft)*: most of the goods produced in agriculture and manufacturing were consumed inside the producing units themselves. This does not mean that trade was nonexistent, but that it involved only a small part of production. The second stage is that of *Stadtwirtschaft* (urban economy): the great majority of goods were distributed within the city, and [p. 17] passed directly from the hands of the producers to those of the consumers. The third stage is the national economy (*Volkswirtschaft*), where goods go through a series of exchanges before being consumed. In Bücher's view, these three logical stages were assimilated into the existing chronological periods—antiquity, the Middle Ages, and the modern period—and led to a linear scheme of the economic evolution of humanity. On this analysis, the economic structure of antiquity was entirely domestic, and the later Middle Ages were essentially an urban economy. A national economy did not commence until the modern era.

Eduard Meyer considered this vision too schematic and held that it did not do the ancient economy justice. He wanted to write a Greek history in more modern terms than had been done up to that point. In this version, economy had to preserve its rightful place, and modern terms had to be used to describe it. Accordingly, Meyer did not hesitate to speak of industry, industrialists, capitalism, etc., and to attribute to the Greek cities commercial preoccupations very similar to those in modern times. He also did not believe that antiquity could be considered as a whole: from an economic point of view, some of its phases were more prosperous, or more advanced, than others. What resulted was a cyclical conception of history: each cycle representing a period of growth, a peak, and a decline. Antiquity had passed through such stages and the modern world was in the process of experiencing them, too: Meyer proposed some approximations between the centuries of the ancient world and those of the modern era.

Now, nobody believes in either of these two extreme arguments. Meyer's approach was initially very important for the historians of antiquity, while several major figures in economics and sociology—e.g., Marx and Max Weber—who tended, like Bücher, to favor primitivism [p. 18], did not have any immediate influence on the historians of antiquity. However, J. Hasebroek, a Greek specialist who drew inspiration from Weber's work, reexamined the problem from the point of view of the traders and the relationships that the Greek cities cultivated with the economy. Based on an etymological study of the words designating merchants in the Greek city, he showed that, outside agriculture, economic agents did not enjoy great social prestige. They did not have much influence on urban decisions, since most of them were metics and not citizens. It transpired that, in Greece, democracy did not depend on a commercial bourgeoisie, and that the ancient city did not have an economic policy other than when it came to consumption. It considered its citizens consumers rather than producers. This position has multiple implications: Hasebroek, for example, did not believe that the Greek cities could engage in wars for economic reasons or for economic purposes.

Hasebroek's conclusions were opposed by M.I. Rostovtzeff, who introduced the Anglo-Saxon world to this controversy and its terms. Following Meyer, he insisted that certain periods of antiquity experienced some forms of capitalism, and that it was possible to talk, at the beginning of our era, of the "industrialization" of Italy. The beginning of this great period in antiquity was, according to him, the fourth century B.C.E., and "industrialization" flourished during the Hellenistic epoch (roughly the third century B.C.E.) and then during the Principate (roughly the first through third centuries C.E.). The key to the success of the ancient economy, which was marked by a great growth of manufacturing and commerce, resided in the freedom and entrepreneurial spirit of the elites, whose interests were very varied, and who could be compared, according to Rostovtzeff, [p. 19] to the modern bourgeoisie. This mentality of the elites could, however, evolve towards complacency and towards a strategy of *rentiers,* which threatened to provoke a social crisis. The egotism and the economic passivity of the elites, the misery of the plebs, peasant revolts, and the increasingly totalitarian attitude of the state, resulted in the definitive decline of the Roman Empire and ancient capitalism. Rostovtzeff argued that this decline began in the third century C.E.

This second phase of the controversy, dating to the 1920s and 1930s, concluded, for the Roman side of things, with M.I. Rostovtzeff's predominant influence, stemming from his two massive books on the social and economic histories of the Hellenistic and Roman worlds, although note should also be taken of T. Frank's important work. Though Frank was definitely less "modernizing," he did not participate directly in this sort of debate.

The third major phase of this controversy began in the 1970s, dominated by the work of M.I. Finley, a specialist in Greek history, whose major work on economic matters, *The Ancient Economy*, was published in 1973. This book marked a decisive turn; it was the source of the wide distribution of "minimalist" ideas, especially in Great Britain and in English-speaking countries. Even though the most recent studies have contradicted its conclusions, it still represents an important point of reference. Vis-à-vis social and economic questions, in the 1970s and 1980s, Finley and his disciples' line of thought played a role analogous to that which historical psychology and anthropology had played in the religious and cultural fields.

Finley treated the ancient economy as a whole. He judged that, despite chronological and geographical differences, it presented the same general characteristics from the Greek archaic period in the eighth to sixth centuries B.C.E. to late antiquity (fourth through seventh centuries C.E.). The notion of economy, as we understand it today, did not exist as such during antiquity and, Finley believed, this was not a coincidence: economic logic, as understood today, did not exist. The word "economy" [p. 20] is of Greek origin; it did not have the same meaning in antiquity, however, when it meant the management of estates. There was of course an economic life, but one that we cannot explain with economic science. In fact, this economic life was neither organized nor conceived in an autonomous manner. Finley borrowed sociologist and economist Karl Polanyi's idea that the ancient economy, like all preindustrial economies, and unlike that of our era, was "embedded," that is to say ingrained, inserted in the social edifice, in its hierarchies and statutes.

According to Finley, concrete economic life in antiquity tended, before anything else, toward self-sufficiency. Its main source was agriculture, and trade represent ed but a small part of the gross product. The following factors explain this situation: production facilities were relatively the same everywhere, the costs of transportation were high, the products traded were—before anything else—luxury items, and the demand for such products was low. In the same way that this volume of traffic was limited, the status of the traders was not very elevated. The local elites, even in such prominent ports as Carthage, Aquileia, or Alexandria, preferred agriculture over trade. The city was a place of consumption rather that one of manufacturing and commerce. Finally, what dominated, from a social point of view, were not classes based on means of production, but on "statuses": this was a less precise category, in which cultural values and social rank mattered more than economic power.

During the 1970s and 1980s, Finley figured prominently in the intellectual landscape of the discipline. However, the vision he proposed of the ancient economy and especially of the Roman economy is no longer dominant today. After the years during which his conclusions continued to spread, notably in the Anglo-Saxon world but also elsewhere (with the exception, perhaps, of Italy and Spain), [p. 21] a fourth phase of the controversy developed in the 1990s. The questions this phase posed still bore the marks of Finley's intellectual influence, but the solutions were increasingly different from his. Even the concept of "ancient economy," as he proposed it, is more and more open to question, as the comparative studies of H.W. Pleket and L. De Ligt, for example, show that the originality and coherence of classical antiquity are much less evident when certain ancient cases are compared to those of the Middle Ages.

Currently, all those interested in the ancient economy are, at least partially, aware of this debate. The methods of explaining it—the "models" used to do so—tend to multiply, and the conclusions vary in detail. Some of Finley's closest disciples remained faithful to his thought, but displayed some flexibility, or engaged in new ideas for research. Others distanced themselves. Of late, his adversaries are no less virulent than in the past, on the contrary. Increasingly his ideas are losing their audience, and the old modernism regains ground. This situation is fueled by economic arguments, like those of P. Temin, who analyzes antiquity using the measure of economic science as is currently taught. Others, however, like R. Descat and A. Bresson in the Greek field, have tried to make use of various trends in the history of economic ideas, and in particular those of neoinstitutional economics. Others insist on posing the problem differently. This is the case for P. Horden and N. Purcell who, on one hand place the Mediterranean area, with its geographic and climatic particularities, at the center of their analyses, and on the other hand consider economic history as a whole, from the beginning of antiquity to the end of the Middle Ages. This is also the case for P.F. Bang, who tries to resituate these topics by comparing [p. 22] Rome with empires such as the Mongol Empire, and draws on anthropologist Clifford Geertz' work. In the process, though, he ends up coming very close to primitivist thought.

Generally speaking, at present we have departed from the Manichean period of the controversy between the partisans and the adversaries of M.I. Finley's work. This is fortunate, since this opposition between the two systems of thought and between the two coteries slowed the impetus of research. Minutely comparing ancient terms and concepts with modern ones, ceaselessly searching, in antiquity, for all possible signs of archaism or modernity, has resulted in a reductionist vision. Such an approach has another effect in providing to current institutions and situations intellectual justifications that they do not deserve, and reinforcing our reassuring and naïve (but illusionary) impression that they are eternal, or at least immutable, because we have now entered the modern era.

Yet, we should not believe that the "Bücher-Meyer controversy" is finally defunct. While it may seem so, this is only a superficial impression: it is continually being reborn from its own ashes. Thus, the material that informed *The Cambridge Economic History of the Greco-Roman World*, edited by W. Scheidel, I. Morris, and R. Saller, remains readily faithful to Finley's vision, as well as to some of his conclusions.

Conversely, the writings of P. Temin and a part of W. Harris' fall within the modernist tradition. Also, the grand themes of A. Schiavone's *The End of the Past* are themselves very closely connected to those of this controversy.

II. The Current Themes of the Controversy

The debates that make this controversy were, and still are, focused on certain themes. Schematically, we can identify seven principal sources of contention. [p. 23]

1. Economic rationality and "embeddedness"

These two terms, very closely related to each other, are at the heart of the problem of preindustrial economies, even though their extreme difficulty has meant that they are not amongst the most discussed. Here, I will only touch upon them briefly, especially in the context of work by M. Weber and K. Polanyi.

Above all, "rationality" has to do with economic behavior in the ancient world: did they have implicit economic goals like early modern and modern men and women? And, did they align their behavior to these objectives in a manner similar to our contemporary practice? Was there such a thing as economically specific behavior in antiquity? The same question was raised by scholars including the Marxist anthropologists Maurice Godelier and Claude Meillassoux in connection with non-European peoples before colonization. This problem of economic rationality could be approached from various angles. One of them is the study of accounting. On this subject, the documentation is certainly not very extensive, but the works of agronomists (Columella's in particular) and certain papyri are very relevant and have given rise to substantial inquiries (like that by Dominic Rathbone on the Heroninos archive).

The notion of "embeddedness," borrowed by Finley from Polanyi, is related to the question of "rationality," but it deals with the connection between economic and noneconomic, and it is primarily concerned with the totality of social and economic structures and the ways they are conceptualized. Did the ancients have an autonomous view of "economy"? To what extent did existing social traditions suffocate the emergent economic innovations? [p. 24]

2. *From an economic point of view, should classical antiquity, both Greek and Roman, from the archaic period to late antiquity, be considered as one unit?*

Finley insisted strongly on such unity, but this does not seem, to me, a well-posed question: it all depends on the sector we are talking about and how we envision economic life. This book will provide much evidence on this subject (and has already questioned it in the Introduction), but without addressing it up front.

3. *Can we say that Rome had an economic policy?*

This is a very important question, to which chapter 6 is dedicated in its entirety. Up to what point was the city, and then the Empire, involved in the economy and in what way? What influence did the economy exert over Roman political life and especially over its external policies? In the case of ancient states it seems to me impossible to speak of a true economic policy, in the sense that we currently attribute to it. As we shall see, such a position depends on what we call "having a policy"!

4. *Market and markets: the intensity of economic exchanges and the role of competition*

This important question, which continues to figure prominently in the debates, is addressed in chapter 5, section I; it is also the subject of chapter 4, section IV, on the credit market. [p. 25]

5. *The nature and extent of the economic interests of members of the elite*

This is another intensely debated essential subject, particularly in Italy, and on which I have published several articles. It constitutes the larger part of section III of this chapter, and it is addressed again more briefly in chapters 3, 4, and 5.

6. Can we say that antiquity experienced a "technological roadblock"? No!

Did Greco-Roman antiquity experience a technological roadblock, due (for example) to the important role of slavery, which explains the archaism of its economy? This idea, formerly very widely accepted, must be abandoned. During the last two or three decades this has been one of the points on which the progress of research has been the most tangible and inarguable. Section IV of this chapter is dedicated to this topic, which is also addressed in other parts of the book.

7. The notions of "consumer city" and "producer city"

The debate over the "consumer city," a notion borrowed from Weber by Finley, has been and continues to be very vigorous. The model of the "consumer city" had a lot of currency in Anglo-Saxon countries. In my opinion we are looking at a badly formulated question, but one that did shed light on the relations between the city and the countryside, which in itself is an essential historical problem. For this reason, I am not discussing it in subsequent chapters but am addressing it below as a historiographical issue, so that we can examine some of its secondary implications. [p. 26]

Three of the grand themes of the debate are therefore discussed in detail in this first chapter: the nature and extent of economic interests of the elite members of society, the absence of a technological roadblock, and the notion of the consumer city. I am addressing these themes now since they are important and relevant for many of the later chapters. At the same time, the first of these themes gives me the opportunity to present several general remarks on the structure of Roman society and a few others on the "epigraphy of the *instrumentum*," that is, the whole evidence of inscriptions on objects used in daily life and in various professions (on kitchenware and table ceramics, terracotta lamps, amphorae and their lids, bricks and tiles, objects of glass or metal, ingots, anchors, pipes, metal or bone labels or tokens).

After the three sections that detail the large themes noted above (sections III, IV, and V), the end of the chapter will address two points that are not equally relevant to the controversy, but are related to it and reveal more precisely problems connected to methodology: models and the study of quantities.

III. The Nature and Extent of Elite Members' Economic Interests

Throughout its history, Roman society was politically and economically dominated by a minority that derived its power from land ownership and was animated by an aristocratic mentality. At the end of the Republic and during the Principate, this minority consisted of two privileged categories, the senators (around six hundred during the Empire) and the equites, members of the equestrian order (whose exact number remains unknown, but was likely around several thousand.) This elite never exceeded ten or twenty thousand heads of household, together with all wives, children, close relatives, and dependents.

Apart from this elite, there were other notables, who imitated the lifestyle of the senators and the equites, possessed similar estates, and sometimes effected equal or lesser influence in society. These [p. 27] notables formed the dominant class in the various cities of the Empire, regardless of the legal status of these cities and their inhabitants. At the top of the Roman social pyramid, therefore, there was a relatively homogeneous elite that could be considered the ruling class. To distinguish the senatorial order and the equestrian order, which were the most prestigious, the richest, and the most educated segments of this class, from other socially significant groups, I refer to this ruling class using expressions like "notables" or "the notables' elite."

It is impossible to determine the limits of this elite of notables with precision. All the *decuriones* and the *bouleutes* (town councilors) of various cities of the Empire did not belong to this class. Some of them, especially those living in small cities, did not have the wealth, the cultural attainments, or the lifestyle necessary to belong to it. On the other hand, wealthy citizens whose personal status excluded them from membership in civic hierarchies—e.g., certain freedmen—could belong to it.

The notables derived great revenues from agriculture and livestock. It is clear that some senators and equestrians received further important legal, or sometimes illegal, revenues from their political, military, and administrative roles—positions for which they had paid exorbitant prices. To these political and administrative revenues we need to add those that certain equestrians received from taxes, especially at the end of the Republic. Certain notables also conducted activities loosely related to cultural and entertainment endeavors (schools of rhetoric, lectures, publications, gifts and indemnities—legal or not—from legal practice, etc.). Such people might also benefit from advantageous matrimonial arrangements as well as the management of kinship and friendships, which provided important inheritances. [p. 28]

Most notables had other private interests, apart from those in agriculture and livestock. These interests of a nonagricultural nature have been much discussed in the framework of the "controversy." Some of these interests were the result of one-time operations (this is what Paul Veyne called the *Gelegenheitshandel* or the *Gelegenheitsunternehmungen*, that is, one-off opportunities of private or corporate enterprise, using words borrowed from Werner Sombart). On the other hand, some developed into regular and continuous activities. The challenge is to know the extent and the nature of these economic, nonagricultural interests. Traditionally, the "primitivists" believe that these interests were limited and that the greater part of the revenues received by the notables came from agriculture and livestock: the "modernists" believe the opposite is true.

Does it matter if a certain economic sector is dominated by the notables, the merchants, or the artisans? Does the social rank of the actors, i.e., the entrepreneurs, matter in economic history, or is it purely a social subject? Like Weber and Hasebroek, Finley insisted on the economic importance of the social rank of the entrepreneurs, on their "status." He insisted that these social components distinguished the ancient economy from the modern one. This modality of situating the problem has predominated in the academic debate, at least from the 1970s to the 1990s. Even a great part of those who oppose his conclusions, have, like Finley, paid close attention to social ranks. Like Finley, they were, and remain, convinced that it was impossible for the status of economic agents not to have consequences for economic life as a whole. Between two enterprises of the same size, the one that was undertaken by a landowner of aristocratic lineage would be exploited in a different manner than that belonging to a freed slave, or a freeborn artisan.

Another question connected to the preceding one is whether the prosperity and modernity of an economic sector are proportional to the social rank [p. 29] and wealth of the entrepreneurs who dominate it. When considering the situation in antiquity, Finley responded in the affirmative. He thought that the closer the economic agents of nonagricultural sectors were to power, the more they identified with the aristocratic ruling elite, and the more the economy had opportunities to prosper. This was one of the conditions, or the elements, necessary for "modernization." On the other hand, the sums of money invested by small artisans were, necessarily, limited, and similar to the volume of their affairs.

Finley thought that in both Greece and Rome the majority of the merchants and artisans had an inferior status; he pointed to the difficulties they had in climbing the social ladder, even when they had the means to do so. J.H. D'Arms, on the other hand, thought that when it came to Rome, the opposite was true. He was convinced that, even outside of agricultural and livestock activities, the most important figures of both Rome and other cities of the Empire belonged, contrary to appearances, among the most active entrepreneurs and were especially involved in commerce. In the same manner, D'Arms worked on minimizing the handicap represented by the status of a freed slave, a freedman. He insisted on the relative social prestige of the rich freedmen who, according to him, had no difficulties infiltrating the higher orders or, at least, enabling their sons to do so.

Did the notables, and the senators in particular, disguise some of their own economic activities considered less appropriate to the requirements of their ranks? What did their eventual interventions consist of, exactly, when they involved themselves in production (artisanal and manufacturing), moneylending, banking, and commerce?

Scholarly work carried out during the last quarter of a century veered more and more towards archaeological and epigraphical documentation and in particular towards the "epigraphy of the *instrumentum*" (see above p. 12). [p. 30] These inscriptions consist either of marks imprinted at the moment of fabrication, or of painted inscriptions that could be connected to the marketing phase of the product, or of graffiti-like marks painted or incised on clay after baking. Some of these materials provide more information than others. This is the case, for example, for bricks and tiles from the Roman region between the end of the first century C.E. and the time of the Severans (third century C.E.). It is also the case for the Baetican oil amphorae (known as "Dressel 20" because they were thus numbered by Heinrich Dressel in the typological table of amphorae he developed at the end of the nineteenth century).

As I will show in the chapters devoted to economic sectors, great progress has been achieved during the last three decades through the study of the *instrumentum*. There has been a debate regarding what kind of evidence these inscriptions provide for the role of the notables, and especially those of the senators and the equites. Some (mostly the "anti-Finleyites") have insisted on active roles for members of the elite; others (the most favorable, or the least unfavorable to Finley's theses) have tended to reduce or place emphasis on the indirect character of this role.

Archaeological and epigraphical studies have vastly enhanced our knowledge of the ancient economy, and they have enabled the formulation of several conclusions regarding the role of the notables. Archaeological and epigraphic evidence shows that their roles varied from sector to sector. They were more important in activities connected to land ownership and rural locations; for example, they were very likely important in the fabrication of bricks and tiles. Above all, the notables considered themselves owners, and landowners in particular. Their reasoning was based on their value as owners, as was shown in the works of "agronomist" writers like Cato, Varro, [p. 31] and Columella. This does not mean that they considered the exploitation of a stone quarry or a deposit of clay as being a kind of agriculture. Varro is very clear on this point: in the countryside, it could have been very profitable to develop the mines, the stone quarries, or the clay deposits, and even to set up a hostel, if the land was close to a well-traveled route. Varro does not oppose involvement in these activities, but he does not believe that they belonged to agricultural activities (Varro, *On Agriculture*, 1.2.21–23).

Some scholars have especially argued for commercial interventions by the notables, and in particular those of the senators and equestrians. I am not convinced by some of these arguments, unless they refer to indirect participation (like moneylending or maritime lending). In my opinion, the role played by the members of the two great orders—and in particular by the senators—in certain sectors of manufacturing was more substantial than the role they played in commerce. The evidence pointing toward the intervention of the senators in commercial activities is very scarce (with the exception of one or two atypical cases). Thus, we should not confuse the selling of agricultural products and livestock with commerce; most of the agricultural producers sold part of their products, yet these activities did not make them traders.

In a very clear way, other categories of evidence show the opposite, namely the existence of traders who were neither producers nor producers' dependents. This is the case of the ingots on the Iberian peninsula that were studied by Claude Domergue. It is also the case for the Baetican oil contained in the Dressel 20 amphorae. The names of the traders, painted on the curves of the amphorae, did not match those of the landowners from whom these products originated. The traders cannot be confused with the oil producers, who owned the land in question, and this was also true for the dependents of these producers. Several literary texts follow the same direction, for example [p. 32] a passage in Diodorus who, in connection with the sale of Italian wine in Gaul, in the first century B.C.E., makes an allusion to the Italian traders (*emporoi*), but not to the producers or their associates (Diodorus, 5.26.3). In his work, Pliny the Younger talks of wine sales on the estate, in a place where traders (*negotiatores*) met to buy the wine (Pliny, *Letters*, 8, 2).

If the commercial role of the notables—and especially of the senators—remains debatable, their financial role is clear, and they did not attempt to conceal it. While lending with interest was not from a moral point of view considered a very respectable activity (far from it!), I note that those involved talked about it freely, and made no secret that they were doing it. I have to conclude that lending with interest was a very widespread practice. This is an important fact that should not be neglected while studying the interests of the elite: most of their interventions consisted of financial loans. During the famous banquet described in the *Satyricon,* Trimalchio describes how, at a certain moment of his life, he decided to retire from *negotiatio*, from trading, from affairs, and how he started to lend money to freedmen, his own or others': *coepi libertos fenerare* (Petronius, *Satyricon*, 76.9). As *fenerare* could hardly be considered a transitive verb, some scholars suggested the following correction of *coepi per liberos fenerare*: "I started lending money through my freedmen." D'Arms used this phrase to show how Trimalchio's economic role was still active. To tell the truth, however, both these readings of the text amount to the same thing: Trimalchio lent to economic agents (traders or artisans); he did not act himself, except for the operation of his vast rural domains. There were several ways of participating in trading and manufacturing: either by direct involvement (developing an enterprise or concluding a company contract) or by lending out money. [p. 33]

Besides the notables, there were two main distinctive socioeconomic groups in the Roman world: the peasants, about whom we know the least (who will be discussed in chapters 2, 6, and 7); and the professionals, who belonged to urban occupations. Most of them were men, but there were also women in this group. If the notables were defined by their estates, that is to say by property in all its forms (lands, houses and residences, livestock, slaves, valuable objects, money hoarded or lent out), the professionals were defined by their activities and qualifications, and their technical competence, of which—according to several funerary inscriptions—they were particularly proud (on this topic I recommend Nicolas Tran's remarkable book). The topic will be addressed again in chapters 4 and 5.

It is necessary to make three additional remarks in relation to these important social and economic categories. Even though the notables and the members of the urban professions were very distinct classes, acting separately, there were also some zones of interaction between them. The first zone of interaction is related to the connection between slaves and freedmen: some professionals were the slaves or the freedmen of the notables. In practice, not all freedmen were connected to their patron in the same way. These relationships vary greatly, from absolute dependence to total independence. In one way or another, some of these professional men succeeded in becoming rich and a small number of them, or their descendants, became notables themselves. To accede to the rank of notable they had to acquire wealth and lead a lifestyle suitable to the rank. It is necessary to consider long-term implication: social environments were [p. 34] distinct, but some moved from one environment to the other; to do so required passage through intermediary stages.

The second additional remark is political. It is likely that the senators had nonagricultural interests that were much less important than those of the equites and the members of the municipal elites because, on average, the senators were much more involved in social and political activities. There were further differences within the equestrian and senatorial orders, but they are too complex a topic and will not be discussed here.

The third additional remark concerns the role of the slave managers. The master could give a slave property or properties, from which the slave derived advantages even if, legally, these properties remained the possessions of the master. Such was the slave's *peculium,* which, with a few exceptions, did not provide much profit to the master. However on the other hand, the master could, by virtue of a "proxy" (*praepositio*)—a kind of legal agreement—charge the slave for the use of a workshop, a boutique, or a ship. In this case, the master was involved directly, as the slave in that case used to earn wages, and would render a statement of accounts for the enterprise to the master. According to these proxies there is no doubt that from an economic point of view the slave owners were personally involved in the activities of ateliers and trades, in which they did not personally engage on a daily basis, but from which they derived profits and for which they were responsible. This element of the Roman system of slavery allowed the rich master to multiply his activities and profits through the actions of his slave managers. We do not know, however, if the activities performed by slaves were very profitable; the effective and consistent control of the slaves and freedmen was an important variable. We should avoid concluding that the notables were involved in many activities and that they became permanently wealthy simply because of the appearance of their names on amphorae and bricks. [p. 35]

IV. Was There a "Technological Roadblock"? No!

The history of technology itself maintains close relationships with the debate we have just examined, but it follows its own trajectory. Nineteenth-century scholars felt great admiration for the technological abilities of the ancients. By the first decades of the twentieth century, however, the idea that Greco-Roman antiquity experienced a veritable "technological roadblock" emerged, and it was prevalent until the 1970s. The notion involved the proposition that there were important technological advances in the ancient Near East and in the Middle Ages but that there was a large gap in technological development between these two time periods. The main task was to explain the absence of important innovations during this period. Among the most common explanations are widespread slavery, the disinterest of the elites and the public powers in technological research, and the lack of interaction between theorists and technicians.

It cannot be denied that there was a lack of regard by ancient scholars for practical applications, and also a lack of connections between ancient scholars and their contemporary artisans or technicians. A scholar of the Roman era such as Ptolemy proclaimed that science is made of two distinct parts: one theoretical and one practical (Claudius Ptolemy, *Almagest,* 1.1). On the other hand, the contemporary divisions between "scientific" and "literary," between the history of science and that of technology, have strongly contributed to keeping these fields apart.

Moses Finley's 1965 article on ancient technology and his book *The Ancient Economy* both reaffirmed this orthodoxy and, at the same time, coincided with the beginning of its end. The last three decades of the twentieth century were marked by a vivid reaction to these ideas inherited from the first part of the century. Technology historians (like M.-C. Amouretti and F. Sigaut [p. 36] in France, G. Raepsaet in Belgium, etc.), economic historians (H.W. Pleket, J.-M. Carrié), and archaeologists (in France, C. Domergue for mining extraction and metallurgy, P. Leveau and J.-P. Brun for hydrology) have demonstrated the falsity of this belief, on the basis of numerous archaeological discoveries.

The evolution of technology has to be studied in its entirety. It is not sufficient to compare antiquity to the most recent periods: we must try to learn the evolution of various preindustrial societies and take account of each region's particular geographical conditions. Some textual sources could be erroneous, so we should not presume an equivalency between the actual practices of the peasants and artisans of the ancient world and the Greek philosophers' accounts of them. In ancient societies, technical knowledge did not depend on scientific knowledge: they evolved independently.

Fernand Braudel noted that, in preindustrial societies, resistance to innovation was the norm, writing that "all new inventions had to wait years, even decades, before they were applied in real life." If we take into consideration this general remark, it is the number and the importance of ancient innovations that should strike us, more than the stagnation of ancient technology.

It was once believed that the Greco-Roman world did not know about the water mill or that it was used rarely, that the water mill did not become a familiar sight until sometime in the Middle Ages, especially as regards the countryside. In the last ten or fifteen years archaeological finds have proved that this view is false. The impressive Barbegal water mill, excavated in Provence, has been dated to the second century C.E., and not to the fourth, as was previously thought. In addition, a considerable number of water mill installations [p. 37] or hydraulic wheels have recently been found in several regions of the Roman west, particularly in southwest France, Switzerland, and Italy. These water mills were installed in the countryside, frequently in the context of large rural areas.

Another especially spectacular example of the evolution of the history of the ancient technology concerns the history of animal harnessing. In two important books,

Lefebvre des Noettes, formerly an officer in the French army, asserts that the harness system was rather deficient in the Greco-Roman world because Greeks and Romans used what he called the "throat collar" or the "withers yoke": the flexible collar rested on the throat of the horse, strangling it when it went too fast or when its load was too heavy. This type of collar prevented the horse from being able to pull a load larger than about 500 kg. According to Noettes there was no other type of harness in antiquity. A careful reexamination of archaeological and iconographic documents, as well as the results of experiments with reconstituted harnesses, allows us to refute his conclusions and to show that the traction system was not lacking at that point in time. Thus, even if the "shoulder collar" was not developed until the ninth or tenth century C.E., there were before this period several other types of traction systems, not just one as Noettes believed. We know, for example, two different types of harnessing that evolved slowly into modern forms: the neck-yoke, frequent in the Near and Middle East, and the back yoke, whose presence was well attested in Greece. In the second case, the yoke pushed against the entire chest, and the animal pulled using its whole chest. Ancient horses, which were much smaller and lighter than modern horses, could pull a load of about a metric ton. Thus, the results achieved in antiquity were on a par with those obtained in other preindustrial or traditional societies. [p. 38]

These two of the supposedly flawed technologies of antiquity—the absence of a harness economically comparable to the medieval version, and the water mill—disappeared at about the same time from historiography. In the field of naval construction, modern advances in marine archaeology have permitted us to observe the progress of Roman nautical technology at the end of the Republic and under the Empire.

Contemporary historians of technology insist that technological progress is not necessarily tied to machines, and that the evolution of tools and technical accomplishments could constitute important progress. This being said, certain machines, particularly those used to move water (as in mines and irrigation) were developed or perfected during the Hellenistic period and, under the Roman Empire, spread more broadly than before. This is the case for Archimedes' screw and for the water wheel. There was much enthusiasm over the "Gallic harvester" (*vallus*) of the Treviri (which was probably used to harvest spelt, a grain to which it was well adapted, but which did not necessarily constitute progress in itself), but much less so over the diffusion of elevating machines.

Technologically speaking, Greco-Roman antiquity (considered as a single unit, since the Romans greatly contributed to spreading the innovations they inherited from the Greek world) is far from being stagnant. It is true that at the beginning of the Middle Ages, fields like architecture, construction, mining, and naval construction abandoned technological methods pioneered by the Greco-Romans. As a consequence it is clear that recent discoveries in the field of technological history do not validate Finley's theses—quite the contrary. In more than one way Finley's thought, [p. 39] which played an important role in problematizing research and which exercised a great influence in the 1970s and 1980s, now belongs to the past; it is part of the historiographical traditions. At the same time it is important not to revert, purely and simply, to old "modernist" views, which hold limited intellectual and scientific interest. Consequently, based on recent discoveries and research, we need to adopt more of a comparative method: comparisons between Greece and Rome, of course, but also between Greco-Roman antiquity and the other preindustrial economies, inside and outside western Europe.

V. Consumer City

In principle, the urban center was only the administrative center of the city-state. It was the theoretical center, and it provided the framework for the city's political and judicial life. And in principle, this function does not make the urban center a social environment different from the countryside. The citizens in the towns and those in the countryside had the same rights and the same obligations; slaves had the same status in both locales. This is how ancient municipal laws constituted the city, and most Latin writers confirmed this theory. The manner in which Cicero, for example, talks of the countryside, properties, homes, slaves and their abuses, never suggests that the urban center could live at the expense of the countryside, or that the latter had formed an autonomous society, separated from the urban elites.

Despite this institutionalized vision of the city as a perfect unit in which the urban center was the county seat, historians and archaeologists agree without exception on the social and economic specificity of the urban center, and with good reason. They might differ on the specific roles of the town and the countryside, but most of them considered the city as composed of two heterogeneous milieus. [p. 40]

To schematize, there are three basic approaches. The advocates of the first approach, and Finley foremost, are the ones who began the debate. According to Finley, the ancient town did not produce anything for the countryside, but thrived at its expense. It paid for its own facilities and maintenance not from the results of its economic activity, but by appropriating a significant portion of the surplus created through the work of the peasants, which was collected by the notables. This was the very essence of the "consumer city" term likely borrowed from W. Sombart and perhaps from M. Weber, too. Or, if we prefer to use a more provocative expression, we could use that of the "parasitic city." Certainly, Finley's comments do not apply only to the city of Rome. In the last centuries of the Republic and under the Empire, the city of Rome had become gigantic, attaining a population that was in the neighborhood of a million inhabitants, and becoming, according to an expression used by C. Nicolet, a "mégapole." Even though the inhabitants of Rome were not idle, even though the city had very lively commerce and artisanal activities, Rome's functions and size meant it could not avoid being a consumer city and especially a big consumer of agricultural products. With some exceptions he admits to, Finley's comments were intended to apply to the ancient cities in general, or at least to the great majority of them.

The second approach had as its main proponent P. Leveau, to whom we may join D. Engels and K. Hopkins: Leveau insists on the activity of the urban center. The resulting model is what we may call that of the "organizer city." Leveau thinks that through the deployment of levies, the urban elite developed exchanges between the countryside and the town, and thus integrated the peasantry in a new system that created a surplus, which was primarily consumed in and by the town. In the trade exchanges between the town and the countryside, the town had the organizing role. Leveau also showed how, in the case of Cherchell for example, [p. 41] the urban elite organized and transformed the countryside to meet its own needs and ideals.

The third tendency, represented by A. Ferdière, is formulated independently, and without contradicting the other two. It emphasizes the autonomy of the rural districts, the perceived permanence of rural history which, while changing, was only tangentially dependent on "big history." Paying close attention to the Roman forms of land ownership and exploitation, Ferdière notes convincingly that "the city could not exist without its territory." He does insist, however, on rural continuity: in a way, the Gallo-Roman rural world existed at the edge of the city, certainly under its control, but maintaining its own cohesion.

The model of the "consumer city" is still debated often and even defended (it is the topic of several passages in the 2007 edition of *The Cambridge Economic History of the Greco-Roman World*). But then again, in my opinion, it does not take into account in a satisfactory manner the functioning of the ancient city. Since the publication of Finley's book, several cities have been discovered in which, during the Roman period, there were substantial manufacturing operations, for example textiles—in second-century B.C.E. Fregelles and in imperial Timgad (chapter 3 will explore textiles in more detail). The model that is most faithful to such ancient conditions is Leveau's "organizing city." Besides, a large range of activities related to agriculture actually take place in the town, such as milling, the manufacture of oil and honey, and the handling of meat and fish. R. Bagnall emphasizes this situation in his book on late Egypt (starting in the third century C.E.), but such practices are found in other places and time periods.

We need to add that the model of the "organizing city" and that of the rural area espoused by Ferdière are not mutually exclusive, at least not when we consider [p. 42] their relationship as being dynamic rather than static. This is especially true because the urban elite was never fully successful in organizing the entire countryside. In fact it could not do this even in Italy, let alone in the great majority of the provinces. On the other hand, given the system of ownership, the existence of the cities, the fiscal system, and all the forms of control exercised by the Roman state, rural autonomy could never play a primary role. Ferdière's ideas are not valid unless we do not push them to their limits. As to the notion of the "consumer city," it should not be maintained if a Finleyite model of parasitism is used to characterize the relationship between the town and the countryside. It is true that the town was a privileged locale for consumption, but the organizing power of the town and its role in consumption are not mutually exclusive. Besides, the social groups that consumed the most were also the ones most involved in organizing the land.

By considering consumption as being exclusively responsible for economic activity and innovation, Finley has misconstrued the problem. The proof that this is the case resides in the fact that certain phenomena could be interpreted in a contradictory manner: for example, the function of information. If information was concentrated in the urban center, could this be taken as a sign of its organizational activity, or as an advantage of a situation from which it profited, and which accentuated its dominance? And what of commerce? The Latin texts, written by the members of the social and political elite, have little to say on the subject. When they do (as for instance in the *Satyricon*, or Apuleius' *Metamorphoses*), commerce appears as an urban activity, even though it seems to be focused on agricultural products. At the beginning of the *Metamorphoses*, merchants' actions are expended in connection with towns, and they travel from town to town in order to sell honey or cheese. What role has to be assigned to the development of such trade? Leveau, for example, saw in these activities proof of the organizing role of the urban center. And he is surely correct. However, couldn't we also consider trade as one of the ways [p. 43] in which agricultural surplus was redirected towards the town and appropriated by it for its own consumption, at the cost of production in the countryside?

The urban center and the countryside were engaged in a social relation of the classist type, exhibiting the key elements of such a relationship: on one side, the economic activity of the dominant classes (activity which brought benefits to the entire society, but evidently in an unequal way); on the other side, important levies at the expense of the dominated strata, and finally, a great social inequity, provoking sometimes active but mostly passive resistance on the part of the dominated social layers, which tried to escape the control and direction of the dominating class. All preindustrial historical societies functioned this way. Depending on which of the three aspects of this relationship we focus upon, we will arrive at one or another of the three tendencies described above. The three are distinct yet complementary ways of analyzing the same problem. The model of the "consumer city" hardly helps us understand it.

VI. The Study of Quantities

Some of the topics we will be considering require that we understand quantities and their evolution. Those who insist on the economic discontinuity of the ancient period make use of quantitative variations, which are sometimes probable or even certain, but which are, most of the time, questionable. Archaeologists like G. Pucci and J.-P. Morel have rightly noted that the quantities of artifacts found in excavations or survey campaigns of sites from the second century B.C.E. were much larger than those of preceding periods. On the other hand, relying on M. Crawford's work, K. Hopkins showed that, between the middle of the second century B.C.E. and the middle of [p. 44] the first, Rome increased its minting production considerably and that, henceforth, the coin quantities produced had nothing in common with the coins produced in a city like Athens in the fifth or fourth centuries B.C.E. (Migeotte, pp. 47–52).

These quantities do not merely show economic progress or contraction in commercialization: they are also relevant to understanding cultural or social differences. Thus, the relative importance of the black-glaze ceramics, whose presence was attested on almost all of the protohistorical sites dating to the last centuries B.C.E. and found in what is now the Midi of France, allows us to distinguish between Greek and indigenous inhabitants of the respective areas. In the same regions, during the first two centuries C.E., rural areas preserved lesser quantities of sigillata (stamped) and slip ceramics than did urban areas. Such typological and inventory studies align archaeology to the interests of economic history and those of cultural anthropology; the study of ceramics could learn much from studying the evolution of dietary habits.

For this reason, much effort in the last ten or fifteen years has been placed on producing a more developed quantification. A long time has passed since scholars like T. Frank and R. Duncan-Jones gathered evidence of prices, production, and output from the ancient texts (numbers are quite rare, and occasionally not very credible). In recent years, two other methods, which the British call "inductive" and "deductive," have been used extensively to establish other quantities. They could be used either to discern trends or tendencies, or to establish the ranges—the minimum or maximum usage of an item—or even to propose absolute numbers.

The "inductive" method consists of counting available objects, usually archaeological finds (but the method could also count coins, inscriptions, etc.). It presupposes [p. 15] an analysis of the methods of counting, of the results obtained, and of their historical significance. The great specialists of this method, who contribute effectively to the history of production and commerce, are clearly the archaeologists, as well as some numismatists.

The "deductive" method attempts to come up with hypothetical quantities, not based on the available documentation, but informed by other quantitative data, based on similarities, analogies, and comparison. Finley's disciples, Hopkins in particular, were especially responsible for popularizing this method. Let's look at a specific example. W. Jongman was interested in finding out if the city of Pompeii exported as much wine in the first century C.E. as it did in the previous century (he believed that this was not the case). Jongman started by asking how much of their territory the Pompeians had to use to grow the grain they needed. To deduce the answer he based his calculations on the median individual consumption (actually unknown, but on which we had sufficient data to estimate possible ranges, even before Jongman's book). Additionally, he used the size of the population and the median grain production per surface unit, quantities which were also not precisely known, but which could be calculated based on other indices. Further information could be deduced from analyzing the quantities of grains and dried vegetables arriving from the provinces at Puteoli, Rome's greatest port, where the Pompeians were known to shop. Jongman concluded that the Pompeians did not export great quantities of wine.

Because this method greatly multiplies the margins of errors, we can see how it can produce risky conclusions. So while it is quite an interesting approach, it presents a considerable difficulty in that it advances numbers that may seem sound but are in fact very questionable. This method cannot bear fruit unless it is used with great care and in circumscribed cases, e.g., [p. 46] as regards demography, where we can also use sound comparative models, such as UN demographic data.

These quantitative studies were partially inspired by Finley's attempts to develop a "Histoire-problème," or Problem-History. Later, however, they were used to pursue very different objectives. This is especially true of the inductive method, which was employed to show that the ancient economy changed drastically from one period to the other, because the volume of material exchanged either greatly increased or decreased. In the great majority of the cases, its application resulted in casting doubt on Finley's conclusions.

VII. The Models

Like the deductive and inductive methods, the use of "models," or *a priori* schematics that in principle must be checked by examining the evidence, stems from Finley's work. Warmly recommended by his disciples P. Garnsey and R. Saller, often this method proves both stimulating and successful. Paradoxically, it reconciled some scholars of antiquity with economic science which, incidentally, Finley did not consider necessary to understand ancient events. In fact, where could we find better and more diverse examples than in economics?

I will now introduce K. Hopkins' "Taxes and Trade Model," which was later modified and completed by H.U. Freyberg. Hopkins summarized it in several pages without trying to support it with solid evidence. In thus doing he unsettled many a scholar, especially Finley's most loyal disciples (who believed that this model places too much evidence on trade and its cycles, as well as on the role of money and its exchanges). It is, however, the most known [p. 47] of the models on ancient history, and continues to have an influence that cannot be ignored. It is believed that at the beginning of the Empire, in the first century C.E., the commercial balance between Italy and the provinces changed greatly, favoring the latter at the expense of the former. The reality of this observation has been contested (we could, for example, question the representation of the products that are documented: we know a lot about ceramics but very little about the textiles of the time), but over all, recent archaeological discoveries seem to confirm the idea. I will be considering this issue in greater detail in chapter 5.

How can we explain this? Hopkins, reasoning at a macroeconomic level, has linked the evolution of trade with taxation. The regions that paid direct taxes without receiving much in return from the imperial treasury (that is, the provinces without soldiers) increased their sales to compensate for the flux of monetary or nonmonetary values that they lost in that way, in favor of Italy. This is the reason, or at least one of the reasons, why starting in the first century C.E., Gallo-Roman ceramics and those of Proconsular Africa replaced Arretine on all the western Mediterranean sites. Such theses continue to be much questioned, but it is important to keep in mind the relationship between taxation and commercialization.

In themselves, such models have intellectual value, particularly because of their internal coherence: they help generate questions. For example, regardless of what H. Pleket has said, the "Taxes and Trade Model" had enabled a better understanding of the logical connections between taxation and economic life. Some inscriptions and literary texts show that Asia Minor's cities sold textiles outside the Empire and we also know that taxes were in place. But Hopkins' model says more than this. Unfortunately, the biggest problem pertaining to such models about the ancient economy is that they cannot be verified. Hopkins himself did not attempt to verify his models. [p. 48] In principle, in economic science, models need to be verified. Without exception, this is not the case for ancient history, since in its case the models are meant to fill in for nonexistent documentation. And if, by chance, documentation does exist, some model theoreticians decline to use it because they consider it too insignificant and uncertain in relation to the coherence of their models. I do not consider this way of proceeding to conform to good scientific method.

Texts

The Wealth and Greed of M. Licinius Crassus

M. Licinius Crassus was consul in 70 and again in 55 B.C.E.

> The Romans, it is true, say that the many virtues of Crassus were obscured by his sole vice of avarice...For at the outset he was possessed of not more than three hundred talents; then during his consulship he sacrificed the tenth of his goods to Hercules, feasted the people, gave every Roman out of his own means enough to live on for three months, and still, when he made a private inventory of his property before his Parthian expedition, he found that it had a value of 7100 talents. The greatest part of this, if one must tell the scandalous truth, he got together out of fire and war, making the public calamities his greatest source of revenue.
>
> For when Sulla took the city and sold the property of those whom he had put to death...Crassus was never tired of accepting or of buying it. And besides this, observing how natural and familiar at Rome were such fatalities as the conflagration and collapse of buildings, owing to their being too massive and close together, he proceeded to buy slaves who were architects and builders. Then, when he had over 500 of these, [p. 49] he would buy houses that were afire, and houses which adjoined those that were afire, and these their owners would let go at a trifling price owing to their fear and uncertainty. In this way the largest part of Rome came into his possession...And though he owned numberless silver mines, and highly valuable tracts of land with the laborers upon them, nevertheless one might regard all this as nothing compared with

the value of his slaves; so many and so capable were the slaves he possessed—readers, amanuenses, silversmiths, stewards, table servants...

Plutarch, *Crassus,* 2.1–7 (trans. B. Perrin, Loeb Classical Library, 1967)

The *Lex Claudia* or "Claudian Plebiscite" (218 B.C.E.)

He was also hated by the senators on account of an unprecedented law which Quintus Claudius the tribune of the plebs had introduced, despite the opposition of the senate, with the backing of Gaius Flaminius alone of all that body, providing that no senator or senator's son should own a sea-going ship of more than three hundred amphoras' burden. This was reckoned to be sufficient to transport the crops from one's fields, and all moneymaking [*quaestus*] was held unseemly in a senator. The measure, which was vehemently opposed, had been productive of great resentment on the part of the nobles [*nobilitas*] against Flaminius, who had advocated its enactment; but had procured for him the favor of the plebs and afterwards a second consulship.

Livy 21.63.3–4 (trans. B.O. Foster, Loeb Classical Library, 1969)

On this text, see A. Tchernia, "Le plebiscitum claudianum," in J. Andreau and V. Chankowski, eds., *Vocabulaire et expression de l'économie dans le monde antique* (Bordeaux, 2007): 253–78. [pp. 50, 51]

Chapter 2
Agriculture and Livestock

I. Available Resources

Extant information regarding land ownership, soil cultivation, agriculture, and livestock is quite varied. We will first start with the literary texts, almost all of whose authors were (more or less important) landowners interested in discussing such subjects. Cicero, Horace, Pliny the Younger, and Apuleius, for example, in a more or less precise and informed way, allude to the operation of their lands, and especially to the buying and selling of land. A great number of Cicero's works address these topics: I mention here, first and foremost, the *Pro Roscio Amerino*, the *Pro Tullio*, the *Verrine Orations*, the *Pro Cluentio*, the *Pro Caecina*, the *On the Agrarian Law*, and the *Catilinarians*. Latin and Greek historians were led to address agricultural issues, especially when these were responsible for causing social or political crises. This is the case with Livy, Sallust, etc., and especially with Appian, whose *Civil Wars* are an important source of information.

Some authors wrote specialized treatises and technical pieces on the administration of agricultural lands, agriculture, and livestock. Four such treatises are still extant: the *On Agriculture* of Cato the Elder (also known as Cato the Censor), likely written in the middle of the second century B.C.E. at the latest; Varro's *On Agriculture* (written between the fifties and the thirties B.C.E.); Columella's [p. 52] *On Agriculture* (written toward the middle of the first century C.E.); and Palladius' *Agricultural Work* (written at the end of the fourth century, or rather in the fifth). To these names we need to add that of Virgil, whose *Georgics*, written in verse between 37 and 30 B.C.E., treat successively the growth of grain (book 1), trees (book 2), large livestock (book 3), and bees (book 4); and that of Pliny the Elder (third quarter of first century C.E.), whose natural science treatise *Natural History* dedicates long passages to wheat and other cereals, to vines, olive trees, and various livestock animals. One historiographical tradition tended to doubt the accuracy of the information provided by these authors. Some have claimed that Varro, for example, was too literary and had been too influenced by Greek texts to be able to present a credible picture of the agricultural and livestock realities in Italy. Such an opinion of Varro's work, however, cannot realistically be maintained: instead, we should pay close attention to what he wrote.

Another category of technical writers is that of the surveyors (the *agrimensores*), officially in charge of land surveys, who published treatises in which they noted the characteristics and the diverse styles of surveys and different types of properties.

The texts that we still have constitute the *Corpus Agrimensorum*, published in 1848–52 by C. Lachmann and F. Blume under the title *Die Schriften der romischen Feldmesser.*

Various legal texts, such as fragments from the *Digest*, deal with aspects of the interventions of the city, or the Empire, in general matters of ownership, landownership, administration of public lands (*ager publicus*), or the administration of imperial properties. It is also important to note the inscriptions from the major areas of Proconsular Africa, normative texts dating from the second century C.E. and detailing the operation of the imperial domains of the Bagradas valley [p. 53] (today known as Medjerda) and in particular the relations among imperial procurators, the farmers who rented the land (the *conductores),* and the "settlers" (the *coloni*, that is, the peasant farmers): the inscriptions of Henchir Mettich (*CIL* VIII.25902), Ain-el Djemala (*CIL* VIII.25943), Ain-Wassel (*CIL* VIII.26416) and Souk-el-Khmis (*CIL* VIII.10750 and 14464 = *ILS* 6870). The two inscriptions concerning Trajan's and Nerva's food establishments in the cities of Veleia and the Ligures Baebiani also constitute important sources of information on land ownership in these Italian regions.

Several other types of inscriptions are relevant to this chapter. As the Romans did not consider the livelihood of the landowner (or that of the farmer) as professions per se, and the *domini* and the *coloni* themselves did not mention their professional activities on their funerary inscriptions, it so happens that the only related inscriptions from which we can gather information are those of the slave managers (the *vilici* and the *actores*). The documentary evidence of daily practice is equally interesting for the information it provides on lands and their exploitation: among them, the most important are the Egyptian papyri, but also some of the Campanian wax tablets. They mention lands for sale, sales, and rentals, because lands and houses could serve as collateral in loan contracts.

Through two of its biggest subdisciplines—excavations and survey—which have experienced tremendous progress in the last three decades, archaeology is becoming more and more important in the study of the ancient economy, and not just that of agriculture and livestock. The brief remarks I am making here concerning this topic are also valid for the other chapters, such as chapter 3, in which I will not be repeating this information again.

"Survey" archaeology, whether aerial or terrestrial, allows the rapid consideration of more spaces and the location of a large number of [p. 54] sites from various time periods. Aerial survey provides information on the density of the population but cannot add much to its chronology. Thanks to information derived from studying recovered materials, ground exploration, on the other hand, further helps to date sites (or at least a part of their history). At the same time, these materials provide information on the objects used at a site. Informed by survey campaigns in Greece, Alcock's synthesis is very clear on this subject. It is also true that, in the great majority of cases, surveys benefit from later excavations: the results of the survey campaigns thus help identify sites where further excavation can profitably take place, and what lines of research should be pursued.

Excavations can be terrestrial or underwater. Underwater excavations are very important for studying cargo, trade routes, and the organization of maritime trade, and they will be addressed several times throughout the book. Terrestrial excavations provide more information on the plans and organization of buildings (agricultural buildings as well as residential) than do survey campaigns, and land excavations also provide more chronological information about the site. During the last few decades, recent finds of tools and instruments (the remains of plows, wine and oil presses, grinding wheels) resulted in important discoveries regarding ancient agricultural techniques. These finds also provided information on the housing of peasants. Until now, however, very few sites have provided definite or even hypothetical information on housing reserved for slaves.

Finally, it is necessary to give credit to the important studies of flora and fauna, that is, to palaeoenvironmental work. As P. Leveau rightly noted, this research area is composed of several different disciplines. Palynology (the study of pollen and spores) helps to "understand the arrival and the development of agricultural systems and their relationship with their natural ecosystems." The study of vegetative "macrofossils" (pieces of wood, roots, leaves, and stems) and wildlife [p. 55] contributes to our knowledge of flora of the past and provides information on the foodways of inhabitants, much more than on their production. Anthracology is dedicated to the study of charcoal; xylology identifies the particular type of wood in the charcoal; dendrochronology allows their exact dating. Archaeozoology or palaeozoology can help determine what terrestrial or aquatic animal species have been developed through human action (either through domestication and animal husbandry), which of them were hunted or fished, and which animal waste was used as fertilizer in agriculture.

II. Property and Various Types of Land

To understand agricultural activity and the life of farmers and breeders, whether peasants or landowners, it is important to have a clear idea how the ownership of the land was organized. This organization, which varies from society to society, constitutes the juridical, social, and cultural background of agricultural life. The techniques and economic management have, of course, their importance, but only in the context of land ownership and their connection to it.

Traditionally, in Rome, it was characterized by the existence of privately owned lots, of public lands that belonged to the city and were used collectively by its citizens, and of other types of common lands rented to various parties. When, exactly, did this practice start? It is impossible to say with any certainty, but it is a very ancient practice. Could Romulus, the first king of Rome, have distributed to the head of each Roman family a lot of two *iugera* in size, that is half a hectare (the *heredium*), which could be passed down to their descendants? Could it be that some senators from the fifth century B.C.E. (like Quinctius Cincinnatus), from the fourth century, or even the third (M. Atilius Regulus), were owners of very small *fundi*, whose areas did not [p. 56] exceed seven *iugera* (1.75 hectares)? Many scholars believe these details are myths, composed long after the actual events, in order to show off the austerity of the ancient Romans and their disdain for riches. However, if we are to give them some credit, these proportions were very likely a function of the collective lands. And, in fact, Roman citizens, besides using their personal lands, also made use of the lands belonging to the city. This tradition is also present in other Italian cities and, through Roman conquests, was later generalized all over Italy and in the cities of the provinces.

When Rome founded a new city, which was called a *colonia*, the *coloni*, or citizens of this new city, received tracts of land with private titles. The Latins called such an activity the *deductio* of a colony (that is, its foundation) and they talked about a colony being "led out" (that is, founded). The citizens of the colony, those who received these lands, were recruited from among poor free men, and later, starting at the beginning of the first century B.C.E., from among veteran soldiers. I must note here that, in Latin, the word *colonus* has several meanings: it could mean the free citizen of a colony (for example, the citizens of Narbonne were called the "colonists" of Narbonne, because the latter, founded by Rome in 118 B.C.E., had the status of a Roman colony). It could also mean, in some texts, any kind of farmer (the one who farms, *qui colit*). In other texts, it could mean a cultivator who does not own the land but has rented it, like a farmer or a sharecropper.

The historian Appian of Alexandria, who wrote in Greek in the second century C.E., explained that as the Romans conquered new territories, they developed the habit of appropriating a part of the land of the defeated people to found colonies populated with Roman or "Latin" citizens. Appian observed that this method of confiscating the land, [p. 57] very soon after its conquest, was a method of replacing the older way of establishing and maintaining order, via garrisons (*Civil Wars*, 1.1.7). What he meant was that, in the past, when Greek cities conquered other cities, they used immediately to establish garrisons there. This system, however, had limitations, and the Romans did not use it. Several objectives were pursued through the foundation of colonies. In addition to facilitating the exploitation of land, and adding a surplus population which then factored in the spread of Roman influence (what is known as "Romanization"), the foundation of such sites was intended to exert close surveillance on the territories just conquered. The colonies founded this way by Rome were much more numerous in Italy and the western Mediterranean area than in the Greek world. As a result, Hellenistic traditions were not drastically affected by Roman colonization (an important point when it comes to land ownership and the occupation of the soil.)

These colonies were brand-new cities: each one contained a small urban center and a rural territory. The Roman colonies, less vast and less heavily populated, but more egalitarian, played important military defensive roles and were considered, pure and simple, as extensions of the city of Rome. The individual lots belonging to the colonists were very small: in the third and second centuries B.C.E. they did not exceed one, two, or three hectares. In these cases, it is clear that the colonists' families could not survive without supplemental sources of incomes. These were accessible to them, through the use of municipal lands, which they were allowed to use as grazing lands, or even to cultivate. A part of these communal lands was exploited in common, as pastures; another part was rented to private individuals, for fees.

The Latin colonies were more agricultural than military in nature: they were conceived as new communities, and were more autonomous. The plots of land given to the "Latin" colonists were more substantial, [p. 58] yet there was, between them, a greater degree of estate inequality. For example, in 184 B.C.E. the residents of the Roman colonies of Pesaro and Potentia each received 6 *iugera*, that is, approximately 1.5 hectares, and in 183, the colony of Parma received 8 (2 hectares). In the Latin colony of Aquileia, founded in 181 B.C.E., the *pedites* (foot soldiers) received, in return, much more expansive lots: 50 *iugera* (12.5 hectares). The family was able to cultivate 3 hectares (even if it could add to this lot the use of the city's collective lands for livestock grazing). But a supplementary workforce was desirable, or even necessary, when the family's lands approached 10 or 15 hectares. Moreover, if the Latin colonists of Aquileia were given lots totaling 50 *iugera*, the noncommissioned officers, the centurions, received in the same colony lots of 100 *iugera* (25 hectares) and the equites lots as large as 140 *iugera* (35 hectares) (Livy, 40.34.2). Patrimonial and civic inequality went hand in hand with the military hierarchy.

This is not, however, the only manner in which Rome distributed the land of conquered peoples. The public treasury maintained ownership over other lands, a part of which it rented out to its citizens, with individual titles. These areas for (long-term) rent could then be cultivated or used for grazing: they were what they called the "public lands," *ager publicus*. Members of the elite held a great part of these lands for which, it seems, they paid low fees. These practices explain how, by the third and second centuries B.C.E., the area of the domains owned by the elite had greatly increased, and why the number of slaves used in agriculture and animal husbandry grew accordingly.

In the passage to which I have already alluded, Appian clearly describes this particular situation. He explains that, if a conquered area had been ravaged by war, the Romans did not want to invest in surveying it [p. 59] so they

> proclaimed that the fields could be used by anybody interested, on the condition of paying an annual royalty in fruits: namely, a tenth, for the lands to be cultivated, and a fifteenth for the lands with plantations.[…] The rich citizens acquired the largest part of these uncultivated lands. […] The lands and the herds thus made it into the hands of the cultivators and the shepherds who bought them, in order to avoid the inconvenience of military conscription that befell those who were free.[…] As a result of all these particular circumstances, the elites became very wealthy, the slave population in the countryside increased, and the living standards of free people decayed.
>
> [Appian, *Civil Wars*, 1.1.7, trans. H. White, Loeb Classical Library, 1912]

Accordingly, the magnitude of Rome's conquests produced great riches for the city, and in some measure for the citizens, but quite unequally. The elite derived much bigger profits than the rest of the citizens. According to ancient authors, the private domains of the senators of the fourth and even the third century B.C.E. were very reduced. On the contrary, the senators living during Cicero's time (the middle of the first century B.C.E.) quite often possessed hundreds of hectares. Even if the poverty of senators from prior centuries was very exaggerated by the ancient authors (almost always nostalgic for the past), it is undeniable that an evolution took place and that the inherited estates of the rich became increasingly more substantial.

Such extensive territories involved the presence of peasants (whether free or slaves). Such large areas could no longer be cultivated by the owner of the field, pushing a plow, as had been the case in the past. The conquests also enabled the transformation of defeated enemies into slaves. From this time on, the lands of the members of the two top orders, the senators and the equites, which up to the end of the Republic were situated primarily in central and southern Italy, and particularly in Latium and Campania, were for the most part cultivated by [p. 60] slaves. This situation stimulated the slave trade. In the second century these powerful developments resulted in agricultural transformations, which favored several crops intended for trade, especially arboriculture (grapevines and olive trees). Cato the Elder's treatise *On Agriculture* is symbolic of this development, which some consider a revolution.

The last centuries of the Republic were definitely marked by a diminishing number of small citizen-owners, even though the reality of this phenomenon—which inspired the actions of the Gracchi in 133 and 123 B.C.E. and which was much discussed in the ancient sources—was contested by various historians. This does not mean, however, that a class of small property owners did not exist, especially when, in addition to the permanent workforce, the exploitation of the domains of the rich, their *villae,* required the use of a seasonal workforce. This seasonal workforce was composed of small property owners and farmers or local tenant farmers, or of groups of laborers from various regions, who were recruited to do such work by entrepreneurs who specialized in this kind of transaction. The presence of the estates did not cause the disappearance of the modest or poor peasants (and sometimes owners) living in the same area. The smallholders could also find other sources of income either doing artisanal work or in the local or regional trade. Besides, the founding of new colonies constantly renewed the class of small and middle owners. Moreover, Rome's *ager publicus* did not admittedly constitute a great resource for the smallholders during the first century B.C.E.: but the different cities under Italy's rule had, themselves, public lands and some of them were cultivated collectively by their inhabitants.

It is impossible to evaluate the development in the number of smallholders in Italy, or even in Latium or Campania, [p. 61] regions that we know relatively well. Between the third and the first centuries B.C.E., in the Italian peninsula, this class of small property owners was always present, but its numbers were very probably reduced: politically and socially, this class had ceased to be the backbone of the Roman city. Additionally, it is very likely that on the lands of the smallholders and on the plots of the *coloni* (as tenant farmers) the number of slaves was the lowest; however, in some cases, even a smallholder or *colonus* could own one or two slaves, who worked alongside him in the fields.

Just like Rome, the other cities of the Empire owned land. Besides the cities, however, there were other communities with a lower status, i.e., village communities that also owned land; some formed part of a city, and some did not. In some provinces, the so-called tribal communities were also involved in land ownership. During the Principate could there have still existed, in some of these communities, the kind of collective land ownership that was very probably more widespread in previous times? It is not impossible. Yet, without exception, we can't know how land ownership was organized in these communities. For example, this is the conclusion that M. Wörrle reached after studying an important inscription in Oenoanda, in Asia Minor, in the vicinity of Caria, Pisidia, and Lycia. This inscription, dated 124–25 C.E., concerns the organization of animal sacrifices. Within the territory of the city there were about thirty villages, most of them bearing indigenous, non-Greek names, and which collaborated in furnishing oxen. If, in that city, the major part of the territory was composed of villages, it is correct to assume that the cities' notables received some of their revenues from these territories. We do not know, however, either the relationships existing in everyday life among the villagers [p. 62] and the inhabitants of the urban center, or the manner in which land ownership was organized within the villages.

Another very interesting if also damaged inscription dates from the first or the second century C.E. and concerns Kastolos, one of the villages (*kome*) of the city of Philadelphia, in Burnt Lydia. In this village there was a council of the elders (*gerousia*), which organized the assembly of all villagers (*kometai*) in order to distribute common lands. The council must have been in touch with the magistrates of Philadelphia who, in one way or another, were certainly involved in the affairs of the village (*OGIS*, 488, also see L. Robert 1937, pp. 159–60). Did all the lands of the villages consist of such common lands, as Briant suggested? He opined that they were subject to a "periodic distribution of the plots among the different families composing the village." In this case, individual land ownership in the village was either strictly enforced, according to rigid collective customs, or did not exist at all. It is also possible that the lands belonging to the village were not at all distributed this way. This is Debord's opinion; he expressed doubt about the existence of such a "communitarian egalitarianism." According to him, besides these collective lands, there were individual plots that the owners could use freely and could sell. Unfortunately, the inscription does not provide us with this information.

III. The Cadaster System

Surveying, measuring lands, determining their boundaries, defining their various categories—these are not Roman inventions. They are found in other cultures as well, for example in Greece and Etruria. The Roman tradition, however, developed specific forms of surveying, made known to posterity through the writings of specialized [p. 63] surveyors (*agrimensores*) and which were analyzed by M. Weber in his *Römische*

Agrargeschichte (1891). These surveyors could equally be called *gromatici*, after the instrument "groma," a cross mounted on a bracket, which fitted into a staff, and was designed to survey straight lines and right angles, which enabled them to perform orthogonal, cross-referential measurements, as each one of the four branches came with a plumb line.

When a new colony was founded, the lands that constituted it were surveyed and, so, received a grid of orthogonal lines, which was marked onto the land itself by way of ditches and paths. These lines formed squares or rectangles. One of the figures was a square of about 710 m long per side, called a *centuria*. In the oldest Latin colonies, the division of the land was made *per strigas et scamna*, a Latin expression very difficult to translate and which meant that the operation of cadastration was determined by long rectangles, oriented either one direction or another. These squares and rectangles did not represent plots of land for individual usage: instead, they represented structures within which smaller plots were later assigned to the *coloni* and their families.

Not all the lands of a colony were thus assigned, nor were they necessarily "centuriated" (i.e., surveyed according to this network of orthogonal lines). On the contrary, the Roman public powers surveyed lands that were then distributed with individual title to Roman citizens, without founding a colony. These cases were called "viritane assignments" (from the word *vir* = man, an individual of masculine sex). This is what happened in the *ager Falernus*, in northeast Campania, probably around 318 B.C.E. Other lands which were not assigned were also surveyed: either lands that did not become part of the new colonies, or lands that embraced the territory of several cities. On the other hand, nothing stopped an owner of extensive property from ordering [p. 64] surveying operations within his domains, if he considered that the exploitation of his properties could benefit from such a practice.

Depending on the nature of the land, its geographical particularities, and local and regional history in later times, some of these orthogonal lines marking the Roman urban landscape disappeared completely, while some have been preserved to the present day. Other types of surveying lines, connected to agricultural exploitation and to livestock operations (enclosures surrounded by trenches, traces of previous land work, etc.), may also have left visible marks on the land. The Roman era is not the only one to have left its mark on the geographical landscape, even though the orthogonal forms preferred by the Romans and their regularity are much easier to spot than those associated with the Middle Ages or the modern era. In Gaul, for example, some of these still-visible traces belong to the Iron Age, while others belong to a period of time later than Roman antiquity. On the Iberian peninsula, they seem to have been preserved more in the north than in the south; those in the Andalusian colonies are no longer visible. For several decades, specialized studies focusing on the identification and delimitation of the Roman surveying operations and their chronology have been conducted by vertical and oblique aerial photographs, geographical maps, survey campaigns, and satellite images. The optical filtering technique has greatly helped this type of research, which has become a veritable sub-discipline of archaeology.

Several questions are important to consider at this point. Could Rome impose successive cadaster operations with different orientations of the same territory—and at relatively short time intervals? And did it proceed to survey large territories at the same time? Could we be sure that some linear conglomerations and some orthogonal forms did indeed belong to this time period, and that they were not produced more recently?

Despite our fascination with the discovery of these disturbing vestiges from the distant past, [p. 65] the remaining questions are numerous. Some cadaster sites are of course Roman, but the identification of other traces is problematic, and it is necessary to rely on the expertise of more qualified specialists (two publications by Chouquer and Favory are mentioned in the bibliography).

When the cadaster was followed by the founding of a colony, it greatly disturbed the balance of landownership in the area: the previous owners, either dead, enslaved, or reduced to the status of peasants without land, were replaced with new ones. In other cases, the cadaster was only a simple operation of measuring the lands, and did not infringe on the status of the previous owners. On the other hand, it did not later prevent lands from changing hands and being incorporated into larger properties. The persistence of certain traces on the landscape, and particularly of certain orthogonal geometrical forms, does not mean in any way that the borders of such properties remained the same for a long time, or that the land was exploited the same way throughout time.

IV. The "Slave-Run Villa"

How were the domains of the middle and large landowners exploited during the end of the Republic and under the Principate, that is between the second century B.C.E. and the third century C.E.? The works of the agronomist writers Cato, Varro, and Columella discuss in great detail a type of estate called the *villa* (a word that, more widely, means a rural property) and which appears to have been ubiquitous in central and southern Italy, and especially in Etruria, Latium, and Campania, primarily during the second and the first centuries B.C.E. In their works, these writers explain the modus operandi of these enterprises and give advice to their intended readers, i.e., the landowners above all. In the villa, several cultures were always in practice since the peasants [p. 66] (either free men or slaves) made their living, partially, from its activities. When it was located near the coast the villa's territory was often planted with grapevines and olive trees, since wine and oil were important trade products.

The villa was not necessarily very expansive: sometimes about ten to fifty hectares, sometimes more, but without ever attaining gigantic dimensions. In his treatise *On Agriculture*, Cato discusses a specific villa, situated in the region of Casinum and Venafrum, which had twenty-five hectares of vineyards and sixty hectares of olive trees. Was this particular villa a real-life example, or a fictitious one, imagined as the prototype? Regardless, the information Cato provides about it seems valid, and in tune with other such descriptions of the time. Based on his excavations near the Orbetello

Island, Carandini evaluated the area of the lands dependent on the Settefinestre villa as being between 100 and 125 hectares. J. Kolendo held that the presence of slaves required a strict system of surveillance, and that the costs of controlling the workforce increased with the area of the lands, not in a proportional manner, but progressively. A domain cultivated by slaves did not necessarily have to be of large proportions; otherwise they were in danger of being mismanaged (but then again, it was possible for all domains to be poorly managed).

According to these treatises, the permanent workforce of the villas was essentially composed of slaves. This is the very reason why a great number of contemporary historians call them "slave villas" [*villas esclavagistes*]. The slaves working there were managed by a steward, also a slave, called the *vilicus*, who was an important person: he was part of the elite rank of slaves. From the twelve books that compose his treatise on this subject, Columella dedicated one to such a personage and another to his wife, the *vilica*, and mentioned that the vilicus was the stand-in for the master himself. The vilicus implemented the owner's orders, directed and supervised work activities, bought or borrowed the materials necessary for daily operations—the slaves' clothes [p. 67] and the food not produced on the premises. In addition, he ensured the security of the domain and he had an important role maintaining order. The downside of this relationship was that his master had to keep a close eye on him. Both Cato and Columella insist on this particular aspect of the relationship between the master and his steward. The latter compares the vilicus to an officer who commands troops in battle. And, in fact, historians have often remarked that there were many similarities between this agricultural villa and the military barracks, or even the prison.

Cato estimated that thirteen slaves were necessary to work olive groves, including the steward and his wife, and sixteen to tend a vineyard, including the steward to ensure smooth operation. Cato estimates that five of the thirteen who worked in the olive grove had no special training, and ten of the sixteen who worked in the vineyard did not. The great majority of other slaves were employed in livestock activities. Actually, in such villas, there was no cattle-breeding as such, but there were animals grown and used for labor and transportation, for grinding operations in the mills, and for meat. So, there one could find slaves in charge of such animals: cowhands, swineherds, donkey drivers, and shepherds. The actual breeding practices took place in separate areas.

This was a system of direct exploitation: the operation was conducted for the direct benefit of the owner and under his orders, even though he did not cultivate the land himself, and he had a steward who performed daily tasks for him, and in his place. The originality of the system resides in the fact that the slaves worked collectively, under the orders of the steward. If there were a lot of slaves to be managed, they were grouped in teams (sometimes called decuries), under the orders of other slaves, the team leaders (the *monitores*). Therefore, we can speak of "slavery by teams" [*esclavage par équipes*]. Some scholars also use "plantation slavery," but this expression evokes the slavery of the New World and it risks implying the existence of vast spaces dedicated to monoculture, which was not true for Roman Italy. So, it may be better to avoid this expression. [p. 68]

It seems that, according to Cato's treatise, only one woman was allowed among the slaves of the villa (the *familia rustica*) and she was the steward's wife. A century later, Varro advised the opposite, namely that the best slaves and shepherds should each be given a companion (also a slave) with whom they could then have children. Varro saw the shepherds having families and children as a positive thing: when they did, they became more attached to their herds, and their children increased the *familia* of slaves. According to Varro, the steward was not the only one to receive a *peculium* (discussed in chapter 4); it had also been granted to the team leaders, and even to the other slaves. What was its value in most of these domains? The absence of women seems very unlikely, especially under the Principate, but also at the end of the Republic, since the replenishing of the slave population could not have been achieved solely through prisoners of war and the slave trade. Internal reproduction within the domain itself seems to have been indispensable. Among the Latin authors who discuss the management of the lands, Cato is, without a doubt, the harshest on the peasant slaves. Varro, Columella, and particularly Pliny the Younger were less tough and a little more tactful. This harshness has as much to do with the times as with Cato himself. Between Cato's and Pliny's times there had likely been a change in the conditions of the slaves, and particularly in the lives of peasant slaves.

Some slaves were chained. These shackled slaves, to which a part of the owners used to resort, but not all of them, constituted what Cato in his treatise called *ergastulum*. The word ergastulum designated both the shackled slaves and the place where they were held. This underground holding cell had narrow windows, placed very high, so that the slaves could not use them to escape.

Among the thirty slaves that Cato speaks about, only the two stewards and their wives could reasonably hope to be freed one day. [p. 69] Very few of the peasant slaves were freed, especially during the Republican era. In the first and second centuries B.C.E., the great majority of slaves had no hope of ever being freed, and a large number of them must have known it. Their condition, however, varied greatly, from one category to another: together with the mining slaves, the peasants and shepherds were most certainly among the most unhappy slaves, from the material point of view.

There were, and there continue to be, debates on the geographical extent of the slave villa model. Some tend to believe that it was very dominant all over Italy and even outside Italy. Others insist on the diversity of the possible models of exploitation. The important role that agronomists attribute to this mode of exploitation shows its social and economic importance, but does not attest to its widespread practice throughout the Roman world. While the slave villa was very common in central Tyrrhenian Italy, it was certainly less frequent an occurrence elsewhere.

In the 2006 volume that Raymond Descat and I wrote together (*Esclave en Grèce et à Rome*), the "slave villa" phenomenon prompted an investigation of notions like "slave society," "means of production," and "slave economy." On that occasion, we made a distinction between slave societies and slave economies. The notion of slave society is primarily social. It is informed by the place that slaves occupy in society and, most of all, by the influence that the existing slave system exerts on the modes of thinking and practices of society as a whole. In this sense, then, it seems to us that Greco Roman antiquity was a slave society.

On the other hand, when it comes to determining the nature of the ancient economy (the Roman, for example), it is not enlightening to define it as a "slave economy." To be sure, slaves were an integral part of all, or almost all, economic sectors. But their numbers varied greatly, depending on the sectors and the historical periods: some segments and levels had many more slaves than others. In Belgian Gaul, in Lyonnaise Gaul, in Britain, in Egypt, [p. 70] the economic role of the slaves was less important than in Italy, and especially in its central and southern regions. Moreover, the slaves did not play the same role in production: they did not all have the same kind of relationship with their masters; neither did they have the same lifestyle. They did not form a social class of their own. In many sectors, the presence of slaves did not radically change the organization of production or the services that were offered. The mere fact that the domestic help working in the grand households of the Roman world were primarily slaves is not sufficient to consider this modus operandi as a category of domestic service in itself.

Should we then understand that the ancient economy was dominated by slavery? Should we infer that the "slave-based mode of operation" has shaped the entire economy? In the book I published in 2006 with R. Descat, the answer to these questions was no.

Between 50 B.C.E. and (approximately) 100 C.E. there were lots of slaves working in Italian workshops producing terra sigillata; a great number of them were managed by potters who were themselves slaves. This artisanal organization, or rather manufacturing unit, had nothing to do with "slavery by teams." They were small groups, not large teams of slaves. We find an almost identical situation when the labor force was composed primarily of free workers (freed slaves or freeborn citizens)—or when the great majority of the potters were free, as was the case in Gaul. In the production of Italian sigillata the presence of slaves was massive, but this fact did not result in the formation of a specific mode of production. The same was true for the mining workforce. Consequently, I do not believe that the mechanisms of the ancient economy were dominated, or determined, by the existence of slavery and of servile work. The social relationships were indeed affected by slavery, but economic life, in its entirety, was not. So, in this case, we cannot speak of a "slave economy." [p. 71]

The Roman economy was a preindustrial historical economy that used, in certain sectors and regions, a great number of slaves. This fact does not imply, however, that it should be considered different from other preindustrial economies because it was a "slave economy" and others were not. It is necessary to compare the details of the various economic structures, and not classify them *a priori* based on the dominant mode of production.

Yet, sometimes slavery could represent the backbone of a specific sector of production or commerce and could have, within a given field, determined the formation of certain specific modes of production, as well as engendered equally specific social relationships. This is what happened in Italy for teams of slaves, during the last centuries of the Republic and the beginning of the Principate. In fact, in the Italian peninsula and in Sicily, slavery played a central role in agriculture as well as in animal husbandry. The slaves of an agricultural undertaking were involved in all its operations; they were divided in groups according to principles similar, in some measure, to those used in the military, and they were commanded by slaves, team leaders, and *vilici*. There were also slave colonists, who had received a piece of land and were cultivating it the way small farmers and free sharecroppers did. P. Veyne insisted on the existence of this category of slave colonists, but available evidence suggests, however, that, by the end of the Republic and the beginning of the Principate, their numbers were reduced. Despite the great diversity of situations and cultures, what for the most part dominated during these years, in central and southern Italy, were teams of slaves. We are thus presented with a specific organization, founded on slavery, which existed sporadically, or not at all, where the main labor force was composed of free men. This type of organization had its own rules of operation, which have been described in great detail by, e.g., A. Carandini in his study of the Settefinestre villa. Slavery was not, however, the keystone of the entire economic system. [p. 72]

V. The Demographic Question

The spread of the slave villa system is connected to the question of numbers of slaves. The ancient cities of the Roman Empire were very mindful of the numbers of possible soldiers, taxpayers, and their fortunes. There were regular counts: this happened for example at Rome, and it was called the *census,* the population count.

Almost nothing of these numerical data has survived to us. Demography constitutes one of the most problematic aspects of ancient history because of this lack of numerical documentation. Not all the individuals were required to take part in the census in person: only the heads of the family participated and they declared the number of members of their respective households. They made known the number of dependent men, women, and children who lived with them: they also declared the number of their slaves, as well as the rest of their property. It does not seem, however, that the government made great efforts to find the total population of the Empire. Nothing suggests that the total number of slaves living in the Empire was calculated, starting with the census numbers. In fact, for fiscal reasons, it was more important to know who owned slaves and how many slaves each paterfamilias owned; in contrast, knowing the total number of slaves seemed to have no utility.

However, there survives to us a rather incomplete evidence regarding the numbers of Roman citizens for the last two centuries of the Republic and the reign of Augustus. One can therefore infer the number of slaves as a function of the number of citizens, using this information. But alas, by themselves, these numbers do not suffice. For the period of time between the beginning of the third century B.C.E. and the reign of Augustus, an entire compilation of numbers of citizens [p. 73] from various censuses were mentioned by various Latin authors, especially by Livy. In the second century, starting in 169–68 B.C.E., between 300,000 and 400,000 adult males were counted: 312,805 in 169–68; 337,022 in 164–63; 324,000 in 154–53; 318,823 in 131–30; 394,336 in 114 B.C.E., etc.

During this time not all free adults in Italy were citizens. In 89–88 B.C.E., after the Social War of 91–89, the free Italians of the peninsula (up to the Rubicon and the city of Lucca) received Roman citizenship. Not surprisingly then, the census of 70–69 B.C.E. showed a visible increase in the number of the citizens, which jumped to 900,000 or 910,000. After this date, no other census was finalized before the beginning of Augustus' reign in 28 B.C.E. Augustus explains in his *Res Gestae* that he conducted a census three times (in 28 and 8 B.C.E., then in 14 C.E.). He indicates that there were 4,063,000 citizens in the year 28; 4,233,000 in the year 8 B.C.E.; and 4,937,000 in the year 14 C.E.

How can we explain the way in which, in forty-two years, the number of citizens jumped from 910,000 to 4,063,000? It is true that during the period of Caesar's dictatorship Roman citizenship was granted to northern Italy: i.e., Cisalpine Gaul. Even allowing for the increase in the number of Roman citizens outside Italy or the founding of colonies for veterans, how can we explain this quadrupling? According to the most common opinion, that of Beloch and Mommsen, supported by Brunt and Nicolet, the counting method had changed during Augustus' time: after it, the women and children of citizens were also included, whereas before, only men were counted in the census. Following the lead of T. Frank, Lo Cascio has been recently promoting a new theory, namely that the number of adult male citizens had, indeed, grown from 910,000 to more than four million. [p. 74]

These divergent interpretations have very important consequences for the ways the total population of Italy is calculated. For the Augustan period, Brunt estimates the total population at 7,500,000 inhabitants (slaves included); Lo Cascio estimates a total population of thirteen to sixteen million (13,500,000 in 28 B.C.E., 16,400,000 in 14 C.E.), which is double! The enormity of these numbers led him to believe that the number of slaves was not as important as previously thought: for 28, he offers a number of 1,250,000 slaves (the free population, including women and children, was then about 12,250,000 inhabitants); and for 14 C.E. he suggests the existence of 1,930,000 slaves (and 14,470,000 free people).

Because of its economic wealth, which was connected to its political influence, peninsular Italy was at this time the region with the highest number of slaves. The density of the slave population in Italy was, without a doubt, greater than those of the western provinces. In the eastern Mediterranean, provinces like Egypt, for instance, did not have many slaves. At the end of his *Natural History*, Pliny the Elder engaged in a panegyric on Italy: "The land, which, among them all, is the most worthy of the best place in nature, is Italy, queen and second mother to the universe, thanks to its men, women, generals, soldiers, slaves, artistic superiority, and the celebrity of its geniuses…" (Pliny the Elder, *Natural History*, 37.76.201).

The proposed assessments are not numerous; in fact, there are only two principal ones. After long and laborious arguments, some scholars concluded that a range between 30% and 40% is acceptable. For others, the number of slaves in Italy during the Augustan period was much lower than this. According to Scheidel and Lo Cascio, the number was not higher than 10% or 15% of the entire population. While these two scholars agree on the percentage of the slaves, they disagree on their absolute numbers because, according to Lo Cascio, the population of Italy [p. 75] was much more important than according to Scheidel. The latter estimates Italy's population at around 7,000,000 inhabitants and does not think that the number of slaves could be more than 1,000,000. Lo Cascio settles on a higher number (during the Augustan period, between 1,250,000 and 1,930,000), based on a population that he also estimates as much larger in number. Brunt himself concluded that there were about three million slaves in Italy during the time of Julius Caesar and Augustus, and this is the number with which I agree, too. If Brunt is correct, the slave villa was certainly much more common in Italy during this period than Scheidel and Lo Cascio have suggested.

VI. Other Forms of Agricultural Exploitation

In the case of direct exploitation, even when the permanent labor force was composed of slaves, wage-earning workers were often involved especially for seasonal work. The landowners also could choose to have their lands worked by farmers (who paid them a fixed amount of money or produce) or by sharecroppers (who paid them a share of the harvests). The word *colonus* could be applied to both these categories with the amendment that the Latins distinguished these two categories less neatly than we do in modern or contemporary history. Yet, when a distinction was made, *colonus* was primarily used to indicate sharecroppers or peasant farmers, who were the poorest people, while the appellation of *conductor* ("successful bidder") was used to distinguish the larger farmers. In a much cited letter (*Letters*, 9.37), Pliny the Younger explained that he would be forced to lend his Tifernum Tiberinum lands to sharecroppers because the colonists had stockpiled more and more important arrears (*reliqua*), despite the fact that he had given them several reductions (*remissiones*). [p. 76]

It was also possible that the owner had part of his lands cultivated by colonists and the rest were worked in direct management by slaves led by a *vilicus*. Regardless of what we might say, this division of the estate was not very common: in the Roman period, the estate was not composed of a "reserve" and of "tenures" (as will later be the case in the Middle Ages).

Scholarship about the ancient world often regards the intensive and extensive exploitation practices of the land as being opposite to each other. The cultivator practicing intensive agriculture would not hesitate to invest large sums in capital and work, in order to achieve his goal of maximizing the productivity of his lands. Extensive agriculture, on the other hand, would be characterized by a relative reluctance of the owner to increase spending beyond what the harvests and land at a minimum required, even if the harvests might be reduced as a result. The agronomists provide very little information regarding extensive agriculture. They criticize the owners who do not take good care of their lands, who neglect them because they are absorbed by living the urban life (see for example Columella 1.3.10 and 1.3.12). Such negligence, however, cannot be confused with extensive agriculture. Extensive agriculture is a conscious strategy, and not the effect of disinterest or incompetence.

Many Roman authors, especially Columella, Pliny the Elder, and Seneca, criticized those who owned extensive lands but were not interested in their proper use, and who neglected or even abandoned them, deriving no benefit from them. These critiques have led historians to question the economic and social importance of what, in modern times, we call the "latifondo." These were very large territories belonging to absent owners, which were underexploited, abandoned to wild animals and extensive grazing, and had very low productivity. When we think of the modern "latifondo" the Latin word *latifundia* is often used. [p. 77] This term should be avoided because it is quite rare in Latin texts (only a dozen or so instances of it) and also because, in spite of appearances, it does not have the same meaning as the modern word. Capogrossi Colognesi has insisted on this point, and with good reason. When the Latins spoke of large territories subjected to extensive agriculture, they did not use this particular word: they used, e.g., the word *saltus,* which designated a vast space planted with trees and grass. The word *latifundia* was neither precise nor technical. It designated very large estates or farms, but it did not specify the particular crops planted on them. It is not true either that, during the Roman period, large, poorly managed territories (which could be compared to the modern "latifondo") were connected to slavery. They were no more related to slavery than the modern "latifondo."

VII. Evolution During the Imperial Period

As conquests expanded Roman territory, Italians moved to the new provinces to conduct affairs and some remained there permanently. In addition, old or new local elites became more and more important and some of them, upon acquiring Roman citizenship, reached the equestrian order and then moved on to the Senate. In most of the western provinces this evolution was accompanied by agricultural and land management changes. Great rural establishments appeared in the center of large land areas: we usually call them villas, as did the Latins. But how many of them were cultivated by slaves? To tell the truth, we most often ignore the composition of their workforce. These establishments did not necessarily resemble the villas described by Cato or Varro. It is difficult to gauge with precision the area of these estates; the archaeological surveys certainly overestimate [p. 78] the role of the large estates, since the smaller ones are more difficult to locate.

Most often, the foundations of these villas, massive and of good architectural quality, contained both the residence for the owner (*pars urbana*) and the work areas (*pars rustica*). Their very existence is connected to that of a commercialized agriculture. They are not limited to just one crop, primarily because the workforce had to be fed from the harvests of the estate itself. They did, however, favor one specific crop more than others—sometimes wheat, sometimes olive trees or vineyards. The North African population seems to have grown considerably under the Principate—it enjoyed great prosperity starting in the second century C.E.—and it is an impressive example of such crops. In the first century of the Principate it was already playing an important role in supplying Rome with wheat, but in the second century, in central Tunisia, immense olive orchards grew: their existence has been confirmed by the discovery of oil presses in the countryside. At the end of the second century and the beginning of the third, Tripolitania experienced similar progress in the production of olive oil. It was clearly an item destined for trade that was transported by boat, from Carthage and other African ports. Not all Africa, however, had such commercial crops. Leveau has shown that, in Caesarea (Cherchell), the provincial capital of Caesarean Mauretania, beside the Romanized countryside that was populated by such villas, there was a second type of countryside where the indigenous traditions endured and where we cannot find much evidence that commercialized agriculture was practiced.

It is difficult to outline the evolution of the rural domains under the Principate, and it is not the same in every region. Could we speak of Italy's decline? Could we speak of a decline of slavery and of the exploitation system founded on slavery (the slave villa, slavery by teams)? These questions are discussed in chapter 5, section IV, and [p. 79] in chapter 7, section II. As to the number of slaves under the Empire, it had probably declined in Italy. But did it also decline elsewhere? It is difficult to say.

On the other hand there was a tendency in the imperial period to accumulate lands, to increase the size of the estates (which did not constitute one single uninterrupted estate and were composed of several farms), and to enlarge the extent of such farms. I will discuss these topics again in chapter 7, section II.

VIII. The Grains

The crops raised in these estates were quite varied. They included legumes and green vegetables; fruits; fiber-producing plants (which I will discuss briefly in chapter 3) and all the plants used to produce perfumes or medicines. Despite this diversity, the famous Mediterranean trilogy of products prevailed: grains, olive trees, and vineyards. It is not solely because of the amphora that oil and wine often take the main stage, in ancient texts as much as in modern scholarship.

Traditionally, the Roman diet was based on grains and legumes (for example broad beans and root vegetables). Among the grains, wheat was preferentially used in Italy, formerly as a porridge (*puls*), and then as bread. In the archaic epoch durum—or hard shell wheat—and especially the *far* were popular. During the Republican period, these types were replaced by new categories of wheat called "new" or "nude," which were either soft or hard.

As conquests continued, the city of Rome grew considerably, until it numbered close to one million inhabitants. It has been calculated that at the beginning of our era, the city consumed between 260,000 and 130,000 metric tons per year. It is not surprising then that the city, and then the emperors, were [p. 80] very mindful of the need to stock enough food for the Roman population. The aediles surveyed the markets and, in times of shortage, special grain committees were named, then special magistrates—the curators of the *annona*, who were charged to address the problem of purveyance. Starting with Augustus, an equestrian administrator called the prefect of the *annona* was charged with this duty on a permanent basis.

Beginning with the tribunate of Gaius Gracchus (in 123 B.C.E.), wheat was distributed at a reduced price to free adult men living in Rome; these distributions, which gave rise to violent political debates, became free of charge starting with P. Clodius Pulcher's tribunate (58 B.C.E). This is customarily called the *annona* in classical scholarship, and by preference the Romans called these the *frumentationes*, or distributions of wheat. The wheat distributed this way came partly from taxes on the crops of certain provinces that produced a lot of grain—first Sicily and Sardinia, then Africa and, starting from the reign of Augustus, Egypt. Certainly, the distributions to a part of Rome's population required such a quantity that the Roman state had to buy other wheat from private producers and traders. In addition, people who produced wheat in Italy and in the provinces helped to ensure that the capital was fed. The problem of the wheat supply was approximately the same for the other important cities of the Empire, that is Carthage, Antioch, Alexandria, Ephesus, and later Constantinople.

The problems caused by the grain crops, and particularly wheat, were not limited only to provisioning Rome. Wheat was cultivated everywhere, and a large number of the smallholders and the colonists fed themselves and their families from the grain they cultivated themselves. Additionally, several documents show that, in small or average cities, the [p. 81] sizable landowners were important producers of grains and were selling quite a significant percentage of their harvests locally, even though they risked being accused of cornering the market, whether rightly or wrongly. In case of famine, the probability of hoarding was very high, and it was the duty of the authorities to take vigorous measures and impose sanctions if needed. At the top of the list of suspects were of course, the owners of extensive lands. Evoking the situation of Aspendos under Tiberius' reign, Philostratus wrote: "The rich have acquired all the wheat and have locked it away, to sell clandestinely outside the country" (*The Life of Apollonius of Tyana*, 1.15). The goal of this operation could also have been to sell the wheat locally but only after the prices went up. Several decades later, there was a shortage in Prusa in Bithynia, and two major landowners, one of whom was Dio Chrysostom, faced the ire of their fellow citizens for doing so (Dio, *Discourse* 46). Another episode of the fight against cornering the market has come to us via an inscription from Pisidian Antioch, in Asia Minor. This is the edict of the legate L. Antistius Rusticus (governor of the provinces of Cappadocia and Galatia), which dates from 93 C.E. I will revisit this document in chapter 6, when discussing the interventions of the Roman state and its representatives in reference to economic policy.

It has often been alleged that Italian grain cultivation had been sacrificed to the higher profit that arboriculture produced: it is necessary, however, to consider the nuances of this argument as M.S. Spurr has suggested. Although Italy did not pay taxes on agricultural products and its landowners did not have to pay wheat to the tax collectors, it cannot be said that they were not interested in wheat and other kinds of grain. Pliny the Younger, for instance, who owned vineyards and openly spoke of them in his letters, admitted to being interested not only in vineyards but also in crops of wheat, barley, broad beans, and other legumes (*Letters*, 1.20.16). [p. 82]

IX. Arboriculture

According to Pliny the Elder, two liquids could please the human body: wine on the inside, and oil on the outside (*Natural History*, 14.29.150). In addition to this connection made by Pliny between the two liquids, there are other reasons for studying both viticulture and olive crops. Together with grains, vines and olive trees constitute what is frequently called the "Mediterranean trilogy." In addition, the latter two were the object of great investments by owners of large estates and, in certain regions and periods of antiquity, they were the predominant crops (even if we still cannot speak of monocultures). The instruments and tools used for making oil and wine were partly similar, and they have been marketed extensively, across long distances. Finally, both oil and wine were transported and stocked in amphorae, which are found in great quantities in excavations and in survey campaigns.

Similarly, altitude and climate do not create a sharp distinction between vine and olive crops. Certainly vines could adapt to cooler and more humid climates than olive trees, which experienced more difficulty as they were planted away from the Mediterranean coasts. The olive tree, however, provides us with an excellent example when we want to see at one glance the importance and complexity of geographical determinism. Mitchell wrote an excellent chapter about the presence of the olive tree in Asia Minor, showing how important it is to take into account climatic factors and altitude, but arguing that some historians had given them too much influence.

In his works, Pliny related Fabianus' belief that the olive tree does not grow either in very cold or very hot regions—which is true (*Natural History*, 15.2.4). The same Pliny, however, also wrote that during his time the olive tree was cultivated in the northern Alps and had reached the [p. 83] center of Gaul and Spain (*Natural History*, 15.1.1). In Syria, olive trees in antiquity were cultivated at around 700 m (Mt. Hermon), at around 850 m in Jerusalem, at 1,000 m in Jordan (Kerak) and up to 1,200–1,300 m on the Iberian peninsula. The olive tree was certainly absent in the greater part of Asia Minor. Strabo wrote, however, that at an altitude of 1,000 m, the plain extending for sixty stades before Synnada in Phrygia was planted with olive trees. At least two other ancient texts mention the olive trees of Synnada in Phrygia, among them Claudian's poem *Against Eutropius II*. Strabo also alluded to the olive trees of the Melitene region, in Cappadocia, and to the region of Selge, which is situated at an altitude higher than

1,000 m (Strabo, *Geography* 12.2.1 and 12.7.1–3). At the beginning of the 20th century, T. Fischer wrote a book about the historical geography of the olive tree. He insisted on the importance of geographical factors (altitude and climate) and ethnic factors: the nomads of the Asian steppes, who had established permanent locations in Asia Minor, were not interested in growing trees; they were interested instead in securing pastures for their livestock; the olive tree was a crop more amenable to the Greek character. This train of thought could lead to the idea that the olive tree was not cultivated in Asia Minor until the present day. In 1975, on average, the Turks consumed 2.7 liters of oil per person per year, and the Greeks consumed 20 liters per person per year.

T. Fischer's ideas were very influential on those examining the cultivation of olive trees in Asia Minor: Louis Robert was one who adopted them. Following other erudite writers and travelers, he believed that the writings of Strabo and Claudian about Synnada were not credible: he also rejected the former's writings on Melitene. In addition to his emphasis on the geographical framework (rightly so, but a bit extreme in this particular case), Robert attributed a sort of economic permanence to Asia Minor (which became part of the Ottoman Empire, later Turkey) from antiquity until the first half of the twentieth century. He did not take into account [p. 84] that cultural factors (called by Fischer ethnic but which are, rather, cultural) could powerfully alter economic practices. In certain cases, landscape and climate do not very tightly determine the ethical mores and sensibilities of the diverse societies. More recently, archaeological discoveries have shown, without any doubt, that Strabo was correct. In Asia Minor, the olive tree was definitely a more common crop during antiquity than in the twentieth century. An ancient oil press was found in the eastern part of Cappadocia and the counterweights from presses were found in the territory of Sagalassos, in northern Pisidia, located at an altitude of 1,400 m. In the southeast part of the Sagalassos territory, in Gravgaz, palynological analyses have confirmed the presence of olive trees between the fourth century B.C.E. and the seventh or eighth century C.E. This example shows that we should not attribute too exclusive an influence to geographical factors (climate and landscape). It also shows that, quite often, despite their technological limitations and the gravity of their social hierarchies, preindustrial historical economies were very different from one another. It is easy to assume that economic life has not changed much between antiquity and the nineteenth-century Ottoman Empire, but this is a problematic way of looking at things and it could be absolutely false. Profound transformations were possible and not only because of the arrival of Christianity or Islam.

The manner in which oil and wine were marketed and traded across large distances, transported from specialized regions, has been the subject of various studies and reflections. While D.J. Mattingly, who has studied oil production extensively, mainly in North Africa, focused his analyses on the Empire's provisioning activities and conceived it as an entity with great consumption needs, others like P. Ørsted and P. Leveau insisted on the regional character of the production areas. They were, quite correctly, opposed to the idea of a monoculture (of vineyards or [p. 85] olive trees). They emphasized that for the producers, the development of arboriculture could have very easily been a way to promote their city and their province (before being a response to the demands of the Empire). They also remarked that certain regions seem to have been very prosperous, although they did not export anything of great importance or value—at least according to what we know so far. Following P. Ørsted's work, P. Leveau has called this "the passing from the ideal of commercial economy to the reality of the regional economy."

That said, because of some other factors, the histories of vineyards and of olive trees are not entirely parallel, since wine and oil do not fulfill the same cultural and social needs. After the fall of the Empire in the west, olive oil ceased to be consumed in some of the historical provinces in the northern Mediterranean area, but viticulture continued to expand up to the present.

In addition, we should not forget that wine could also be transported in barrels. The barrel or cask (*cupa),* which was widely used in the Celtic world and which, during the Principate, had gradually succeeded in replacing amphorae as storage and transportation containers and was represented on two different monuments: the columns of Trajan and of Marcus Aurelius. It did not spread as quickly in Italy as it did in the Rhine or the Danube areas. It is not widely attested there until the third century: in Rome, however, by the fourth century, it had become one of the ubiquitous objects of daily life. It is important to consider these facts when studying the evolution of the production and commercialization of wine since, unlike amphorae, the barrel is almost entirely absent from the archaeological evidence.

Between the third and the first centuries B.C.E., wine consumption greatly increased and viticulture and the role of wine changed. In Italy, starting with the time when "soft" wheat became predominant and bread replaced porridge in the Roman diet, wine became an essential dietary item, [p. 86] for the rich and the poor alike as it could more easily accompany dry foods than wet foods. At the beginning of the Principate, Rome had almost one million inhabitants, including children and slaves. A. Tchernia has estimated that the city's annual wine consumption was between 1,450,000 and 1,800,000 hectoliters—that is, on average, more than 1.5 hl per person per year. Of course, not everybody drank wine, or drank only wine. The soldiers received water mixed with a bit of vinegar (the *posca*). In the months following the harvest, Cato gave his slaves *lora*, the "second wine" obtained from passing water over the grape dregs produced by the press. In the Mediterranean world, almost all free men and women drank wine. It is important to mention, though, that it was mixed with water, and that the wine-drinking restriction for women was lifted only as of the second century B.C.E.

Amphorae enabled the preservation of wine and prevented it from spoiling. In the second century B.C.E., vintage wines became increasingly appreciated. It is also from around this century and the beginning of the next that the taste and reputation of certain vintages developed. At the end of the Republic, the most reputable Italian vintages were the Caecuba, near Fondi and Terracina, the Falernian, in northern Campania, and the Alban, the closest to Rome. A little later, those from Sorrento and Mount Gaurus, near Puteoli, were also appreciated. The oldest and most important wines were sweet, but drier wines were preferred during the imperial era. In Italy, all the best vintages were white while red wines were not produced. Red wines existed and were produced, however, in Greece and Gaul. I have remarked elsewhere that the Romans liked certain Greek wines very much, like those from Lesbos and Chios, which were an import staple. [p. 87]

Viticulture techniques progressed greatly in these same periods. The producers compared the different ways of culturing the stems (low vine, high vine, vines joined to trees). They grew careful not to mix the different grapevines and chose them on the basis of their objectives. Columella and Pliny the Elder classified grapevines in three categories, based on their aptitude for aging well, the nobility of the wines they produced, and also their fertility. After the great vines, which produced the best vintages, came those that were of secondary quality but were also productive and whose wines were of good quality. Lastly came the vines notable only for their productivity.

Recent archaeological discoveries have shown that wine- and oil-making equipment had also greatly improved during that time. This is an important fact to remember when considering technological progress in Greco-Roman antiquity. The treatment of olives required one more processing step than the handling of grapes. Both olives and grapes have to be pressed but, before this operation, the former have to go through an additional grinding process, which transforms the olive and its kernel into olive paste. The same equipment could be used for the pressing process for both products. The lever-operated press, which appeared in the Bronze Age in the eastern Mediterranean region and was later used for the processing of the grapes as of the Greek archaic period. As J.-P. Brun noted, Cato's *On Agriculture* showed that during his time, "the press that crushed the dregs weighed several tons and its maneuvering required, on one hand, a powerful supporting system of wedges, and, on the other, a complex system of pulleys and hoists." This equipment made possible the great wine and oil production of the entire Roman era, even though it went through several improvements later on—for example, the adoption of vertical screws, which [p. 88] replaced the hoists and the cables and allowed rapid raising and lowering of the lever without risk to the operator.

At the same time, mills with circular motions used to crush the olives were spreading to southern Italy; they dated in the Greek world from the fifth century B.C.E. onward. Cato described them in his work and they became ubiquitous in peninsular Italy. These grinding wheels were either hemispherical (*trapetum*), or cylindrical (*mola olearia*), and they allowed the efficient crushing of great quantities of olives (Columella, *On Agriculture,* 12.52).

Social differences, however, were extremely important. The social hierarchy was duplicated in the hierarchy of wines. Not all the producers used the most advanced techniques: these were reserved for the most fortunate and the most highly placed producers. Using simple tools, small family-sized productions endured in every region; yet, most of the time, archaeological remains offer little new information about it. Nevertheless, its production was probably not negligible from a quantitative point of view, and it was not always limited to the consumption of the producer and his family.

Viticulture and olive crops, which produced substantial profits when they were cultivated on a grand scale by means of adequate equipment, were mainly the crops of the elite. They belonged to wealthy notables who needed huge revenues and who paid attention to managing their lands, and also to adventurous businessmen who wanted to become wealthy and attain a better social position. Among these businessmen we should count the freedmen to whom Pliny the Elder paid tribute in his writings. Acilius Sthenelus, for instance, was a freedman who had very successfully managed a fifteen-hectare vineyard in the Nomentum territory and then helped grammarian Remmius Palemon replant the vineyard of a grand domain in the same city. The results were so impressive that [p. 89] after eight years the harvest of a single year was sold for 400,000 sesterces, which represented two thirds of the purchase price of the property (Pliny the Elder, *Natural History*, 14.5.48–51).

The senators and equites were all landowners, and the great majority of them owned vineyards. This was the case at least in the wine-producing regions. For example, at the end of the Republic, Publius Sestius, whom Cicero defended in court in the *Pro Sestio*, owned lands in the city of Cosa. It was probably Sestius' villa, or that of a neighbor, that A. Carandini and his students excavated at the site of Settefinestre. The remains of the villa showed clear signs of the presence of vines and olive trees. After talking about Remmius Palemon, Pliny the Elder added that Seneca later bought, for a very high price, these very vineyards whose productivity had been increased by the good care of Acilius Sthenelus. His nephew, Pliny the Younger, owned vineyards in the Tiber valley, at Tifernum Tiberinum, and thought about buying others, close to the lands he already owned (Pliny the Younger, *Letters*, 3.19). These senators and equites did not live on their lands but they visited them from time to time and especially during harvesting. The fact that they lived in the city, and most often in Rome, does not mean that they had no interest in their lands and the revenues they received from them. It is true, however, that some were more interested in these lands and their management than others.

A hypothesis has caught on during the last decades, according to which the owners of vineyards and olive trees actively participated in the commercialization of their productions: this was particularly true for senators or equites. The archaeologists of Settefinestre have said and repeated it as for the senator Publius Sestius. I am not convinced by this hypothesis: in any case, not as it applies to the senators. When it comes to wine and oil no reliable evidence supports the idea that the producer also played the role of the merchant, or that the merchant was usually a dependent of the producer. This topic was also addressed in chapter 1, section III, and the reader is asked to consult that section. [p. 90]

Olive oil served several functions. Obviously it was part of the daily diet, but it was also used for body care (men covered themselves with it before physical exercise, and massages with or without perfumes were used after the bath), for pharmaceutical purposes, and in veterinary care. It was also used as fuel for oil lamps, and as grease to lubricate leather, etc. Different types of oil had different uses. For example, oils from green olives were used primarily in perfumes and pharmaceuticals; oil made from mature olives was reserved for human consumption; and the oil used in lamps was usually the result of a second pressing.

Most of the time, amphorae were used to transport and preserve wine, olive oil, and fish products (salted fish preserves and fish sauces), but certain amphorae could also be used to store fruits. A certain type of amphorae from the Lipari Islands and used for transporting alum has recently been identified and studied. In this section we are only discussing oil and wine amphorae: we will address those used for curing and for fish sauces in the last section of this chapter.

The pioneering scholar of Roman amphorae studies was the epigraphist Heinrich Dressel, whom Theodor Mommsen asked to study the inscriptions on the *instrumentum domesticum* of Rome, at the end of the nineteenth century. After reading the marks and the painted inscriptions on a great number of amphorae found in Rome, and especially those from Monte Testaccio that were known at that time, Dressel published his findings in volume 15 of the *Corpus Inscriptionum Latinarum* (*CIL*). Monte Testaccio is a hill 35 meters high, formed at the end of the harbor area of the Tiber River by the accumulation of the remains of Baetican oil amphorae. Dressel attached to his publication an illustrated list of the types of amphorae he studied: this visual representation of the Roman amphorae, known as Dressel's Typological Table, [p. 91] is still widely referenced today; it represents the first attempt to classify the various types of Roman amphorae.

The marks inscribed on pottery before firing were usually the name or initials of the producer of the amphora's contents or the manufacturer of the amphora itself. The painted inscriptions, added after the amphora was fired, provided information on the commercialization stage of the container: the names of the merchants, and sometimes the nature of the products transported. In the last thirty or forty years, our knowledge of the types of amphorae has experienced great strides, thanks to excavations on land and of shipwrecks. The study of the forms and inscriptions was supplemented with findings informed by the study of pastes contained within. In addition, many ateliers manufacturing amphorae were found: they provide substantial information on the origins of these different categories of amphorae.

The first wine amphorae manufactured in Italy were called "Greco-Italian" and, at the end of the third and during a part of the second century B.C.E., they were used to transport wine produced on the Tyrrhenian coast of Italy, from Etruria to Campania. In the 130s B.C.E. they evolved into a different type, the Dressel 1, which was produced in the same regions and which dominated the market for almost a century before being replaced by the Dressel 2–4. It is during the period of Dressel 1 that the export of wine produced in the Tyrrhenian part of central and southern Italy reached its peak, especially in the direction of Gaul. Excavations of the Saône riverbed at Chalon-sur-Saône, and also at the Atax and the site of Old Toulouse brought to light hundreds of thousands of fragments of Dressel 1 amphorae. A great part of these wine amphorae exported to Gaul were intended for the use of Roman soldiers, but many of them were found in the Gallic *oppida,* indicating that the Gauls had consumed their contents. [p. 92]

The Gauls were very fond of wine, and particularly so their chiefs who, during this period, found in it a method of displaying their wealth and generosity, in militaristic and religious rituals and large festivals of redistribution. Diodorus Siculus evoked these practices and emphasized the great profits that these exchanges (developed well before Caesar's conquest of Gaul) brought to the Italian traders. On this point see the text "An Unequal Exchange: An Amphora for a Slave (First Century B.C.E.)," included at the end of chapter 5 below (Diodorus, 5.26.3). At the same time—the end of the second century and during the first—the Adriatic coast (Picenum and Apulia) also produced wine that was transported in amphorae called Lamboglia 2, widely exported in the east: on the eastern coast of the Adriatic, the Aegean Sea, Thrace, Asia Minor, and even in Egypt.

Starting with the beginning of the Principate, the shapes of Italian amphorae changed, and the products exported did not necessarily originate from the same regions. After Apulian oil, which was transported in amphorae named for Brindisium, it was the Istrian oil that was later exported in Dressel 6B amphorae. On the Adriatic coast, the new wine amphorae were the Dressel 6A, and on the Tyrrhenian coast, the Dressel 2–4, which were an imitation of the Cos amphorae. The fundamental characteristics of this latter type were widely adopted both inside and outside of Italy, but with enough regional variations to allow an identification of their place of origin. At the end of the first century C.E., as the Dressel 6A started to disappear, various types of amphorae with a flat bottom started being produced in northern Italy and the Tiber valley, and they were used until the third century.

As has already been mentioned above, wine and oil production spread to various provinces, causing several types of amphorae to appear in these regions. For oil, the best known ones are the Tripolitanian amphorae and particularly Dressel 20, which were used to transport the oil from Baetica. Starting with the end of the Republic, for wine, Pascual 1 amphorae appeared in Tarraconensis, [p. 93] followed by the Oberaden 74 with flat bottom and the Dressel 2–4. In Gaul, a type of amphora with flat bottom, the Gauloise 4, became the most used starting in the middle of the first century C.E., and it was widely exported.

Taking into account the number of amphorae found in various archaeological sites, in Italy (particularly in Ostia and Rome), in Gaul and elsewhere, it is possible to estimate the importance of various exporting regions—not in absolute numbers, but comparatively—and to appreciate the evolution of their roles. It is particularly fascinating to know the origin of the products consumed in the great megalopolis that was Rome and its two ports, Ostia and Portus. For the last thirty years, this topic inspired the main research of amphora specialists like C. Panella. When analyzing wine amphorae, it is certainly important to remember that during the Principate, the barrel played an increasingly important role, too. It is also important to remember that certain wines consumed in Rome were produced in the center of Italy and arrived in the capital via the Tiber River, which means that their presence could not be discovered in Ostia or in the southern part of the city. In addition, the results of counting have evolved as new excavations had to be taken into consideration. But these methodological limitations being taken into consideration, these counts provide us with suggestive evidence. They show that very important changes took place between the first century B.C.E. and the first century C.E. Looking at wine, for example, the extensive exports to Gaul from central Tyrrhenian Italy greatly diminished starting with the very beginning of Augustus' reign. It was the end of the Dressel 1 amphorae and of the boom of Tyrrhenian wine.

This change is comparable to the case of oil, even if Italian oil was never sold as extensively as wine in the period of Dressel 1 vessels. At the end of the Roman Republic, it was the Campanian oil—especially that from Venafrum—used in the perfume industry that was the most famous in Italy. On the other hand, the Brindisium amphorae, containing oil made in Apulia, were exported outside Italy, [p. 94] and 600 stamped handles are presently housed in the Alexandria Museum in Egypt: other oil amphorae, "the ovoid amphorae of the Republic," were also exported. After their disappearance during the Augustan period, Dressel 6B amphorae used to transport Istrian oil were documented up to the first half of the second century (but in the direction of Magdalensberg or the Danube, and not in the Mediterranean area). In the course of this same period certain provinces acquired an increasingly important role in supplying regions in central Italy, including Rome, Baetica (with the Dressel 20 amphorae), then Tripolitania, Proconsular Africa, and Mauretania. The production of Baetican oil is well known thanks to various texts (Pliny, *Natural History*, 15.3.8, and Columella, 5.8.5), from inscriptions by *diffusores* or *mercatores olearii* (see for example *CIL* VI.1625, 1935, 29722), and most of all, thanks to very numerous spherical amphorae (Dressel 20) that served to transport oil to Rome, in the Rhone valley, in the Rhine area, and everywhere else in the Mediterranean basin. I have mentioned earlier that debris from this type of amphora formed an entire hill in Rome, known as Monte Testaccio. Baetican oil was sold in very large quantities in these amphorae and, starting with the reign of Septimius Severus, it was distributed free of charge to the plebs. North African oil, partially provided as tax (Caesar, *The African War*, 97) was transported in cylindrical amphorae whose dissemination started at the end of the first century C.E. and which became predominant in the course of late antiquity. This extensive production required the presence of a multitude of manufacturing sites situated in towns (Thuburbo Maius, Madaurus) and in the countryside, where there were many large manufacturing sites containing six to twelve presses, especially in Tripolitania, Proconsular Africa (Henchir el Kousset, Bir Sgaoun), and in Mauretania Sitifensis.

These observations on the evolution of sales of Italian wine and oil are important to remember when considering the issue of possible commercial competition between Italy and the provinces in general, or between Italy [p. 95] and specific provinces, and especially when considering the theory of an eventual Italian economic "crisis." We will revisit this topic in chapter 5, section IV.

X. Livestock

Varro carefully divided livestock in two categories: field livestock (*agrestis*), and farm livestock (*villatica*) (*On Agriculture*, 3.1.8). The first category is what we now call large-animal breeding: horses, bovines, sheep and goats, and pigs. The second category includes small-animal husbandry: poultry, bees, fish, birds (thrushes, peacocks, pigeons, doves, etc.), dormice, snails, and even game (hares, wild boars, deer) when they were kept in gaming reserves. Honey was an important product because it was the only available sweetener. During Varro's time, the whole of this small-animal husbandry had become very profitable, especially if the breeders owned lands near important cities like Rome. A part of this product was used in luxury items. If Varro called it *villatica pastio*, that meant it was practiced in farm buildings or near them, and thus close to its agricultural activities. On the contrary, according to Roman tradition and in many regions of the Empire, larger livestock were separated from agricultural endeavors: the grazing grounds of the livestock were sometimes far away from cultivated fields. This is a characteristic of ancient breeding and a reality that has been often emphasized. To some degree, this preference made the use of manure difficult and made the presence of burden beasts necessary in the agricultural areas of estates. As is also true in the modern period, having such animals handy was very important to farmers.

Nevertheless, in the studies carried out in the last two or three decades, less emphasis than before has been placed on the lack of manure for agriculture [p. 96] and on the lack of fodder to feed the animals. Archaeozoology, which studies ancient animal remains, has revised some of the previously accepted theories. Likewise, transhumance also constituted an important object of study, and rightly so, since many questionable ideas are connected to it. In the past, it received too much importance. In fact, some scholars tended to believe that, in antiquity, all forms of large livestock involved transhumance—which is incorrect—or that long-distance transhumance was a constant phenomenon and, so to speak, eternal, which is also not true. In Spain and in southern Italy at the beginning of the modern era, transhumance was greatly developed, as per the demands of the reigning political powers, and primarily for fiscal reasons. When transhumance was practiced in antiquity it was sometimes done over very small distances. Thus, after discussing sheep traveling from Apulia up to Samnium, Varro moves on to discuss the mules of Reate, whose trip was, by contrast, very short (*On Agriculture*, 2.1.16–17).

Often, various types of livestock could be found sharing the same areas. Strabo, for example, mentions bovine breeding in Baetica, even though it was wool that the area was famous for (Strabo, 3.2.6; Pliny the Elder, 8.73.191). On several sites in Catalonia, evidence was found indicating the presence of bovines, as well as that of sheep, goats, and pigs. Surely, archaeozoology very often supplies more information on consumptive practices than it does on the livestock themselves. After all, information on consumption is enabled by the presence, in those respective locations, of gaming and breeding activities. On the other hand, archaeozoology is less developed in Italy, Greece, and Turkey than in the more northern regions (Germany, Holland, England, and France). Thus, even though it draws its origin from Greece and Italy, the development of livestock practices is presently better evidenced in the northwestern provinces of the Empire. In these latter regions, the study of animal remains has shown that bovines and [p. 97] horses of the Roman era had developed into bigger sizes than their counterparts in the Iron Age and the Middle Ages. It also showed that bovines, although traditionally raised as beasts of burden, were also raised for their meat. In the regions of central Italy, pork certainly mattered more than beef, and gourmands like Apicius priced pork over beef: in Diocletian's *Edict*, the price of beef was lower than that of pork. Despite this fact, however, the studied remains showed that under the Empire the consumption of beef was not negligible.

As to horses, which were not used for human consumption, they were very likely fewer in numbers, but it is important not to underestimate their value, notably for transportation and in wars.

Up until the beginning of the Principate, the breeding of pigs in Italy was a kind of monopoly of the Cisalpine region. Numerous pieces of evidence show that, later, under the Principate, it increased as the place of meat in the daily diet also grew. Columella, for example, accorded more importance to these practices than his literary predecessors. The Emperor Aurelian added pork to the public distributions of wheat, and this act shows the increased importance, starting in the third century, of this animal in the diet of the capital's inhabitants.

A significant portion of the meat for consumption came from the animals sacrificed during religious rites (but not the whole of it). After the sacrifice, this meat became profane again, meaning it lost its sacred or religious nature and, as the jurisconsult Trebatius noted, "returned to the provision and propriety of men" (Macrobius, *Saturnalia*, 3.3.4). It passed into the hands of butchers and was sold at the daily meat markets, that is, at the *macellum*, in the cities that had such a marketplace. [p. 98]

XI. Fishing and Preserving Fish

To the products of agriculture and livestock we need to add those from fishing, which was practiced both at sea and in rivers and lakes. Naturally, fishing ensured that fresh fish was available for consumption, but it also provided the necessary products for the preparation of salted and dried fish, of salted fish preserved in brine and smoked fish, not to mention for the preparation of fish sauces.

The preparation that is most cited in ancient texts is *garum*. It was a sauce roughly resembling the Vietnamese "nuoc-mam," and it was very much appreciated by the ancients. It was the product of the autodigestion of pieces of various fish (for example tuna, mackerel, or sardines) by the diastases present in their own digestive tracts, treated with an antiseptic—salt—to prevent further putrefaction. The proportion of salt to that of fish had to be between a quarter and an eighth part. From these numbers it is clear that the factories in which such sauces were made generally existed near saltworks. The brine was placed in large containers, outdoors, and the *garum* was extracted after a certain time. Such fish-based sauces were transported in amphorae, some of which were marked with inscriptions indicating their specific contents. Some of the words that could be discerned include *hallec* or *allec* (which is mentioned in Plautus' comedies and designated the garum's residue, a product that enjoyed low esteem and was consumed by the poor), or the *muria* (a particularly salty sauce, much less expensive than garum), or *liquamen* (a variety of garum, whose defining characteristics we do not know).

In addition to sauces, palaeoichthyological studies and studies of amphora inscriptions have shown the importance of fish preserves, in salt or in brine—preserves of which the ancient texts speak much less than they do of sauces. Traditionally, both these types of fish by-products have been prepared in the Crimea and on the coast of [p. 99] the Sea of Azov. They were transported by the Phoenicians and then produced by the Punics (Polybius, 4.38.4). Later, they were manufactured in various regions of the Mediterranean and even on the Atlantic coast. In the western part of the Empire, one of the most renowned manufacturing regions was the Iberian peninsula. Sites of production have been identified in the southern part of the peninsula, from the mouth of the Sucro River, south of Valencia in Tarraconensis, up to the mouth of the Tagus, in Lusitania. Some more sites have been discovered in the northwestern region of the peninsula, in the Spanish provinces of Pontevedra, La Corona, Lugo, and Oviedo. Robert Étienne, who together with F. Mayet studied these Iberian fish preserves and sauces, was particularly interested in a very famous type of garum called the *garum sociorum* (that is, the "garum of the associates"). Étienne believed that this product was manufactured, in any case, at the end of the Republic and beginning of the Empire, by a company of publicans who had received exclusive development rights for the Iberian saltworks. In fact, the preparation of these fish preserves and sauces required great quantities of salt, and was thus closely dependent on the salt production.

But the Iberian peninsula is not the only region where we are cognizant of such activities. We know that garum and other sauces and preserves were prepared in the west, on the Campanian coast, at Pompeii (by the business of A. Umbricius Scaurus, in the first century C.E.), on the shores of Languedoc, and in Mauretania. In the east, the fish products of the Euxine Sea and the Propontid continued to be very famous during the Principate, and cities like Sinope, Amastris, Tieion, Heraclea Pontica, and Chalcedon were famous for these activities. Together with oil and wine, fish preserves and sauces are the best-known food products from antiquity because of the amphorae in which they were stored and transported and the epigraphical information the amphorae provide. Even though they played a small part in family budgets, it is necessary to [p. 100] pay close attention to them because they were greatly appreciated in antiquity and they represented an important product for long-distance commercial transport, from one corner of the Mediterranean to the other.

Texts

Raising Sheep in Lycaonia (Asia Minor)

> [Wild asses graze there,] though there is a great scarcity of water; and even where it is possible to find water, the wells are the deepest in the world, just as in Soatra, where the water is actually sold (this is a village-city near Garsaura). But still, although the country is unwatered, it is remarkably productive of sheep; but the wool is coarse, and yet some persons have acquired very great wealth from this alone. Amyntas had over three hundred flocks in this region… In this neighborhood is also Iconium, a town that is well settled and has a more prosperous territory than the above-mentioned ass-grazing country. This place was held by Polemon.
>
> Strabo 12.6.1, translated by H.L. Jones (Loeb Classical Library, 1969)

Rebates on the Price of Grapes in Italy

This regulation dates to the start of the second century C.E. On this text see A. Tchernia, "La vente du vin," in E. Lo Cascio, ed., *Mercati Permanenti e Mercati Periodici nel Mondo Romano* (Bari, 2000): 199–209.

> Caius Plinius to his dear Calvisius:
>
> Other people visit their estates to come away richer than before, but I go only to return the poorer. I had sold my grape harvest to the dealers, who were eager to buy, [p. 101] when the price quoted at the time was tempting and prospects seemed good. Their hopes were frustrated. It would have been simple to give them all the same rebate, but hardly fair, and I hold the view that one of the most important things in life is to practice justice in private as in public life, in small matters as in great, and to apply it to one's own affairs no less than to other people's. For if we say with the Stoics that "all offenses are equal" the same applies to merits. Accordingly I returned to everyone an eighth of the sum he had spent so that "none should depart without a gift of mine." [Virgil, *Aeneid* 5.305] Then I made a special provision for those who had invested very large sums in their purchase, since they had been of greater service to me and theirs was the greater loss. I therefore allowed everyone whose purchases had cost him more than 10,000 sesterces a tenth

of anything he had spent above the 10,000, in addition to the original eighth which was a sort of general grant.

I am afraid I have put it badly; let me try to make my calculations clearer. Suppose someone had offered the sum of 15,000—he would receive an eighth of 15,000, plus a tenth of 5,000. Moreover, in view of the fact that some people had paid down large installments of what they owed, while others had paid little or nothing, I thought it most unfair to treat them all with the same generosity in granting a rebate when they had not been equally conscientious in discharging their debts. Once more, then, I allowed another tenth of the sum received to those who had paid. This seemed a suitable way both of expressing my gratitude to each individual according to his past merits, and of encouraging them all not only to buy from me in the future but also to pay their debts. [p. 102]

My system—or my good nature—has cost me a lot, but it has been worth it. The whole district is praising the novelty of my rebate and the way in which it was carried out, and the people I classified and graded instead of measuring all with the same rod, so to speak, have departed feeling obliged to me in proportion to their honest worth and satisfied that I am not a person who "holds in equal honor the wicked and the good." [Homer, *Iliad* 9.319]

Pliny the Younger, *Letters* 8.2
[p. 103]

Chapter 3
Manufacturing Activities

When ancient authors talk about different economic activities, they usually make a distinction between agriculture and commerce, or between agriculture, animal husbandry, and commerce. Most frequently, however, they ignore what we call handicraft, manufacturing, industry, or more generally, the secondary sector, that is, the activities connected with manufacturing from raw materials. In the preface to his *On Agriculture,* for instance, Cato the Elder compares agriculture to commerce and to moneylending, but he does not say anything about manufacturing activities. Enumerating the possible occupations that a future slave could pursue if he was not killed at the moment of his capture, Horace mentions agriculture, raising livestock, and trade (Horace, *Epistles*, 1.16.70–72). In the fourth century C.E., Basil of Caesarea, in one of his letters, distinguishes only two substantial kinds of occupational activities: trade and agriculture (*Letters*, 2.2). In another work (*Letters*, 18), he distinguishes three, but always ignoring manufacturing: agriculture, maritime transportation, and military mercenaries. In a passage from the *Spartan Sayings* (*Agesilaus*, 72), Plutarch talks about blacksmiths, carpenters, masons, and other men of business (*technai*), but he does not group them in one category of artisans. And, while it is interesting to note this way of thinking, explaining it proves quite difficult.

According to ancient Roman traditions, manufacturing activities took place within the home, in the family. Nevertheless, the early appearance of certain professional colleges (as early as the reign of Numa Pompilius, according to some Latin texts) suggests that [p. 104] early in the archaic period, manufacturing activities were also carried out for the public, by specialized workers, as occupations per se. And, based on recent archaeological finds, we know today that, as early as the eighth century B.C.E., there were potters and specialized bronze workers in Latium. Later, alongside these domestic and professional artisans bigger ateliers developed, particularly starting with the third and second centuries B.C.E. Artisanal activities usually took place in city-centers and second-rate towns, and the resulting products were, quite often, sold in the same premises where they had been produced. As to the big workshops, which—without exaggerating—we could call manufacturing facilities, they could be found in the countryside (especially as part of the great rural domains), or in the middle of the big cities—according to the sectors of activity and regions. The elite land owners were, on average, more interested in workshops and premises located in the countryside than in those situated in the crowded urban areas. For example, the fabrication of the amphorae, bricks and tiles took place preferentially in the countryside, while the fabrication of tableware took place in the cities. We should not, however, consider this distinction to be firmly fixed.

When considering these activities, should we label them as artisanal, as manufacturing, or industrial? Of course there were many artisans in the Roman Empire, but to use the word "artisanal" to label this entire secondary sector seems to us reductive. On the other hand, to call them "industrial" brings to mind unwanted modern overtones. It is for this reason that we have chosen instead to speak here of "manufacturing" and "manufacturing activities," terms through which the different aspects of the secondary sector in antiquity can be accurately expressed.

Such activities are very varied, and the abundance and the nature of the documents that address them differ greatly, according to the sectors. When a part of the objects described was conserved, as was the case with terracotta, glass objects, and ingots, the available documentation [p. 105] was more abundant than in the case of perishable objects like textiles and wood. Among the products that have persisted to our time, some carry marks, painted inscriptions or graffiti more or less visible and more or less substantial, which could not have happened with the other products. The marks, called "stamps" in English (both "estampilles" or "timbres" in French, "Stempeln" in German, and "bolli" in Italian), were printed on the objects before baking. The bricks and the tiles were often marked with such stamps, which are particularly interesting in the Rome region, in the second and third centuries C.E. Arretine sigillata were also similarly marked. Unlike them, the African red slip ware and certain types of oil lamps were not marked at all.

On the other hand, literary and legal texts, inscriptions in stone, writing tablets, and papyri offer more information on some activities than others. The varied sources are the objects of different areas of scholarship: general examinations of manufacturing during the Roman era are not very numerous, and they are sometimes too generalized, too removed from the specific problems raised by the specific documentation. In this chapter, we are trying to avoid this pitfall. The opposite pitfall would of course be to detail each activity minutely, but without managing to go beyond the juxtaposition of the studies of details.

So, how could we classify the different manufacturing sectors? We will be successively discussing five of its sectors, some which appear to have been particularly important, and some of which are relatively well known. These are: textiles, glass, mining and metallurgy, stone quarries and building trade, and finally, terracotta objects. The latter are themselves divided into three categories: bricks and tiles, oil lamps, and ceramic tableware. [p. 106]

Of course, there are other less central but similarly interesting sectors that we could consider, sectors that have benefitted from recent discoveries. However, in the limited space of this volume, it is impossible to mention all manufactured products. Apart from the five sectors which we have noted, we will also discuss tanning and the perfume industry, albeit briefly. Archaeologically speaking we know very few places where tanning was practiced: one in Liberchies (Belgium), perhaps one in Saepinum (Italy), and one in Pompeii (I, ins. 5). This last was identified with certainty because of the tools characteristic of the trade, and the alum amphorae, that were found there.

Like dyeing shops, tanneries used alum. P. Borgard's recent discoveries on the uses of alum have greatly contributed to our knowledge of tanneries, as well as of fabric dyeing. We will shortly speak of it again, in connection with fabric dyeing.

J.-P. Brun's most recent studies focused on the manufacture of perfumes: he has identified and studied perfume factories at Delos and Paestum. Beyond locating perfume factories and their manufacturing techniques, Brun was interested in the price of perfumes (based on information provided by ancient authors), and the social rank of the professionals who made them (called, e.g., *unguentarii*). Under the Empire, the most expensive perfume was the Judean Balm, extracted from the sap of the balsam fir tree, that was apparently introduced in Italy in the first century C.E. (Pliny the Elder, *Natural History*, 12.54.111–13). According to Pliny, it cost roughly two hundred denarii a liter. Even a relatively modest perfume like Campanian Rose cost eight denarii a liter, which was the equivalent of four days' salary for a farmhand. (The liter was, of course, not a Roman unit of measure: I use it here to illustrate my point.) [p. 107]

I. Textiles

We start with textiles, the first of the five sectors mentioned above. We know how important this sector is for the study of medieval economics or of early modern times. For antiquity, unfortunately, textiles are less in evidence: until recently, relevant archaeological remains were nearly unknown. Information began accruing, though, starting with the most recent excavations like those at Hadrian's Wall (in a damp preservation context) and those in the eastern Egyptian desert (an arid context). Technical studies of the textiles themselves have greatly progressed in the last quarter of a century under the guidance of J.-P. Wild. An Oxyrhynchus papyrus, commented on by P. Van Minnen (*P. Oxy*. Hels. 40), suggested that the quantities of clothes produced were much higher than previously believed. In addition, the collection of the available texts has been recently studied in greater detail.

Most often, it was the women who worked in the textile industry since such work entailed spinning; weaving was a more complex process and was done by men. Some women of high social rank practiced spinning and even weaving in their own homes: these activities were considered their prerogative (see Suetonius, *Augustus*, 64 and 73). Others, slaves or free individuals, worked in actual professional workshops. Pausanias, for example, wrote that one could encounter many women in Patras, the great majority of whom made a living working with linen (7.21.7). It would be incorrect to believe that, under the Empire, the majority of the population produced their garments in their homes: even in the poorer environments this was not the case. Spinning was a more domestic occupation than weaving. It is also important to remember that, in antiquity, garment making was not separated from weaving. As J.-M. Carrié notes, "the ancient garment was born directly from [p. 108] weaving, as a unique piece shaped from the beginning according to the use for which it was destined" (*Antiquité tardive*, 12 [2004]: 20).

On the other hand, several other types of textiles existed in antiquity: wool, linen (which, in Egypt at least, was much more expensive than wool), and hemp. Of these, wool was the most common. Flax crops were very well adapted to the marshy lands close to the coasts—for example, in the Nile Delta, or in Colchis (Herodotus, 2.105). Besides being well situated for the cultivation of flax, the location of these coastal regions meant that they were also well positioned for the export of flax via maritime transportation.

In *The Corrupting Sea*, P. Horden and N. Purcell observe that, in preindustrial economies, while textile production could be very important, as was the case later in the Middle Ages, this does not require us to conclude there should be a march toward an industrial revolution. The textile sector is one of those where the teleological tendency has been the most sensitive and had the most damaging effects. In antiquity, this tendency was most visible vis-à-vis the "consumer city" model that I talked about in the first chapter, which prompted the question whether producing cities existed during this time.

In this regard, as a note of caution, please note that when the ancients praised the products of a city, they were considering the entire territory of the city. Ancient cities were composed of an urban center (often very small) and the surrounding rural territory. Fabrics or vases were not necessarily produced in the city center: the production ateliers could, very easily, be found in suburbs, in villages or in the rural territory that belonged to the city. Such testimony does not provide accurate information as to the location (urban or rural) of the manufacturing processes. When sufficient evidence exists, we can see that both cases are possible: in Britain, textile production seemed to have been mostly rural; in Gaul, it took place mostly in towns and villages; in Egypt, between the second and the fourth centuries, the village economy [p. 109] went through a great depression as specialized activities concentrated, henceforth, in the cities.

However, regardless of the urban or rural territory that produced them, it is clear that some cities were important textile centers, and that their production exceeded local needs. Was this the case with Pompeii, as W.O. Moeller suggested, and then W. Jongman refuted? It is not certain. However, for the second century B.C.E., F. Coarelli found signs of such an activity at Fregelles, and for a much later period, A. Wilson also found evidence of its presence at Timgad, in Numidia.

At Timgad, excavated between 1908 and 1913 by A. Ballu and in the 1930s by M. Christoflé, twenty-two establishments displaying signs of textile activities were found, representing double the amount found at Pompeii. Seventeen of these establishments were found in the same area: the northeast quarter of the city, which seems to have been almost entirely dedicated to such activities (which could be explained by odors and prevailing winds). As was customary during the time when these excavations were performed, no stratigraphic survey was done. So, for the moment, it is very difficult to date these manufacturing premises. They do not go as far back as the foundation of the colony of Timgad (100 C.E.) because some of these premises occupy half of an "islet": at the city's early stages the islets were divided into eight sections, not two. They seem to have functioned at the same time. The *terminus ante quem* is the destruction of Timgad in 535 C.E., following the Aurès' revolt under Vandal king Honoric. It is also possible that they date from a much earlier time, like the third or the fourth century C.E.

In addition, two inscriptions were found at Timgad concerning a *forum vestiarium adiutricianum* (*AE* 1909, 4), which indicates that another textile center existed there previously (because of the meaning of *adiutricianum,* "auxiliary," "complementary"). The placement of these textile centers is not self-evident, but the problem of their location is less important than even their existence. Did the spinning [p. 110] take place in Timgad? In any case, this textile production does not seem to be intended for this one city: and the laundry facilities discovered there could not have been intended for the use of the city alone. The region was also home to sheep transhumance. Garments made in Numidia are mentioned in Diocletian's *Edict.* The nearby presence of Lambaesis, where the Third Legion was stationed until the Tetrarchy, makes it safe to assume that Timgad was supplying the army.

At Cuicul an inscription was also discovered confirming the existence of a fabric market (*basilica vestiaria*). As to the Syrian province, the local wool was worked in many cities of the interior. In Asia Minor, the presence of textile occupations (dyers, fullers, wool weavers and merchants, linen and silk workers) is attested in many places. Additionally, cities such as Ephesus, Thyatira, Laodicea, and Tarsus are well known for their textile activities. In the *Description of the Whole World and Its Peoples,* a very rhetorical and laudatory piece of writing, which is intended to praise the cities it mentions, a certain number of these cities are described as "having distinguished themselves through the abundance of their [textile] productions" in various provinces of the Empire.

A not-inconsiderable part of textile production took place in ateliers in private households, or having the same size as that of households. This is actually one of the reasons why we have difficulty finding traces of this kind of activity: textile production spread around the city is difficult to document if extensive excavations are not undertaken. In Timgad, the workshops were grouped in a quarter, as at Sabratha the dried fish premises were established, but this was not always the case elsewhere.

On the other hand, it is important to distinguish carefully between ordinary and luxury textiles (of which we know a little more). The former were manufactured widely (which, as we have just seen, did not exclude the existence of more important centers), and especially close to [p. 111] the coast, hence the significant role of islands like Djerba or Malta. Depending on the evolutionary patterns of the population and its concentration in certain centers of consumption, textile production increased or decreased. Recent studies appear to show that while complex and innovative weaving methods were used under the Principate to produce daily items for the general public, the production equipment itself did not necessarily go through a major transformation.

Textiles of quality were characterized by a very great variety, and they were preserved for a long time (this is what M. Lombard has called the "hoarding of fabrics" for the Middle Ages). Tax rates such as that of Zarai and price-lists such as Diocletian's *Edict on Prices* illustrate the great variety of luxury fabrics (45% of the *Edict* is dedicated to textiles, garments, and their accessories). Such fabrics were manufactured in specialized centers. From the fourth century B.C.E. silk fabric was made in Cos; by the end of the Republic and the beginning of the Empire, these Cos-produced fabrics were famous all over Italy. Other fabrics, whose weft contained gold thread, were the specialty of the old kingdom of Pergamum (Pliny, *Natural History*, 33.19.66).

In addition to the textile operations, we need to mention dyeing facilities. Three types of colorants were used, depending on the manner by which the dye was fixed in the fabric. Some ("the substantive dyes") fixed themselves based on the natural affinity between the coloring agent and the material to be dyed. Some ("the colorants containing mordant") needed the help of mordant agents to affix themselves to the cloth: alum was such an agent. Finally, certain colorant agents needed a chemical reaction to affect the color of the material durably: they are the so-called vat dyes. Our present knowledge of textile dyeing was greatly revolutionized [p. 112] by P. Borgard's discovery. He understood that the amphorae labeled "Richborough 527" were used to transport alum produced on the Lipari Islands. In the places where many such amphorae are found, textile activities necessarily took place as well (even though alum could also have been used in a tannery, as was mentioned earlier). This mordant agent was also found at Pompeii, in the dyeing facility V 1, 4, and in the tannery I, ins. 5; it was also found at Padua, which Strabo described as a big textile center. On the other hand, a large quantity was found at Arles, which is surprising: could this discovery be somehow connected to the sheep being raised at Crau?

II. Glassmaking

Glassmaking and metallurgy have one factor in common: they both use a technological process composed of two distinct and successive phases. In both cases, the first phase (primary glassmaking and primary metallurgy) results in an intermediary raw material: masses of unrefined glass for glassmaking, metal ingots for metallurgy. From these intermediary materials the final products are then shaped: perfume vases, tableware, small containers, window panes, etc., in the case of secondary glassmaking and spoons, knives, pipes, weapons, etc., in the case of secondary metallurgy.

These industries share another thing in common: once used, or used and broken, both glass and metal objects could, as much as possible, be recycled to create other objects. Certain ancient texts mention this glass recycling practice (for example, Martial, 1.41.3–5). At Pompeii, in the Pisanella villa, a basket containing broken glass was found. It follows that the quantity of glass objects discovered during excavations is usually very low [p. 113] compared to the quantity of fine ceramics, whereas in a Roman household during the Principate there was very probably more glass than fine ceramics. J.-P. Morel's observations about Pompeii, where the broken glass used just before the eruption could not yet have been recycled, show it clearly.

Glass is obtained from fusing together a mix of silica (which is the liquefying agent), sodium oxide, potassium oxide, and lime. It first appeared in Mesopotamia in the third millennium B.C.E., but it was toward the middle of the second that glass started to be used in the fabrication of containers and tableware, in the Near East and, it seems, also in Egypt. Several techniques were used to make these objects: cold-cutting an object from a glass block; molding them with open or closed shapes, fabricating them from a core of sand or terracotta. Beyond Mesopotamia and Egypt, starting with the seventh century B.C.E., glassmaking also spread to Syria, Rhodes, Cyprus, within the Greek peninsula, and then Italy.

The Roman period is marked by a far-reaching technological innovation—that of blown glass—which was produced in Egypt and in Syria-Palestine, likely during the first century B.C.E. and whose diffusion had major consequences, including for daily life. It became widespread from Augustus' reign, and objects of blown glass were found at Pompeii. The glass produced in the eastern Mediterranean regions remained the most famous until the end of antiquity, and even later. The blocks of unrefined glass (primary glass-making) were not produced in the same ateliers, or even in the same places as the finished glass objects (secondary glassware), even in Egypt or in Syria-Palestine where these activities are well documented. Admittedly, in the western Mediterranean regions, unrefined glass was also produced because, according to Pliny the Elder (*Natural History*, 36.66.194), the white sand found on the Campanian coast, from Cumae to Liternum, allowed a very pure type of glass to be manufactured. However, in the great majority of the Roman west, [p. 114] the workshops known to archaeologists were focused on secondary glassware. This is the case, for instance, in Gaul and Britain. There they used either recycled objects or blocks of unrefined glass transported from the eastern Mediterranean. The presence of crucibles is indicative of the existence of a factory for secondary glassware. Since crucibles were often made out of refractory clay, the crucibles withstood the heat necessary to melt a block of unrefined glass or broken glass, but very likely could not take the higher heat needed to liquefy sands.

We can then say that, starting in the eastern Mediterranean region, there was commerce in unrefined glass. Indeed, shapeless blocks of glass of various sizes have been found, as in the shipwreck on the Sanguinaire Islands, off the coast of Corsica (third century B.C.E.), which contained more than 550 kg, and especially in the West-Embiez 1 shipwreck (the end of the second or third century C.E.). For the latter, which foundered near La Ciotat and was no doubt on its way to Arles, approximately 17 metric tons of unrefined glass were found. In this case, the crude glass represented the main cargo; in the case of the former, the quantities were much smaller, and unrefined glass was clearly an accompanying cargo (on accompanying cargo, see below at the end of this chapter). Both wrecks also carried objects of finished glass (the West-Embiez 1 contained glass goblets, window panes, and footed glasses). All of these products came very likely from Syria-Palestine. It is estimated that during the fabrication of glass objects, one third of the weight of the blocks of raw glass was lost. It is not easy to discern the evolution of glass-trading patterns as, in all epochs, Syria-Palestine and Egypt predominated. As regards the fabrication of glass and glass objects, Italy did not hold the prominent place that, up to the first century C.E., it held in the production of terra sigillata.

Window glass was used, and there were several techniques employed to make it. At the beginning of the Empire, cooling and pulling glass was the most common. The crude glass was poured on a horizontal surface [p. 115] that served as a mold, then it was spread using tools that left traces on the top surface of the glass, while the lower part was less smooth because of the support marks. During the imperial period, the windows of the bathhouses, the palaces, and certain villas were closed up with tens or even hundreds of panes of glass. In the form of windows, besides glass, specular, or selenic, stone was used. According to Pliny the Elder, this mineral was extracted in Cyprus, in Cappadocia, in Sicily, and also in Hispania Citerior, a "thousand steps" (74 km) from Segobriga (*Natural History*, 3.3.30 and 36.45.160).

Under the Roman Empire, glass production varied greatly. There were window glass; glass vessels, whose forms were inspired by those used in ceramics and included small cups, bowls, and goblets; ointment and perfume vials; bottles, some of which contained wine (Petronius, *Satyricon*, 34); scarabs, beads, buttons, statuettes, rings, etc. The forms of all these objects were very homogeneous from one region to another, and even from one half of the Mediterranean to the other.

The custom of marking certain glass objects with stamps is associated with the invention of blown glass: before this invention, we do not see such stamps. A percentage of these marks, written in either Greek or Latin letters, were men's names (Ennion, Eirenaios, Sidonios, Iason, etc., in Greek letters; Aristo, Arta, M. Licinius Diceus in Latin letters). Others represented expressions of desire or exhortation, like *Katachairei kai euphrainoi*, "be welcome and be charmed." The place of the origin of some of these objects is problematic, since they are found both in the western and eastern Mediterranean. At this point, there is another question: were some containers made for specific contents? Is this, for example, the case of the "balsamaria," destined to contain ointments and perfumes? If these balsamaria carried a stamp, did this designate the [p. 116] manufacturer of the glass, or the product it carried, or a wholesale trader who purchased large quantities of the product, repackaged, and resold it? In most cases, this third possibility can be eliminated because the names appearing on the vases are never the same as those of the Italian traders whose names are known from stone inscriptions (the Trebonii, the Faenii, the Popillii, etc.). Most likely, then, the marks on the vases designate their manufacturer. On the other hand, as some would note, no solid evidence exists that the senators and the equites acted as glassware entrepreneurs. Certainly, moneylending can never be ruled out, but such loans are not mentioned in the evidence we have. Generally speaking, in this economic sector, there are no traces attesting to more direct involvement. Glassmaking seemed to be the prerogative of artisans, professionals with great technical competence. This does not exclude, however, the eventuality that some of them also acquired great fortunes while becoming great masters of their trade.

Another question, connected to the preceding. The secondary glassware shops validated by archaeological evidence are small and quite modest in size, especially in the western Mediterranean. Among other locations, I am thinking of Avenches (dating from the first century C.E.), Sentinum, in the Marches (between the first and the third century C.E.?), and Cesson-Sévigné, close to Rennes (the end of the third and the fourth centuries). There is, however, a great homogeneity of forms, from one region to another. Did the most frequently mentioned glass artisans, like Ennion for example, move from Syria-Palestine and Egypt towards the western part of the Empire? Were some secondary glass ateliers offshoots of other ateliers situated overseas, the "branches of a large center from which the artisans emigrated," as D. Foy suggested? These legitimate questions have been asked repeatedly, but for the time being it is impossible to answer them satisfactorily. [p. 117]

III. Mines and Metallurgy

While venerating Mother Earth for furnishing them with metals, the ancients did not shy away from digging mines, from ripping metals from the ground by force. "The ancient tradition is therefore unanimous in condemning this activity" (R. Halleux), as was obvious in the passages of moral inspiration written by Seneca and Pliny the Elder (Seneca, *Natural Questions*, 5.15.1–4 and Pliny, *Natural History*, 33.21.66–78). This did not however stop mining and metallurgy from being among the most impressive achievements of the Roman economy, and from currently being one of its best-known sectors.

Copper was extracted from the island of Elba during the period of Etruscan independence, then iron, beginning in the fourth century B.C.E.. Near Populonia, copper and iron slag from the metallurgical processes of these metals have been found. Italy, however, was extremely poor in mines. Yet, between the last decades of the third century and Trajan's reign, Rome's successive conquests provided it with numerous deposits some of which were very rich situated outside Italy in addition to the gold found in the territory of Salasses in Piedmont. Among these deposits were the mines in Sardinia; Macedonia; the Iberian peninsula (first Cartagena, i.e., Carthago Nova, then Sierra Morena and the southwest and, finally, northwest Spain during Augustus' reign); Asia Minor; Gaul Narbonnaise, then the three Gauls; Thrace; during Augustus' reign, those in the Danubian provinces and Lower Germany; in the eastern Mediterranean, Cyprus and Fenan (copper); as well as those in Egypt (gold); and finally, the lead, silver, iron, and copper mining sites in Britain, and gold in Dacia. Starting with the conquest of the Iberian peninsula and continuing until the second century C.E., these were the most important and productive mining sites. At the beginning of the third century, however, [p. 118] Iberian production seems greatly to diminish or even stop, and this is true for all metals. The mines exploited during the third and fourth centuries were located in other regions of the Empire and they are, for now, less well known.

Metallurgy that is extractive, or primary, consists of the separation of the target metal from the rest of the ore collected in the mine: the final results are ingots or metal bars. Most of the time, this operation took place on the site of the mine itself, or very close by. The practice varied from one metal to the other. Nevertheless, to simplify greatly, we can say that the process consisted of the further separation of ore from the rock that contained it, first using physical methods (crushing, grinding, washing), then heating, which allowed the transformation of the resulting salts (lead and copper sulfides, etc.) into oxides, and finally, reducing these oxides in bottom-heated stoves fueled with charcoal, to obtain the metal itself.

One of the most important aspects of Roman technology concerns the exploitation of consolidated alluvial deposits that contain gold and are found in northwest Spain. Since the gold content of these alluvia was very reduced, great quantities of soil from the deposits had to be displaced using the hydraulic method in order to make the operation profitable. First crushed by workers, if the deposits were less thick ("comb sites"), or pierced by long galleries, if they were deep (*ruina montium*), the alluvia were swept away by water, and gold was separated using "sluices." These gigantic operations carried away hundreds of millions of cubic meters of material, which greatly impressed Pliny the Elder (*Natural History*, 33.21.66–78), and left spectacular scars in the landscape of the region that are still visible today. C. Domergue and G. Herail have conducted impressive studies of these formations.

The machines used to lift water (to which I alluded in chapter 1, section IV) were another strong element of the [p. 119] mining technology. Generally, they were considered Hellenistic inventions that were first used for irrigation, and later used by the Romans to evacuate water from mines. First and foremost were Archimedes' screws and the revolving bucket wheel, both of which were described by Vitruvius (*Architecture*, 10.4.3–4) and traces of which are still found at several mining sites (in the Iberian peninsula, in Great Britain, and in Romania).

In the Roman world, there have always been mines that belonged to cities or to private individuals (Crassus, for example, owned silver mines). Nevertheless, the most important deposits were, without exception, public property. At the end of the Republic they were contracted out and therefore underwent indirect management. For a long time, it was believed that the *publicani* played a great role in exploiting mines. Most recently, however, scholars like A. Mateo and C. Domergue have presented very strong arguments supporting the idea that the role of the *publicani* was restricted to collecting royalties on behalf of Rome, and that mining itself was leased to individual private entrepreneurs, or sometimes entrepreneurs who belonged to ordinary private companies. Thanks to inscriptions on lead ingots from Cartagena, we know of several such successful concessionaires who lived in the first century B.C.E. It is possible, or even probable, that in Cartagena the concessionaires, some of whom were equites or were later accepted in the order, did not themselves develop the concessions they received. They would have sent freedmen to Cartagena who were charged with the smooth functioning of these operations, but it seems that later these freedmen put down roots in the province.

Under the Principate, mines were part of the imperial treasury, and they were managed by equestrian procurators who were charged with the financial operations of the province or who were responsible for the mining district itself, if the latter was sufficiently important. We know, for instance, that there were procurators for the silver mines in Pannonia and the gold [p. 120] mines in Dacia. The mining district was located outside the cities of the region. Some procurators, subordinates to equites, were imperial freedmen. A part of the district was exploited under direct management, by procurators and their colleagues, using the indigenous labor force (this was the case in northwest Spain). In other cases, the management was indirect: the procurator offered mining concessions to certain private persons (individuals or private companies), according to rules described on one of the two bronze Vipascan laws, at Aljustrel (in southern Portugal). These two inscriptions on bronze, discovered in 1876 and 1906, contain regulations: the first, on the organization of the mining district, the second on the leasing of wells and the links between the concessionaires and the authorities. Finally, in the second century C.E., we note the existence of very large districts, awarded by the Empire to major mine owners, the *conductores*. This seems to have been especially common in the Danube region.

Some senators and some individuals close to the emperor owned mines, but this was not the most common situation. As to the contractors, their social and financial rank was clearly proportional to the size of their concessions. Those in Vipasca, e.g., were all modest. On the contrary, the marks on the ingots from Cartagena, dating from the end of the Republic as we have just said, show that a certain numbers of their contractors were already equites, or were about to reach that status. In Cartagena then, the concessions were definitely more substantial than in Vipasca, but this situation does not imply that some senators were contractors.

Concerning the private metals trade, inscriptions on the ingots and inscriptions (funerary and others) of the *negotiatores ferrarii* and the *negotiatores aerarii* provide us with important information (*CIL* II.1199; *CIL* VI.9664, 9665, and 9666; X.1931; *AE* 1922, 82). [p. 121] C. Domergue has clearly showed that, generally speaking, in the case of ingots from the southern Iberian peninsula, the producer (whoever was conducting the mining operation) was a different person from the merchant: the latter bought the ingots from the producer and transported them to Rome via ship where he sold them for profit. This plan shows that, if certain notables were also metal producers, they were not involved directly with trading ingots.

Did the public powers receive their royalties in the form of ingots or bars, or in cash? For the great majority of cases, we don't know. The most likely event is that the financial authorities received directly, from the producers, the metal ingots they needed. This would explain the presence of stamps carrying the emperor's name on some ingots. Despite this, it is impossible to establish even approximately what part of the metal production remained the property of the financial authorities and what part entered private commerce.

Starting in 190 95 C.E., the number of developed sites diminished drastically, and this trend continued into the third and the fourth centuries. The mines in northwest Spain and those in Sierra Morena were no longer open after the beginning of the third century: most of the iron mines in Gaul were closed a bit after the middle of the third century, and the same was true for the silver and gold mines in Dacia. The causes of these closures are not easy to determine, since the larger part of the deposits was not exhausted, far from it. In the case of gold and silver, the production diminished, which must have had some effects on the monetary system. On the other hand, to the degree that we can estimate the quantities extracted, the production of iron and copper did not seem to have decreased and the mines in the eastern Mediterranean continued to be exploited in the third and fourth centuries. [p. 122]

Unlike primary metallurgy, secondary metallurgy (that is, the transformation of ingots and bars into finished objects) took place far, or very far, from the mines. Two situations coexisted in parallel, at the same time and in the same areas: either the objects could be made in the very cities where, then, they were used, or in specialized centers. The first situation is attested pretty much everywhere in the Empire. In his contribution to the fourth volume of T. Frank's *The Economic Survey of Ancient Rome*, T.R.S. Broughton emphasizes that, in almost every city in Asia Minor, we have evidence of the presence of a forge that simultaneously worked in iron, copper, or bronze. The blacksmith made objects used in daily life: tools, weapons, household utensils. He received the metal in raw form and made it into objects. On the other hand, the fabrication of valuable objects, of superior quality, took place primarily in specialized centers with a reputation for such activities, and whose geographical location varied from one era to another. During the Hellenistic period, Cyprus was well known for its production of iron weapons (Plutarch, *Alexander*, 32). Under the Principate, strigils arrived from Pergamum (Martial, 14.51). In these more specialized centers we find associations teaching artisanal skills (which were well represented in these locations). An association of bronze-workers existed at Thyatira; an association of blacksmiths at Sigeion in Hierapolis; one for manufacturers of iron beds at Tralles, and a silversmithing group at Ephesus. The debate over the consumer city has hidden the coexistence of these two modes of production, which we knew very well previously. In fact, some insisted on the existence of large centers of industrial production while others denied it, and it became impossible to realize that the two situations coexisted, partially according to regions, but especially according to the quality and the value of the objects produced. It is essential to abandon such *a priori* ideas completely. [p. 123]

IV. Stone Quarries and Construction

During the Republican period, stone quarries belonged to the city of Rome, to various other cities of the Roman world, and to private owners (individuals or societies). This situation continued under the Empire. The quarries of Mt. Pentelicon, for example, in the second century C.E. were the property of Herodes Atticus. But little by little, the most important quarries—or those that produced the most prestigious stones (marbles, for example)—passed to the imperial patrimony (*patrimonium Caesaris*) through confiscation, purchase, or inheritance. Tacitus and Suetonius both recorded that Tiberius confiscated a series of mines and quarries that previously belonged to cities or private owners. This was the case for the Luni (*Luna*) marble quarries. On the blocks of marble the names of municipal slaves (Philo, Tiburtinus) were later replaced with those of imperial slaves (Eros).

Several imperial quarries of marble or other stones provide abundant epigraphic evidence, but the interpretation is quite difficult. I am thinking, for example, of the marble of Chemtou (Simittu), in Numidia; the marble of Synnada in Dokimeion, in Phrygia; of the granodiorite from Mons Claudianus, in the eastern Egyptian desert; of porphyry from the Mons Porphyrites, also in Egypt. Despite the progress achieved by this branch of the *instrumentum domesticum*, it is very difficult to know in detail how the exploitation of these quarries was organized. It is often said that it was very similar to that of the imperial mines, but this is not necessarily true. The available inscriptions seem to suggest that the organization varied from one location to the other: some sites were exploited by the contractors who had purchased the rights, while others (very likely in larger numbers), were developed through direct management, under the direction of the procurators. Between the first and the third centuries C.E. it is very likely that [p. 124] there was an evolution from leasing to direct management.

The emperor used stones from his quarries for public construction that he oversaw. In this particular case, the producer was also the consumer, and the products from his quarries did not pass through the cycles of trade. The imperial services seem also to have sold a part of these quarried materials to private parties. Certainly, a trade for used materials (whether originally produced by the imperial services or not) existed already, and measures against trafficking in construction materials were taken, particularly in Italy, in the first century C.E. As for the cities, they either continued to own some quarries, though of lesser prestige and importance, or they bought needed materials from private parties. While we have very little evidence of the role played by the members of the imperial and municipal elite in the construction industry and urban building ownership, this role was very likely important. We will also see that this is the case as regards bricks and tiles in the region of Rome. This was also probably true for bricks and tiles produced in other regions but, when they exist, the stamps imprinted on their bricks do not very often allow us to identify the individual they name and, in general, they cannot attest that the names were those of entrepreneurs and not of owners who received a rent.

V. Bricks and Tiles

The use of baked bricks varied according to each region, the availability of construction stone, and the importance of urbanization. In the area near Rome, it is clear that the demand for bricks was very high. Additionally, F. Coarelli has recently shown that baked [p. 125] brick does not date from the final years of the Republic, as was previously believed, but that it had already been widely used at the end of the second century B.C.E. If, in the most rural regions of Italy and the provinces, the use of baked bricks was less frequent and that of stones preferred, in Rome and in its ports, Ostia and Portus, the great majority of the private construction during the imperial period was made out of baked bricks. It is necessary then to take into account the use of tiles, which was widespread.

In the great majority of the regions including Rome, bricks and tiles were stamped with marks made in the clay before baking. Not all the bricks were marked; regardless of the manufacturer, only a small number of bricks were stamped. Sometimes the marks were anepigraphic symbols (circles, stars, crosses); most often they were names, sometimes abridged, or initials. On the bricks and tiles found in the northern regions of the Adriatic Sea, and studied by C. Zaccaria and C. Gomezel, we can also read the following:

- groups of three initials, which almost certainly belong to the three elements of a man's name (*tria nomina*), e.g.: C.I.A., C.P.A., L.R.S.
- abbreviations of the three elements present in the name of a man, like: *T. AE. MA* or *L. ST. IVSTI*
- the names of a man whose family name (*nomen*) was spelled out: *L. BARBI L. F., Q. BARBI Q. F., L. BARBI TI. F.*, etc.

Near Rome, on the bricks and tiles produced in the first century B.C.E. or the first century C.E., we find similar family names (*nomina*), most often in the genitive case: *C. COSCONI* (*CIL* XV.145) OR *L. ATINI (CIL* XV.874). Women's family names have also been attested: for example, *MINATIA*, in Venosa, in southern Italy (*CIL* IX.6388, 2). In all these cases, we could wonder about the role the named person played. Was this name that of the owner of the land and the installations? Did this owner [p. 126] develop the manufacturing site directly (was this done through his dependents, for example the proxies)? Or, was the manufacturing facility lent out and the owner was but a landowner receiving a certain amount of rent from those doing the work? When the bricks contain just one name, it is impossible to answer these questions with confidence.

Commencing with the reign of Domitian and continuing until the time of the Severans, in the Roman region, stamps appeared that were both bigger and much more explicit. We can read the names of the annual consuls, and quite frequently the name of the *figlinae*, which stood at the same time for the clay-pits and the manufacturing equipment used. We could also read either the name of a person (man or woman), or the names of two individuals (men or women). The most specific stamps are circular, with the inscriptions placed on two or three concentric lines. A third of these stamps contain the names of two persons. In this case, the first name is that of the landowner, preceded by *ex praedis* ("from the properties of…") or by *ex figlinis* ("from the clay-pit, or the factories of…"). The bearer of the second name is conventionally called *officinator* by the actual specialists: depending on the case, he is represented in various ways in the inscription. All the emperors from Domitian to Septimius Severus and Caracalla were owners of lands that contained brick-making facilities; half of the rest of the owners were senators (79 out of 161, after P. Setälä). On the other hand, no senators or emperors were found among the "second people" (*officinatores*).

In the area around Rome at this time, the demand for bricks and tiles was substantial, especially in Ostia and Portus, where architecture dating from the reigns of Trajan and Hadrian is extensive. The construction activities seem to have diminished during the second part of the second century. [p. 127] These questions were first studied by H. Dressel and H. Bloch, and then by members of a Finnish team of epigraphists (J. Suolahti, M. Steinby, T. Helen, P. Setälä, etc.), charged by the office overseeing antiquities in Ostia with the inventory of the bricks and tiles stamps of the area.

This volume is too short to address all the problems concerning bricks and tiles. Here, I will only address two topics whose economic importance is undeniable. The first has to do with the specific role of the landowner and the *officinator* in the commercialization of bricks and tiles. The team of the epigraphists was divided on this topic: while T. Helen thought that, in the great majority of cases, the landowner was merely a renter who hired out his lands and equipment to an *officinator*, M. Steinby insisted on his active involvement. She based her claims on the fact that the bricks and tiles from the domains of certain senators and equites were found in the public buildings constructed during their time in office, when they had easy access to these materials. Marcus Rutilius Lupus' example is particularly relevant. An important eques during Trajan's reign, Lupus was the prefect of the *annona* between 107 and 112, then the prefect of Egypt from 113 to 117. At the time he owned the *figlinae Brutianae*, and bricks from this location were found in the buildings of the monumental center in Ostia and in the markets of Trajan in Rome. M. Steinby rightly asked: how could such coincidences be explained if M. Rutilius Lupus did not have control over the commercial use of bricks and tiles in his estates? She presents several other arguments, but those proposed by T. Helen are not insignificant either. Most likely, both types of management were present. Besides, excerpts from papyri and legal texts show that the exploitation of large ceramic factories could be done on location by a contractor (*P. Fayoum* 36, *P. Tebtunis* 342), or on the other hand through [p. 128] a contract stating that the landowner kept the finished goods and commercialized them, according to the model suggested by M. Steinby (*P. Oxyrhynchus*, 3595–97 and *Digest*, 18.1.65 Iavolenus). Nothing required a landowner to use the same management model repeatedly. For certain cases, T. Helen was correct. In approximately two thirds of the cases, however, M. Steinby was probably correct. The manufacturing of bricks and tiles was one of the sectors in which the members of the elite (and near Rome, the senators especially) had much vested interest.

Another fact should be mentioned here: at the beginning of the second century C.E., near Rome, all the landowners represented by brick stamps were private parties; starting with the reign of Marcus Aurelius, the situation was reversed. Henceforth, the great majority of brick factories belonged to the emperor or the empress. Most often, these ownership changes were the result of inheritance or marriage, not confiscation. That was the case with the important brick factories of M. Annius Verus and his wife, Domitia Lucilla, the daughter of Publius; upon their deaths, the factories were passed to their son, the future emperor Marcus Aurelius.

At the same time, in the second part of the second century, construction activities at Ostia and Portus slowed down noticeably. Without a doubt, the same happened in Rome, too, to the point that M. Steinby speaks of "crisis." The word "crisis" incites heated debates and requires thoughtful handling: I will revisit the topic again in chapter 7. Should the word "crisis" be used here, in relation to the brick and tile industry? It is not clear. Should the concentration of brick and tile factories in the hands of the emperor be causally associated with the decrease in production activities? It is rather difficult to identify the criteria that would justify seeing a causal relationship here. In any case, I can, with absolute certainty, reject the idea that this was a case of "nationalization"!

This noted evolution, however, could not have been inconsequential for market activities in Rome and its environs. If the emperor owned all the brick and tile factories in the region, [p. 129] pricing and transaction methods could hardly have escaped being affected. Unfortunately, we lack the evidence that would permit us to estimate the extent of its effects.

VI. Terracotta Lamps

In addition to bricks and tiles, several other types of objects used in daily life were made out of terracotta. In the chapter on agriculture I talked about amphorae, which served to transport wine, oil, sauces, and fish preserves. There are two other essential categories of objects that are extremely important for our archaeological knowledge of antiquity: oil lamps, and table and kitchen ceramics.

Unlike the Hellenistic world, non-Greek Italy and central Tyrrhenian Italy in particular did not begin manufacturing terracotta lamps until relatively late—the second half of the third century B.C.E. According to C. Pavolini, we should conclude that before this time, the populations inhabiting these regions did not use oil for lighting, but instead used other methods, i.e., wood or wood-derived materials (pitch, resin). The oldest lamps from central Italy had a black glaze. Among them we count the "biconic Esquiline type," manufactured from the third to the first centuries B.C.E., and the "cylindrical Esquiline type," manufactured in the second and first centuries B.C.E. Examples of the former were found not only in Rome and in Latium, but also in Campania, in Apulia, and even on other western Mediterranean coasts. The latter was probably made in Latium. A different "cylindrical" type was also made in northern Italy (at Aquileia?), at about the same time. The lamps with so-called radial decoration were made with a mold, from the end of the second to the end of the first century B.C.E., either in Bruttium, or in Sicily. [p. 130]

Later, in Italy and in both the eastern and western Mediterranean, we note the presence of multiple local or regional production sites, which are less polished, and on the other hand a number of products with wide distribution. The question of the organization of workshops and the system of commercialization arose based on this series of best-selling items (well known to archaeologists because in excavations they belong to what are called "guiding fossils"). The "volute lamps" were produced in Italy, and especially in Latium and Campania, starting with the reign of Augustus. During a substantial portion of the first century C.E. they were circulating on all the Mediterranean coasts, even the eastern, but the numerous production workshops seemed to have been of a modest scale. This fact suggests that the central role of connection between production and market belonged to the traders. Such a system of commercialization, which F. Mayet proposed for the Hispanic sigillata (discussed later in this chapter), seems to have been the most likely choice for lamps and ceramics, but also for other manufactured products. Commencing with the Flavian era, however, the success of the volute lamps diminished and production, more uniform but of less good quality, seems to have been focused on more important enterprises. Worthy of mention is C. Oppius Restitutus' stamp, found very frequently on all the coasts of the western Mediterranean, and used from the 80s to the 120s C.E.

Around this time, the production of lamps called "Firmalampen" (or "lamps of firms"), all stamped, and many of them with a small number of well-attested names (Fortis, Strobilis, and Communis), began to be produced in the Po valley. They continued to be manufactured during the second and the third centuries. In the fourth century, red clay lamps became popular that were decorated with a rich Christian iconography inspiring their name, "African Christian lamps." [p. 131]

W.V. Harris wondered if the "Firmalampen" with the same names were all produced in the same area. Taking into account the improbability of these objects being transported over long distances, he concluded that these enterprises had subsidiaries—sometimes far away from the source—that were managed by slave proxies, the *institores*, who used the same stamps as the main manufacturing facility. Harris' theory is consistent with what we know elsewhere regarding proxies. His theory, however, was criticized by P. Procaccini, who believes that long-distance transportation was possible and, in fact, an actuality. Neither one of these two theses can be proven for the time being. The dispute would be settled if archaeological examples of the subsidiaries W.V. Harris mentions were to be found.

VII. Ceramic Tableware

Ceramics are certainly the best-known product of Roman manufacturing. They are divided into several categories. On the one hand, there were fine ceramics, used as tableware, whose clay was in general more finely grained and more homogeneous. These were very often covered with a clay coating, fired at high temperature or not—called glaze or slip—but these were not luxury objects. On the other hand, there was the ordinary kind of ceramic, the surface of which in most cases was not coated with anything. Some of the objects made of this kind of material served as tableware, but their quality was clearly more modest than that of fine ceramics. Another section of these objects was used for cooking (called culinary or kitchen ceramics) or to store food.

The study of fine ceramics has greatly progressed in the last four decades. Precise typologies have been composed for many categories of these ceramic types and their dating is becoming more precise each year. Fine ceramics permit the most [p. 132] efficient dating of the different stratigraphic levels, and thus the various historical phases of a site. At the same time, their dispersion is a very useful indicator that helps us distinguish the economic evolution of various regions of the Empire. The two volumes of the *Atlante delle forme ceramiche* (*Atlas of Ceramic Forms*), published in the 1980s, are an absolutely indispensable source for the great majority of fine ceramics. The *Atlas* contains a detailed bibliography, especially of the sites where examples of this type of ceramic were found.

The study of the stamps that could be read on certain types of fine ceramics (especially on the Italian and the Gallic or the Gallo-Roman ones) is part of the larger epigraphic field of the *instrumentum domesticum*. These stamps show that some potters moved from one atelier to another, and give details of the organization of the production ateliers. We should not, however, disregard the limits of our knowledge, especially when it comes to ordinary ceramic ware which, most often, was not dispersed outside the city or, at best, outside the region where it was produced. Almost always, ordinary ceramic ware was unmarked: exceptions exist, but they are quite rare. Ordinary ceramics were not the only product to have no stamps—this was also the case for many types of fine ceramics. In the absence of these stamps, it is impossible to determine the identity of the potters, and this constitutes a substantial obstacle when it comes to the study of how production was organized.

Between the end of the fourth century B.C.E. and late antiquity, at every period, fine ceramics, which were widely distributed, were produced in the Roman world, whether east or west. One of the traits common to all these categories is that they were manufactured in several cities (at once) and that all these workshops adopted the same repertory of forms at the same time. The color and consistency of the clay, as well as the glaze and certain particularities of form, enable us to distinguish among the productions of the various workshops. [p. 133]

In the western Mediterranean, the first of these categories is the black glaze Campanian ware, manufactured in various Italian cities and in Sicily between the fourth century B.C.E. and the beginning of the imperial era (Augustus' reign). Beginning at the start of the second century B.C.E., three main types of black glaze ceramic, conventionally named A, B, and C, predominated. Type A, made with a red-brownish clay at Naples, was widely dispersed in the second century in the entire western Mediterranean. Type B, made from a beige clay, was manufactured in Etruria in the inner territories (Volterra) and appeared during the first part of the second century, and spread widely during the second half of the second century. Type C, of a brown or gray clay, and of a lesser quality than the other two types, was manufactured in southeast Sicily (the Syracuse region).

In the first century B.C.E., the glaze on fine ceramics changed its color from black to red or orange, as a result of another firing technique. This is the start of the era of the "sigillata," which lasted until the seventh century C.E. The adjective *sigillata*, derived from the Latin word *sigillum* (seal, stamp, hallmark), was not used to describe these ceramics in antiquity. There are two or three possible explanations for the original use of this word. As it is used nowadays in the study of ceramics, it does not have a precise meaning: it is a conventional modern appellation that applied to almost all fine ceramics circulated in the Roman world between the first century B.C.E. and the seventh century C.E.

The oldest sigillata are Italian. They include first of all the Arretine sigillata, whose fabrication started towards the middle of the first century B.C.E. at Arezzo, then at Pisa, Puteoli, and Lyon, and probably in at least two other locations. During the reign of Augustus, it was present on all the Mediterranean shores (but particularly in the western Mediterranean) and in continental regions of the Empire (all of Gaul, the south of England, the Alps, and the right bank of [p. 134] the Danube River). Starting in 15 C.E. the names of the potters on the stamps were inscribed inside the outline of a bare human foot (the so-called *in planta pedis*). Its distribution then substantially diminished: it continued, however, to be produced until the last third of the first century C.E. During the reign of Augustus, other sigillata were produced in the Po valley. After 70 C.E., the "Tardo-Italian" sigillata appeared and it was widely dispersed on all the shores of the western Mediterranean, in Gaul and on the shores of Danube, and manufactured until the second century.

The Italian sigillata were replaced by two other large categories. The first one to develop (starting in 25 B.C.E.) was the Gallic or the Gallo-Roman sigillata, manufactured in a great number of shops and with a glaze usually darker, more of a carmine red, than that of Italian sigillata. This category is subdivided into smaller ones according to the regions of production. The first of these subcategories is that of southern Gaul, whose ceramics were produced in the departments of Tarn (Montans), Lot (Carrade), Aveyron (La Graufesenque), Lozere (Banassac, Le Rozier), Herault (Aspiran) and Aude (Bram, Narbonne). The starting production date for these venues is believed to be 25 B.C.E. and some of them produced until 260 or 270, with their apogee between 30 and 120 C.E. Not all ateliers distributed their products equally, or in the same directions. Those from Bram were only distributed in the valley of the Garonne and in western Languedoc; those from La Graufesenque sold their ceramics in all western provinces and in Italy (except in the Venice area), to some eastern shores (in Corinth, Syria, Egypt) and on the edges of the Rhine and Danube rivers. After 70–80 C.E., these sigillata from southern Gaul were no longer found in Africa and, after 120, they disappeared from Mediterranean shores in Europe completely.

The ateliers situated in the center of France were widely dispersed in the valleys of the Vienne, Loire, and Allier, all the way to the Rhone-Saône axis, and [p. 135] debuted under the reign of Tiberius. Some of them continued to produce until the second part of the fourth century, with the most productive period being between the second century and the beginning of the third. The main production center was at Lezoux (Puy-de-Dôme). The dispersion of the products was variable, according to each workshop, and mostly continental: those from Lezoux were found chiefly in Britain, northern Gaul, Germany, and on the Rhine and the Danube.

In eastern Gaul and Germany, in about fifteen centers (for example those in Boucheporn and Metz in Lorraine, Itterwiller and Mittelbronn in Alsace, those in Rheinzabern in Rhenania), to which we could add several centers in Argonne, the passage of the first century C.E. saw different types of sigillata being produced, the oldest ones being produced during Tiberius' reign. Several ateliers or groups of ateliers were closed at the end of the second (Boucheporn, Mittelbronn), others in the third century or even the end of the fourth century. The most prosperous period of these eastern Gaulish shops was in the second century, between the reigns of Hadrian and Marcus Aurelius: their spread was entirely continental (north Gaul, Britain, the valleys of the Rhine and the Danube).

During the middle of the first century C.E., the production of sigillata started to develop in the Iberian peninsula, too, in the valleys of three rivers: the Ebro, the Duoro and, in the south, the Guadalquivir. The most important production center was the Tritium Magallum (Tricio, in the upper valley of the Ebro). Its best period was the last third of the first century and the beginning of the second. The ceramics manufactured in the biggest centers were then dispersed across the Iberian peninsula, in Aquitania, on the shores of the Mauretanias and Numidia; it was also found at Narbonne, Marseille, and Ostia, but in small quantities. These shops stopped production at the end of the second century or the beginning of the third, but new work commenced during the Tetrarchic period and in the fourth century, in three or four centers including Tritium Magallum. [p. 136]

North Africa has both produced and distributed sigillata, which can be found in great quantities at many sites and whose fabrication lasted until the seventh century C.E. In the 1960s, N. Lamboglia called these "light-colored" (*sigillata chiara*) A, C, and D, since at the time he was not sure of their place of origin. To these three types he added a fourth, the "light-colored" B (which was not sigillata per se, and whose production took place in Gaul). Some other subcategories, and especially the A/C and A/D, were recently added to the three main categories. Now, this "light-colored" sigillata is generally called African red slip ware; it is never marked.

The African red slip ware that Lamboglia has called A, bright orange in color with a thick glaze and thick walls, was produced in north Tunisia, in Zeugitana, in particular at Carthage, and in the valley of Medjerda. Its production started towards the middle of the first century C.E.; the export to Italy and Gaul started in the 70s (when it is found in Pompeii). In the second century, it had spread to all the western Mediterranean basin and could be found at other sites in the eastern Mediterranean, for instance at Antioch. It was produced until the fourth century.

The C African red slip ware was produced in Byzacena, in the central region of Tunisia, also known for its olive tree plantations. It was manufactured for about three centuries, from the end of the second to the end of the fifth century C.E. It was much more dispersed than type A, except in Algeria and Morocco, where it was less common than both types A and D.

Like type A, the D African red slip ware was produced in Zeugitana and possibly also at Tripolitania. It had several forms, and quite often the glaze on the outside walls was missing. Its manufacture started at the beginning of the fourth century and ran until the seventh. It was most dispersed toward the end of the fourth and the first half of the fifth century, not only on all the Mediterranean coasts, but also in northern Gaul, Germany, London, Noricum, [p. 137] inside Syria and Egypt, and along the Nile. The Vandals' capture of Roman Africa in 430 does not seem to have affected the distribution of this type of ceramic ware.

Among the fine ceramic wares of the western Mediterranean, too, I should probably mention the palaeo-Christian, sigillata-derived material formerly known as "Visigoth" or "stamped sigillata." Their fabrication started during the fourth century and seems to have lasted until the end of the fifth century. They were therefore contemporaries of type D, but much less widespread. They were produced in southern Gaul, in what is now Switzerland, in Aquitania, and in Spain.

Fine tableware ceramics were also produced in the eastern Mediterranean. They are called "eastern sigillata" and are divided in several groups. The ceramics from the first group ("eastern sigillata A") were very likely manufactured in the Syro-Palestinian region, but outside the territory currently making up the state of Israel (if they had come from Israel, where research has been more intensive, we would certainly know the place of origin). They were manufactured between the middle of the second century B.C.E. and the end of the second century C.E. Their brilliant red glaze resembles Arretine but they take specific forms, for instance with larger feet. Some of these specific forms have marks imprinted on the clay before firing. The marks consist of unique male names written in Greek letters, without abbreviations, and in the genitive case: for example, Chaireou, Loukiou, Titou, Hermaiou, Taurou, Demetriou (forms 25, 30, 34, 48, and 49). These are the names of potters or of owners of the workshops but, as far as I know, they have not been included in any historical research yet. On the other hand, other marks consist of abstract names (Charis, Charites, Kerdos, Kala, Kalon; forms 33, 34, 35, 37, 38, 39, 48, and 49) [p. 138] or of names of gods (Hermes, Aphrodite; forms 37 and 48) in the nominative case, a phenomenon that we have not observed in the case of western Mediterranean ceramics and that is difficult to interpret. The word *Charis* is especially frequent.

Produced in the province of Asia between the reign of Augustus and the middle of the second century, "eastern sigillata B" was found in great quantities in the excavations at Ephesus and Priene. Many ceramic vases of this type were also marked with the potters' names, in the genitive case (Didumou, Koiranou, Alexandrou, Chariciou, Sporou), or abstract names or the names of gods, in the nominative case (Dôron, Charis, Isis). It is important to mention the presence of the mark carrying the name Arretina, in Latin letters, and of a name in the genitive case which could be found written sometimes in Latin and sometimes in Greek: *Iatrocli* (in Latin letters) and *Iatrokleous* (in Greek letters). The name of C. Sentius, which is attested on eastern sigillata B, was also known in Arretine sigillata in the time of Augustus. These homages to Italy and to its Arretine show that direct contacts existed between the two producing regions, Italy and Asia, and that the former exerted influence over the latter, rather than vice-versa.

Among the "eastern sigillata C" (also called Çandarli ceramic ware), and produced near Pergamum between the first and the third centuries C.E. (remains from an oven were also recovered), we also find sigillata carrying names in the genitive case, but very few of them are abstract names or the names of gods in the nominative case. The Cypriot sigillata, likely produced in Cyprus or Israel in the first and second centuries C.E., also carries marks of male names, but they are fewer in number and no abstract names are mentioned. The same is true for the Pontic sigillata, which are found during the same time on the shores of the Black Sea and which display additional anepigraphic symbols.

The "thin-walled pottery" (which Nino Lamboglia had called "ceramica a pareti sottili") constitutes a particular case. [p. 139] They were small dishes used for drinking, goblets, and cups, manufactured in northern Italy and in several provinces in the western part of the Empire (Baetica and the regions of Narbonne and Lyon). They appeared in the second century B.C.E. and gradually disappeared during the first and second centuries C.E. The growing spread of glassware was very probably the main cause of their disappearance.

When it comes to the way the workshops were organized, the epigraphy of the *instrumentum* provides very important information, but not for all fine ceramics. In fact, the clues found in the stamps applied on the Italian and the Gallo-Roman sigillata before firing are entirely absent on the vases and plates belonging to the African red slip ware.

Based on all this evidence, how can we assess the role played by ceramics in the Roman world? What was their economic importance? They occupied a very modest place in the domestic budget. Based on this reasonable observation, it would be easy to elaborate on the disparity between the existing documentation (very abundant in the case of ceramic objects) and the key products of the economy: grains, metals, and textiles. In any case, we cannot invent documents that have vanished.

However, three remarks are necessary. The first has to do with the connections between the evolution of public building projects and fine ceramic exports. F. Jacques noted that, in the case of Proconsular Africa, the two paths coincide, which shows that these activities represent meaningful indices of the region's economic wealth. We could then, with some caution, assume that the increase or the decrease of a certain type of sigillata also provides important information on the respective economic situation.

The second remark is that—because of their mass, the manner in which they could be dated, and because of their specific placement in the stratigraphy of excavation sites—ceramics constitute an important tool in historical reasoning. For example, they help to formulate [p. 140] hypotheses on the itineraries and the transportation methods by which pottery was dispersed.

The third and last remark addresses the role played by ceramic wares in the cargo logistics of maritime transportation. As a result of the excavations performed on the *Cala Culip IV*, shipwrecked in Catalonia during the time of Vespasian, J. Nieto argued that, in maritime transportation, most of the freight comprised two different types of loads. On one hand there were very heavy objects that occupied most of the ship (amphorae, ingots, stone or marble blocks, blocks of unworked glass), and they represented the main cargo. On the other hand, there were smaller objects, which took less space and added very little weight to the overall weight of the cargo, like dinner or cooking ware and oil lamps. The latter is called secondary cargo by J. Nieto, but I would prefer to call it "complementary cargo" or "accompanying cargo." In the *Camarina A* shipwreck, for example, which sank in Sicily towards the middle of the third century C.E., the cargo consisted of two large marble columns from Chemtou (18 metric tons together), amphorae, and African cooking ware. Similarly, in the wreck *Pointe de La Luque B*, which sank near Marseille in the fourth century C.E., amphorae were found, together with at least 250 terracotta lamps. The importance of the production of fine ceramic ware in a given region, and the export of those wares, therefore indicates in many cases that that region produced and exported other merchandise, e.g., food products, which took a more important role in shipments (and also in the household budget). This conclusion, then, would bolster the merits of F. Jacques' argument, according to which ceramics production is indicative of the presence of other products marketed over long distances. [p. 141]

Because of the practice of complementary cargo, there was sometimes no competition between the sigillata: this concept of commercial competition did not always apply. However, even in this case, competition is an important element to consider when it comes to common ceramics and unique sigillata, or among the common sigillata themselves. Moreover, several sigillata dating from the same time period were found at other sites, including maritime sites. Because of these findings, and despite its methodological promise, I cannot completely subscribe to this fight against the competition idea, which seems to me to have its limits. The practice of complementary freight helps explain the history of sigillata and the manner in which they succeeded one another. It does not, however, account for all the ceramic markets: in fact it is far from doing so. The theory may not be credible when it is applied to river traffic, and surely it does not apply to terrestrial transportation. This being said, I completely reject the idea that, across the whole Roman Empire, there was a unified ceramics market. The best way to explain the presence of ceramics in archaeological sites is to consider that, in their case, some competition existed, but that the ways in which competition manifested itself were dependent on the respective situation (according to the different cities, regions, and epochs) and that the markets were fragmented. We will be revisiting the relationships between competition and ceramics in chapter 5, section I. [p. 142]

Texts

Work Contract from the Dacian Mines, 164 C.E.

Under the consulship of Macrinus and Celsus, the thirteenth day of the calends of June [= 20 May 164 C.E.]

I, Flavius Secundinus, have written this at the request of Memmius, son of Aesclepius, who has declared that he is illiterate. He recognized that he had rented his services, and in fact he has rented his services to Aurelius Adjutor to work in the gold mines from today until the next ides of November [=13 November 164], for a salary of 70 denarii. He will receive his salary in several payments as is customary. He must supply to his aforesaid employer standard work as from a man in good health. If he wishes to leave or to cease work without the consent of his employer, he will pay for each day he will not work 5 sesterces, which will be docked from his salary. If work is made impossible because the mine is flooded, his salary will be proportionately reduced. If the employer does not pay the salary on the usual dates of payment and is late paying it, he must pay the same penalty, except for the first three days that the payment is late.

Written in Immenosum Majus.
Titus, son of Beusas, who is also called Bradua.
Socration, son of Socration
Memmius, son of Aesclepius

CIL III, tablet no. 10, p. 948

See also J. Macqueron, *Contractus scripturae: Contrats et quittances dans la pratique romaine* (Camerino, 1982). [p. 143]

Three Examples of Brick Stamps and Tiles from the Area around Rome

Capital letters are visible on the inscription; I have provided lower-case letters in parentheses to fill out the Latin words or abbreviations. The translation is provided below the Latin, and a description of the figure (*signum*) is provided after that.

1. *CIL* XV.21 (115 C.E.)

M. R(utili) L(upi) BRVT(iana tegula) PEDONE ET MESSALLA COS
(lupus ds. gradiens altero pede anteriore sublato)

A "Brutiana" roof tile of Marcus Rutilius Lupus, under the consulship of Pedo and Messalla.

This mark is decorated with a wolf walking to right, one of its forefeet lifted.

2. *CIL* XV.90b (123 C.E.)

EX PR(aedis) ARR(iae) FADIL(lae) PETT(i) PROC(u)LI
PAET(ino) ET APRONIA(no)
COS

A brick of Pettius Proculus, coming from the lands of Arria Fadilla, during the consulship of Paetinus and Apronianus.

3. *CIL* XV.160 (202–5 C.E.)

OP(us) DOL(iare) EX PR(aedis) C. FUL(vi) PLAUT(iani) PR(aefecti)
PR(aetorio)
C(larissimi) V(iri) COS II FIG(linis) DOMITI(anis)
(gallus ds.)

A brick from the lands of Caius Fulvius Plautianus, praetorian prefect, *vir clarissimus*, consul for the second time, in the brick workshops called *Domitianae.*

This stamp is decorated with a rooster turning to the right. [pp. 144, 145]

Chapter 4
Banking and the Financial Life

I. Different Kinds of Financiers

On several occasions I have explored the idea that Roman financiers could be divided into several categories based on their lifestyle, their financial means, their work methods, and the operations they conducted. For these reasons I used the notion of "work status" and explained it as follows: "The work status is the rapport with one's profession in its broadest sense, both in terms of institutions and representations. The status of a professional banker who runs a shop is not at all the same as that of a notable financier like C. Rabirius Postumus, and neither one of the two enjoyed the same status as a contemporary American or French banker" (*Banking and Business* (1999), 3–4). In the case of Rome-based bankers it is very important to make a distinction between professional bankers and notable financiers (like C. Rabirius Postumus).

The professional bankers were the *argentarii* and the *coactores argentarii,* the assayer-changers and the deposit bankers (who controlled the money, carried out exchanges, received deposits, lent money, and acted as mediators in auctions to lend money to the buyers). In this same category belong the *nummularii,* who were first assayer-changers and then, starting with the second century C.E., deposit bankers. The *argentarii* appeared in Rome between 318 and 310 B.C.E. and disappeared from the Latin part of the Empire in the last part of the third century C.E., when the monetary crisis swept them out. [p. 146] They reappeared again in the last quarter of the fourth century C.E. The *nummularii* appeared in the first century B.C.E. and were also affected by the monetary crises of the second part of the third century. In the Greek part of the Empire there were also assayer-changers who acted as deposit bankers, the so called *trapezitai.*

When it comes to notable financiers, there were some senators, some equites, and other notables who were actively engaged in financial activities that brought them profits, and who lent out money with interest. These financial activities did not constitute their professions; rather they were part of a plethora of different economic activities available to them, but not as primary jobs or occupations. Engaging in these financial activities in their eyes was part of their involvement with the management of their estates. Nevertheless, some of them dedicated a lot of time and means to these activities: they clearly pursued higher profits and even the increase of their properties. Even though lending with interest was generally seen as a questionable practice, it was widely practiced in all social environments and those involved in it did not hide it (except in some specific situations). In addition to moneylending, some of these notable financiers played the role of credit intermediaries (by connecting the moneylenders and those who were looking to borrow), or helped the transfer of funds from one location to another without physically moving cash, or played an active role in maritime loans, etc.

Roman notables, and particularly the members of the two leading orders, were very happy to increase their gains and were very strict when it came to money. It was not considered illegal for them to want to increase their wealth, in fact, far from it: it was seen as reprehensible if they allowed it to diminish by neglect. At the same time, however, these notables were involved in a series of social networks to and for which they were responsible. They were linked to their kinsmen, [p. 147] spouses, and possibly their ex-spouses, to their friends and those close to their friends, their clients, the other members of their orders, etc. Both of these tendencies were considered legitimate behaviors and coexisted: the drive to gain and become wealthier and the obligation to be generous and socially responsible. If we want to understand this aspect of Roman life, we need to take both of them into account. This is what M. Ioannatou and K. Verboven have done in their recent books on financial life during this time.

In addition, there existed other financiers who were neither professional bankers or money exchangers, nor were they notables. For example, there were relatively important businessmen who did not belong to the notables' elite, small lenders and loan sharks involved in short-term loans, and traders who were also involved in financial transactions. Based on the available documentation, it is often difficult to decide to which specific group a particular financier belonged. For example, G. Camodeca placed the Sulpicii from Puteoli, whose financial records were found in the area of Pompeii, at Murecine, in the category of exchange-bankers, while other scholars considered them just specialized businessmen and not involved in the banking occupation.

However, this is not the place to explain in detail all the activities of the members of these various groups. Here, we are interested in the role played by professional bankers and notable financiers in manufacturing and commerce. Unfortunately, the literary texts are not particularly informative on this point. We read a lot about financial operations, especially in Cicero's works, but these operations generally pertain to consumption.

Often, there were loans connected to political life which as we know, at the end of the Republic, made room for extensive financial operations. The same senators did not hesitate to be successively (or simultaneously) debtors and creditors of their peers. Caesar's debts are particularly well known: in 61 B.C.E. they [p. 148] reached the enormous amount of twenty-five million sestertii. The need to spend tremendously during certain moments of one's political career resulted from several factors: electoral corruption, the desire to acquire support by financially helping possible allies, great wealth disparities in the senatorial environment—all contributed to the need for huge financial transactions. Some of them were so influential that they directly influenced the interest rate. It is thus that, in 54 B.C.E., electoral corruption resulted in a doubling of this rate: in Rome, it went from 4% to 8% annually (Cicero, *ad Quintum fratrem*, 2.14.4; Cicero, *ad Atticum*, 4.15.7 and 4.17.2–3).

Political life sometimes provided free loans, but they were not devoid of a different kind of obligations: they were loans that came with political favors. The lender was a politician who expected to derive a political advantage in his career. The interest was small or even nonexistent, precisely because the discounted favor was not of a financial nature. This does not mean, however, that the lender did not benefit from them (at least, he had a hope of benefit). Crassus and Caesar were both glad to take advantage of this type of operation.

We should not confuse these loans "with political benefits" with other political loans that were not disinterested, either, and used to bear interest: these were loans "for political ends." The borrower was a political man who needed money to develop his career, organize an election campaign, and extend certain legal or illegal favors. He used the borrowed money for clear political purposes. In this case, there was no reason for the lender to be indifferent to future financial benefits and the payment of interest made possible by this very transaction.

We could say that these were consumer loans, as they were part of the sums that the senators used in the framework of their political and social life. [p. 149] If they borrowed to buy a luxurious city residence in Rome or to improve the comfort and luxury of one of their countryside residences, these are still considered consumer loans. Likewise, the poor peasant who had to borrow to afford food for his family before the harvest season was also taking out a consumer loan. All these forms of consumer loans were, clearly, part of the economy itself. However, up to now, historians studying the ancient economy have been wondering if the activities of the financiers actually contributed to the smooth running of production and trade. I will make a few remarks vis-à-vis this question before proceeding to address two other topics investigated in the last few years by W.V. Harris and P. Temin: the creation of money and the size of the credit market.

II. Credit and the Economic Life

When it comes to the links between Roman financiers and the economy, there are three important ideas that should be discussed. First, both ancient Greeks and Romans did not make a clear distinction between production loans and loans for consumption. Second, Roman financiers did not direct most of their efforts to production and commerce, in order consciously to create a setting propitious for efficient investment: there were no financial establishments specializing in production loans or commercial credit. But third, despite the previous two statements, it is also evident that Roman bankers and financiers intervened, in one manner or another, in economic life in general, and in commerce in particular. They did play an economic role.

Besides credit, the bankers and financiers provided numerous other services to the economic agents. The assayer-moneychangers were pivotal in exchanges and [p. 150] payments of money. It is not a coincidence that the changers of money were often based in ports and markets and that, in Pergamum during the reign of Hadrian, tensions erupted between them and the merchants (see inscription *OGI* 484 + II, p. 552). It is true that the merchants and the ship owners controlled and exchanged money themselves: touchstones were found in the wreckage of ships. However, the existence of the assayer-changers was very useful to commerce. The bank deposits, for which the bankers were or were not remunerated, were useful to commerce as well. This operation enabled merchants to maintain money in a city where they did not reside but that they often visited, as traders were accustomed to do. As early as the Ptolemaic period, merchants and traders were already part of the bankers' clientele.

When he condemns the widespread practice of borrowing, Plutarch makes an exception for those who had to borrow because they had nothing to eat or drink. But he treats in a similar manner those who borrowed to buy lands or hardworking slaves and those who borrowed because they enjoyed luxury and euergetism (Plutarch, *Moralia*, 830 E). In another passage the same Plutarch talks about borrowing in order to buy wheat fields, vineyards, and olive tree plantations (*Moralia,* 523 F). Such texts as Plutarch's, which mix the possible uses of loans, show two things at the same time: one, that the Greeks and the Romans were not familiar with the idea of production loans (that is, loans destined to finance production and trade), and two, that such loans existed and were in use. Several fragments of the *Digest* discuss the case of a loan that was taken out with the intention of buying land, repairing a boat, feeding the sailors, buying merchandise, etc. (*Digest,* 12.1.4 pr., Ulpian; *Digest*, 14.1.1.8–11 Ulpian; *Digest*, 14.1.7 Africanus). E. Cohen highlighted in one paragraph of his book a phrase of Demosthenes' on the role of loans in commerce, a phrase that was also cited by P. Millett. We find in Seneca's letters to Lucilius a very similar phrase: a man who wants to become involved in business, [p. 151] maritime commerce or public farms, needs to borrow and contact an intermediary to secure the necessary credit (Seneca, *ad Lucilium*, 119.1).

The Roman financiers (professionals or not) did not limit themselves to consumer loans. This does not mean however that the majority of the loans were production loans. How many of these loans pertained to production or commerce? We do not know. Probably, they were a minority. At this point, it is reasonable to concur with E. Cohen's conclusions about the situation in classical Greece, which also reflect those of P. Millett. The latter, in fact, in his book on the loans of Athens, compares classical Greece to modern Indian situations, in which he observes that 30% to 40% of loans were production loans. The ancient Greco-Roman world was not, of course, an under-developed country like India was, thirty or forty years ago (that is, it did not come in contact with a more "developed" country). That being said, it is very likely that a minority of the loans were production loans, but exactly what percentage, we cannot determine.

All categories of financiers were induced to give production loans, and (could) thus influence economic life, but not in the same ways nor at the same scales. In his

1992 article, C. Howgego briefly enumerated these categories of individuals and institutions which, in Roman antiquity, were giving out loans. In brief, short-term commercial credit was practiced by several categories, professional bankers and merchant-financiers in particular. The long-term credit, very likely a less frequent operation, was practiced primarily by the notable financiers and by wealthy businessmen.

Immediately or very soon after the auction, the *argentarii* and the *coactores argentarii* paid the sellers the sums they had to receive, and for a short amount of time (several months, never more than one year, according to the sources we have) used to lend money to the buyers. Often, these auctions were conducted in commercial places like ports, [p. 152] and in wholesale and retail markets. There were several such places in Rome: for example, the *Portus vinarius superior* (which was situated on the Tiber River, upstream from central Rome), the *Forum Boarium* and the *Macellum Magnum*. In Ostia, we have evidence of the existence of a *praeco vinorum*, who was involved in wine auctions. Outside Rome, in cities where fairs took place, such as Cremona, or where *nundinae*, the periodic markets, took place, we could find moneychangers and collectors.

In southern Latium and Campania, all the cities where we know changers and bankers dating back to the Principate have something in common: they are mentioned in the periodic market lists, the *indices nundinarii*. The periodic markets (*nundinae*) formed networks of which these indices provide examples. It is certain that, in Pompeii and in Puteoli, auctions took place on the days of the *nundinae*. When the assayer-bankers and the auctioneers entered the stage, starting with the end of the second century B.C.E., it is clear that such auctions were already commonplace. One hundred thirty-eight tablets belonging to the moneychanger and banker Lucius Caecilius Jucundus (*argentarius* or *coactor argentarius*), who lived and worked in Pompeii during the first century C.E., represent the receipts for auctions that took place during the periodic markets. When he paid the seller of the bid the agreed-upon price (and while waiting to receive the same amount from the buyer at a later date) the vendor gave him a receipt. At the end of this chapter the reader will find a translation of tablet no. 6 from Jucundus' collection. This tablet is different from the rest of the lot: the payment to the vendor took place in installments and not in one lump sum, as happens in the other documents.

In addition to its function as a rural market for peasants and the smallholders of the surrounding area, the *nundinae* fulfilled two others. They constituted one of the places where estate transactions could take place, where the owners, even the most important ones, could sell and buy [p. 153] lands, houses, animals, and slaves, and where they could sell at least some of the products of their properties. At the same time, these were the markets attended by merchants and played a rather nonnegligible role in the commercialization of agricultural productions, routed to the coast, and then transported all the way to Rome. In the *nundinae* taking place on the coast of Campania, the merchants came to auction the products that they had transported or were going to transport via the sea. Tablet no. 100 in Jucundus' collection shows that, in the middle of the first century C.E., a certain Ptolemy of Alexandria sold a lot of flax in the Pompeii *nundinae,* and received a receipt from the banker for the sale.

Of course, situations clearly varied enormously, depending upon whether the seller, the buyer, or both, were consumers, retailers, or wholesalers. For the traders who were buying, the short-term commercial credit provided by the banker meant that they could secure the merchandise without having to pay for it immediately. They could also resell this merchandise before they even had to pay for it. Horace's pseudo-Acron scholion, which attempts to explain the meaning of the words *coactor* and *argentarius,* provides a great example of this type of situation. It mentions olives, which were sold by the *foranei* (merchants installed in the forum or near it? in this case, it would be the wholesalers). The auction buyers themselves were the *circumforanei,* traveling merchants, fairground vendors who would resell merchandise to the surrounding areas at retail prices. The banker (*argentarius*) used to pay the sellers immediately. Through the intervention of the debt collector (*coactor*), he was reimbursed by the buyers, the traveling merchants, to whom he had given credit, and who could, without a doubt, sell the acquired products before they had to pay for them (pseudo-Acron, *ad Hor. Sat.*, 1.6.85–86). For the merchants selling these products, the credit they had gotten from the banker allowed them to replenish their stock more quickly, without having to wait for the buyers to pay for the merchandise that had been sold. [p. 154] Even when the buyer was a consumer, the price paid to the banker was still benefitting the accounts of the vendors.

In other cases, the *argentarii* and the *coactores argentarii* intervened in the auctions connected with artisanal or mining production, and, in this case too, the buyers could be merchants. In Rome, the *coactor argentarius* Aulus Argentarius Antiochus, for example, who conducted his profession *inter aerarios,* was probably doing so in auctions of artifacts produced by bronze-workers (*CIL* VI.9186). The bronze plaques of Vipasca, on the Iberian peninsula, also mention auctions mediated by *argentarii* and *coactores argentarii.* The *lex metalli Vipascensis* shows that mine shafts were sold at auction and so were slaves, mules, donkeys, and horses—that is, the labor force and the beasts of burden needed in the exploitation of the mines (*CIL* II.5181). At Vipasca, the short-term credit provided by the *argentarius* was used by men who exploited the mines.

It could also happen that the products being sold at auction were agricultural (food) products, and that the seller was either a landowner or a farmer. In his *On Agriculture,* Cato mentions such a case and, two and a half centuries later, Pliny the Younger provides another example (*Letters,* 8.2). Pliny himself sold the products of his vineyards at auctions to buyers called *negotiatores.* In this particular case, the *argentarius* is not mentioned. The text of the letter clearly shows that, in this particular transaction, the sum used in the auction by the buyers was not provided by a banker.

The professional bankers, however, were not the only ones providing short-term commercial credit. The Agro Murecine tablets show that Hesychus, an imperial slave, who before had been the slave of an imperial freedman, and who was not a banker by profession, also practiced this kind of short or average term loan, by lending out money to C. Novius Eunus, a wheat merchant. Similarly, a passage written by Paul in [p. 155] the *Digest* describes a slave who, charged by his master to lend money with interest, took it upon himself also to practice commercial lending, and used to pay the barley traders on the buyers' behalf (*Digest* 14.5.8 Paul). Finally, maritime loans were also a form of short-term commercial loans, but a very specific one. Very likely, it was practiced primarily by notable *feneratores*, wealthy businessmen, or by merchant-financiers.

Among the production loans (that is, of loans contributing to production, transportation, or the distribution of goods), medium- and long-term loans are rare (particularly in the documents on this practice that survive to present day). This often seems surprising, but probably it is wrong to be surprised, for the two following reasons.

First, even in eighteenth-century England, such long-term loans were not as frequent or as massive as was previously thought. P. Verley summarizes in the following way the most recent studies on start-up capital and self-financing, as well as on the relationship between fixed and liquid capital: "low demands for start-up capital, rapid growth then permitted a massive reinvestment of the profits, predominantly therefore using internal over external funding, low demand for fixed over liquid capital" (P. Verley, *Révolution industrielle*, 1985, 48–51.) No wonder if such conclusions are valid *a fortiori* as regards Roman antiquity. Self-financing was also present in antiquity.

In addition, Rome had institutions that offered financing choices other than long-term loans. The first of the institutions is what we would call a limited partnership: one of the associates provided the capital to one or a few associates who were in charge of the actual work and asset management. This was well suited to the needs of elite members specially interested in increasing their inheritance. These elite members had the opportunity to extract profits from commercial, industrial, or [p. 156] even financial enterprises without having to live the life of an entrepreneur. As J. Le Goff commented à propos the medieval *commenda*, which resembled this type of association: "The contracting parties were associates when it came to sharing the risks and the profits of the enterprise but otherwise, the relationship was very similar to that between lender and borrower." It is thus erroneous to conclude that, just because a senator participated in such a contract he was a merchant or an industrialist. Even from an economic point of view, this is wrong. The great Crassus partook in such associations, and probably so did Vespasian (Cicero, *Paradoxes of the Stoics*, 6.46; Suetonius, *Vespasian*, 4.6). There were, however, some municipal notables who were involved in such limited partnerships as well. This was the case with P. Alfenus Pollio, identified as such in Jucundus' tablet no. 45, found at Pompeii.

The second institution is the *peculium*: it is very important to make a clear distinction between this term and the *proxy* (*praepositio*), discussed in chapter 3. In the latter case, the master maintains his role as the entrepreneur and the servant is the "manager," to use a term proposed by J.-J. Aubert. This is not the case in the *peculium* situation. Aubert wrote that "even though a slave with *peculium* was legally dependent, his economic activities were practically kept separate from his master's. [...] A slave with *peculium* was not acting as business manager on behalf of a principal" (J.-J. Aubert, *Business Managers*, 4). He was an entrepreneur. In practice, from an economic point of view, the *peculium* was a sort of long-term credit.

However, we have some evidence of medium- or long-term production loans. Some of these loans were granted by patrons to their freedmen. A passage figuring in the *Digest* and written by Q. Cervidius Scaevola mentions such a case, when a commercial loan was granted for a term of several years. Using stones as a pledge, a *negotiator marmorum* borrowed from a lender whose identity is not clear. The borrowed money was used to pay the vendors who had sold the marble to the *negotiator*. The latter, on the other hand, had [p. 157] rented warehouses that belonged to the emperor (*Digest*, 20.4.21.1). This is still another type of loan that served to finance the circulating capital.

To summarize: Roman banking and businesses did not necessarily function as facilitators used to encourage economic investment. Regardless, their economic role should not be entirely dismissed.

III. The Creation of Currency and the Transfer of Claims

In two recently published articles (listed in the Bibliography), W.V. Harris discussed the methods of payment and the money supply. He started with a concrete example: in 62 B.C.E., Cicero bought a house on the Palatine, which cost him 3,500,000 sestertii; how did he pay this amount? At this particular time, very few gold coins were in circulation in Rome. Could he have paid this amount in full, in silver? This would have amounted to a weight between 3300 and 3400 kg. Harris believes that it is very unlikely that such a substantial and heavy sum of money could be transported: besides, few Latin texts mention silver being moved around. Were there other methods of payment? Payments in kind were mentioned in Latin texts, but quite rarely, and they do not refer to large amounts of silver. Gold or silver ingots could have been used as methods of payment, but this was not common: ingots are rarely found in hoards. Among the Republic-era hoards that Michael Crawford considered in his book *Roman Republic Coin Hoards*, only two contained metal bars. In the cities of Vesuvius, no gold or silver ingots or bars have been found.

So, what other payment methods were available at this time? As I have already mentioned, in the great majority of cases, the buyer or the debtor was authorized to pay back the respective amount over a certain period of time, [p. 158] or in several installments, as in the sales at bids, as we have seen above. In the end, however, the buyer needed to pay back. To revisit the case of the house Cicero purchased in 62 B.C.E., we know that he tried to borrow the money, but we do not know in what form exactly he ended up paying for it. We assume that he paid with coins, but in three or four installments: in the first case, each payment would have weighed 1100 kg; in the second, more than 800 kg.

It is for this reason that W.V. Harris insists that the payments were actually made through the transfer of claims (*nomina*). We know for a fact, both from juridical texts and from several allusions in Cicero's correspondence, that a debtor could transfer claims to his creditor. If Gaius was indebted to Titus and at the same time was owed a debt by Marcus, he could transfer his claim on Marcus to Titus. In some cases, the claim (*nomen*) was accepted for the value that had been written on it. In other cases, however, Titus might hesitate to accept the claim, because he had doubts that Marcus would reimburse him later. He could also accept the claim, but at a lesser value. Certainly, to be able to pay by means of claims, one had to have such things. As lending with interest was a widespread practice, it is safe to assume that a lot of men had claims, especially those belonging to the elite. Harris believes that payments by way of claims were actually quite common. Each historian is tempted to use the argument of silence (*ex silentio*) and to use it selectively. Harris, for example, writes that the reason we have little evidence of payments being made in ingots is because such forms of payments were indeed rare. But payments by transfer of claim are also not much attested, yet nevertheless Harris concludes that they were quite common!

Such forms of payment were, indeed, used: we are sure of that. But were they common? Assuming that they were, for the members of the elite, could we by extension assume that they were also practiced in other [p. 159] social milieus, and at every moment between the second century B.C.E. and the fourth century C.E.? Harris wondered if these payments by transfer of claims were not more common before Caesar's dictatorship than after. Many gold coins were minted during the 40s B.C.E. and even more during the Augustan period, to such an extent that cash payments became easier to make. Why not, indeed? Unfortunately, we do not have the means to prove that payments by means of claims were frequent, or the contrary. In this case, the best method is to stay close to the extant documentation. There is no doubt that we have much more evidence supporting the presence and use of cash payments than other types of payments. Why should we then doubt the verity of this information and assume that other forms of payment—which are, in fact, very rarely mentioned in literary and legal texts—were in reality very common?

The question of payments was not the only topic discussed by Harris in these articles. He was also interested in money supply, in the economic sense of the expression. During Roman antiquity, did metal coins constitute all available cash? Like R. Bogaert, I have explained elsewhere that the Roman banks enabled purchasing power, but not the currency per se. Is this distinction between "purchasing power" and "money supply" relevant? Once I believed it so, but recently I am less convinced. The first of the three monetary aggregates discussed in economic science textbooks, the so-called M1, consists of coins, banknotes, and also of most liquid bank deposits. It shows that these bank deposits contribute to the money supply. So, Harris is correct: by receiving deposits, the ancient banks created currency.

Harris is well aware that the number of ancient banks and the volume of their transactions was not sufficient to create [p. 160] a lot of currency. While vigorously maintaining that there was an abundant money supply in Rome, he turned toward the nonbanking claims, which did not concern banks or financial institutions, but private individuals, and argued that this type of claim produced an additional money supply. Yet, in economic textbooks, such claims are never taken into account in the three aggregates, M1, M2, and M3. So how could we then justify the thesis that, in Rome, such claims were responsible for the creation of currency? Harris' arguments fail to convince us that this was, indeed, the case.

He goes a step further and attempts to sustain the idea that the transferred claims I mentioned earlier could circulate freely, and that it was a chain of delegations that moved from hand to hand. At the discretion of this chain, the value of the claims could fluctuate. According to him, these claims had a "market value" and they were traded in a "market *in nomina.*" But the very strict legal constraints were an obstacle to the assignment of these claims: for this reason only, they could not have been as common as Harris notes. The delegation required that a new contract be established, carrying the name of the new creditor or the new debtor. Accordingly, it is impossible to conclude that claims could circulate freely. In addition, we have absolutely no text, in Greek or in Latin, documenting such markets or providing a debt rating, regardless of the type of claim. Harris based his argument on the existence of payments by delegation—which were used, but not nearly as extensively as he claims—and of delegations in series that then developed into negotiable free claims. However, these last two phenomena that he builds his theory upon (delegations in series, negotiable free claims) are never attested in any ancient texts. These successive shifts show just how strong the tendency to modernize the ancient economy is. The Bücher-Meyer controversy is by no means extinct, and it continues to create new myths. [p. 161]

IV. The Credit Market

Interest-bearing loans, which were quite common, regularly produced crises of debt and default. The state, closely monitoring and keenly aware of these situations, tried to resolve them through timely interventions. And additionally, during these critical times and even independently of them, the state often enforced a maximum rate of interest. Under the Principate, when such a rate was enacted, this maximum interest was typically an annual rate of 12%; rates beyond that were considered usurious, and they were illegal in principle. Examples towards the end of the Republic—in particular, in central Italy and in the city of Rome—do demonstrate that, whatever the official maximum rate, the *de facto* rate varied considerably, and was responsive to shifts in the supply and demand for money. And this is to say it is quite proper to speak of the Roman credit market existing at this time.

P. Temin recently devoted two articles to financial intermediation and credit market, the first as sole author, the second in collaboration with D. Rathbone. Temin points out the indisputable presence of financial intermediaries whose job was to connect lenders and borrowers, and he details different ways these intermediaries involved themselves in lender-borrower transactions. He then makes direct comparisons between these various modes of intermediation, which appear during the Roman Empire, and similar modes of intermediation developed in England or the United Provinces (the Republic of the Seven United Netherlands) at the beginning of the eighteenth century. Such comparisons are, of course, very interesting to make; however, they will not be examined in detail here. At any rate, in the conclusion of his second article, Temin also argues that financial intermediation did not play an important role in the triggering of the industrial revolution—a conclusion that seems convincing. On the other hand, as Temin is convinced that the Roman economy was a market economy, he insists that there was a unified credit market, from one end of the Mediterranean to the other. In my view, this thesis of a unified credit market is incorrect—which I will show by analyzing available data on interest rates. [p. 162]

The variations of the interest rate provided by the evidence were, almost without exception, between 4% and 12% per year. It was extremely rare to find an interest rate less than 4% (though in a text by Q. Cervidius Scaevola, *Digest*, 33.1.21.4, there is a mention of a 3% rate). One of the authors of the *Historia Augusta* classified the 4% rate as *minimae usurae* (*Historia Augusta*, Antoninus Pius, 2.8). As to the maximum: except in usurious cases, the 12% rate was almost never exceeded (but yet see *CIL* V.5134). G. Billeter is correct to claim that rates above 12% per year would have appeared usurious, even when the interest rate was not *legally* limited. When, following the battle of Actium, the treasure of the Egyptian kings was brought to Rome and partially cashed out, the interest rate plummeted from its usual maximum to its minimum, falling from 12% to 4% (Suetonius, *Augustus*, 41.2; Dio Cassius, 51.21.5); it thus moved from its highest typical level to its lowest.

I. Shatzman and A. Gara asked another good question: how can we explain the fact that the interest rate was often higher than the land revenues (which, according to ancient authors, did not usually go over 6%)? In these conditions, how was it possible to continue the exploitation of lands? Gara answered these questions by explaining that the ethical and social values of the ancient world prevented the ancients from investing the whole of their properties in moneylending. Very well, then. Yet, we have to consider the risk, too: lending with interest was a much riskier proposition than agricultural operations, for example. When the rich wanted to preserve their existing capital and have it produce a modest but reliable revenue, the land was a much better investment than lending money. With very few exceptions, the land could never be lost, while financial capital could be lost.

Finally, we need to consider that, in the same cities, several interest rates were practiced contemporaneously, without even taking into account the usurious loans. Considering the paucity of our available documentation, this greatly complicates the perception of possible short-term developments. The rate of interest varied [p. 163] based on the personality of the creditor and that of the borrower. The amount of the loan and its duration must also be considered. In addition, the differences in the rates of interest were also dependent on the particular concerns and the strategies of the lenders. Two quite different approaches were possible: the strategy of provident management and secure investments and the—much riskier—strategy of enrichment and quick profits. A passage from Persius' work describes these two strategies side by side, and notes that the former brought in a modest 5% while the latter brought in a whopping 11% profit. This passage shows that in the same time period, in the same location, rates could vary widely, but without reaching usurious levels (Persius, *Satires*, 5.149–50).

At a given time, did the interest rate vary from place to place? Several legal texts suggest that they did. In these examples, the reason for these differences is not always given (unless I am mistaken, it is not explained in *Digest*, 22.1.37 Ulpian). When such an explanation is provided, the cause of the differences is not always the same. Sometimes the text makes implicit references to a limitation provision from the provincial edict (*Digest*, 17.1.1.1.3 Ulpian, *legitimo modo*; *Digest*, 26.7.7.10 Ulpian). In other cases we see that conjuncture also played an important role and that variations depended on the demand and supply of currency (*Digest*,13.4.3 Gaius; *Digest*, 27.4.3.1 Ulpian and probably 26.7.7.10 Ulpian). Thus, Gaius says that, in certain places, the interest was lower and the money supply abundant while in other places, it was higher and the supply was more limited. Sometimes the jurisconsult made references to regional customs, that is, the sustainable local practices were relatively immune to changing circumstances (*Digest*, 33.1.21 pr., Scaevola; 22.1.1 pr., Papinian; 30.39.1 Ulpian). These more or less enduring customs are referred to as *mos* and *consuetudo*. The variations of demand and supply of money were not the only causes for these differences: we need to consider that, in certain regions, interest rates varied little, based on local or regional traditions. [p. 164]

What about the variations in time? In Italy, we are faced with two very different and successive situations. In the last century of the Republic we have several well-known examples of abrupt changes. Under the Principate, on the other hand, we could barely notice any variations, and the rates mentioned in literary and legal texts and on inscriptions are low, most frequently 5% or 6% per year (please refer to Columella, *On Agriculture*, 3.3.9; Persius, *Satires*, 5.149–50; Pliny, *Natural History*, 14.56; *Digest*, 15.4.3 Ulpian; *Digest*, 22.1.13 pr., Scaevola; 22.1.17.6 Paul; 26.7.7.10 Ulpian; 45.1.134.2 Paul; 46.3.102.3 Scaevola).

Between 88 and 62 B.C.E. the usual rate had surely varied repeatedly. At the end of 62, in Rome, it was rather low (6%), but it seems to have escalated during the last weeks of the same year. In 54 B.C.E. as a result of a case of grave electoral corruption, it doubled, from 4% to 8% (Cicero, *ad Atticum*, 4.15.7 and 4.17.2; *ad Quintum Fratrem*, 2.14.4). We notice that before this incident it was very low. The senatus consultum of 51 B.C.E. shows that it had risen considerably between 54 and 51. It is clear that around the time of the Civil War and the debt and payment crisis that marked it the rates did not go down any more. Caesar himself wrote that interest rates always rise during wars, because of the exceptional contributions demanded from everybody: this explanation proves that he was aware of the causal relationship between demand and supply (Caesar, *The Civil War*, 3.32.5). We saw this observation in practice when, in 31 B.C.E., the treasury of the Queen of Egypt was confiscated and the rates fell from 12% to 4% per year.

This ample documentation shows us that the interest rates varied from one province to the other, and from one region to the other, and that P. Temin was completely wrong when he discussed a unified credit market, extending from one corner of the Empire to the other. On the other hand, variations in time, which have been documented, give an idea of the rapid changes in the interest rates—at least in Rome and central Italy, where the aristocratic part of the financial world lived. [p. 165]

We also see that in this region, during the first century B.C.E., the interest rate fluctuations were not contingent upon economic phases, as was the case in modern Europe (on this subject, see pp. 191–201 in J.-Y. Grenier's book, *L'Économie d'Ancien Régime*). It is impossible to place them in a specific relationship with economic life. In general, these rates grew higher around political and military events (civil wars, wartime looting) and during the ups and downs of senatorial political life. Do these valid observations reveal a pronounced archaism of the Roman economy? It is difficult to say because we lack information on the possible economic cycles: the absence of data, however, does not necessarily mean that the phenomena themselves were absent. That being said, the fact that Rome built an empire and its financial life was almost entirely contained within the imperial borders could not have failed to have consequences on such an important thing as interest rates.

Texts

Receipt Delivered by the Slave Salvius to the Banker L. Caecilius Jucundus of Pompeii (29 May 54 C.E.)

Signature of Salvius.

Under the consulship of Manius Acilius Aviola and Marcus Asinius, on the fourth day of the calends of June [= 29 May 54 C.E.], I, Salvius, a slave of the heirs of Numerius Nasennius Nigidius Vaccula, recognize by this writing that I have received from Lucius Caecilius Jucundus three thousand fifty-nine sesterces, for my sale at bid, which I have conveyed with the stipulation of Jucundus; the sesterces that I have received in successive payments as I wished, concluding today.

Written at Pompeii.

CIL IV.3340, no. 6 [p. 166]

Bankruptcy of the Moneychanger-Banker Callistus, at Rome, under the Reign of Commodus

Callistus was a slave of a certain Carpophorus, a Christian who was part of the imperial household. To Callistus, because he was Christian, Carpophorus gave a large sum of money. Furthermore, Callistus had promised to return to him the benefits that would come to him from the bank's business. With this money he founded a bank in the quarter of the Piscina Publica. After a certain amount of time, thanks to the credit of Carpophorus, he received a number of deposits from widows and religious brethren. But since he had squandered the money, he was in considerable financial difficulties. The fact was reported to Carpophorus, who informed Callistus that he wanted an accounting. Understanding this, and suspecting the punishment his master had in mind for him, Callistus fled to the sea. Finding at Portus a ship that was ready to sail, he embarked, not caring about the destination. But he did not succeed in escaping, because Carpophorus learned about it. He arrived at the port and, after directions had been given to him, he tried to enter the boat which, thanks to a delay by the captain, was still sitting in the middle of the bay. Callistus, on board his boat, spotted his master at a distance and understanding that he was to be taken, renounced his life. He determined to make away with himself, and he threw himself into the sea. However, the sailors, leaping into small boats, pulled him from the water in spite of himself; during these events those who were on land uttered great cries. He was thereafter returned to his master, taken back to Rome, and put into service at a gristmill.*

Hippolytus of Rome, *Refutation of All Heresies*, 9.12

[p. 167] *Gristmill: this was the use of a circular treadmill to power a heavy grindstone to mill grain, which was a very severe punishment visited on slaves. After other episodes, Callistus was sent to forced labor in the mines of Sardinia, probably in 188 C.E. Long after he returned from Sardinia and was freed, he became Pope in 217 C.E. and died in 222. Hippolytus considered him to be a dishonest man and a heretic: when he wrote this text, Callistus was already dead. [pp. 168, 169]

Chapter 5
Commerce

We can speak of commerce when, between the producer and the consumer, one or more intermediaries become involved with and part of the exchange. When the producer sells directly to the consumer, we can still speak of a sale, of a market, but not of commerce. Every landowner sold a part of the products of his lands; he did not, however, complete a commercial role, except if he explicitly attended to an operation or a service that usually belonged to intermediaries. A peasant going to a neighboring village to sell his products did not perform a commercial act.

At first glance it seems that this book discusses commerce exclusively in the current chapter. The reader will notice, however, that the topic of commerce was sometimes discussed in the preceding chapters (and he or she will find more information in the last chapters of this book). There are several reasons for this distribution. The first has to do with the fact that the Bücher-Meyer controversy continually addresses the commercial sector. The debates on the exchanges between the city and the countryside, the interests of the elite apart from agriculture, the importance of the market, and the interventions of public powers are all related to commerce, and I have discussed this relationship in chapter 1.

Chapters 2 and 3 are dedicated to production; the extended space allotted to this subject emphasizes the importance of this activity as commerce is made possible by the exchange of a specific good that was previously produced. At the same time, however, these two chapters touched upon additional topics related to commercialization in order to show that this process is partially dependent on specific products. [p. 170] There are also some constants at play, but these constants do not cover all aspects of commercialization. The glass trade, for example, is defined by the fact that it deals with both unprocessed glass and glass objects. The metal trade, too, consists of the same two levels (bars and ingots on one hand, and metal objects on the other), but it is also marked by the strong influence of the State, i.e., the owner of the most important mines and the agent responsible for redirecting a part of these metals into free trade. The tableware trade is characterized by the fact that, when transported by ship, it often fulfilled the role of supplemental cargo. In the construction materials trade (stones, bricks, tiles, etc.) the role of the members of the elite was by no means insignificant. Additionally, a part of these products passed directly from the hands of the producer to those of the consumer, without the intervention of the intermediaries (as, for example, when the emperor's agents purchased bricks and tiles for the construction of a public building). I hope that the passages in chapters 2 and 3 that were dedicated to the commercialization of these products helped comprehension of these specifics.

I also have to note that, every time public officials had to transport their goods (for example, wheat, oil, stones for construction) they used private carriers. The state did not have its own fleet.

The people in the trade were part of a peculiar social milieu, which belonged to what we could call the urban professions. The moneychangers, the bankers, and the debt collectors, to name just some of the financial agents discussed in chapter 4, also belong to this milieu, as do the artisans. Generally speaking, similar comments could be made about both artisans and traders, and in this chapter the two professions will be discussed together. [p. 171]

This chapter is composed of five sections dedicated to the following topics: the notion of the market and the problems posed by it; local and regional trade; the social milieu of traders and artisans; the potential competition between Italy and the provinces; and finally, trade in the east (exchanges between Rome and the regions situated outside the imperial borders, in Asia and eastern Africa).

I. The Market and the Markets

As I have already mentioned in chapter 1, the market, in the abstract sense of the term, continues to fuel one of the biggest debates about the economy of the ancient world. The word "market" has several meanings. S. Kaplan, a modern historian who has extensively studied the food supply of Paris under the Ancien Régime, distinguished between the actual sites where trading took place, the "marketplaces," and the principle of the market, or "market principle" (see S.L. Kaplan, *Provisioning Paris* (1984), pp. 25–29). The market, as a concrete site, is a place where transactions take place, and which is subject to the control and intervention of political authorities: in other words, it is "a location in space and a group of regulations that are linked to this location." The "market principle," however, is not dependent on a concrete location, and

> it implies the existence of a system of relationships within which transactions take place and, wherever the transaction takes place, the impersonal forces of demand and supply decide specific prices […]. The market principle, founded on the idea of a perpetual automatic adjustment at the global level, requires that trade has a freedom of action without interference.

Such "concrete" markets, taking place daily or periodically, were a common occurrence in antiquity, and these two ideas necessarily existed in antiquity as well. A. Bresson, R. Descat, and L. Migeotte have shown how, during the Classical period, the city of Athens had designated special places as market sites, which were subject to strict inspections performed by the magistrates of the city, the so-called *agoranomoi* (Migeotte, pp. 122–27). This seems to also be the case in Rome, [p. 172] even though we have much less evidence on the running of these Roman markets and the exact manner in which the magistrates could intervene in them.

The moment a vendor and a buyer face each other and discuss the price of the merchandise, we can speak of market, in the abstract sense of the word. The price is the product of adjustments between the opposing interests of these two protagonists. This is what R. Guesnerie calls the "stylized market," or, a schema that helps explain various historical situations. This adjustment process, which results in an agreed-upon price, depends on circumstantial conditions, and it can occur in places larger or less large. Thus, in its abstract sense, the word *market* designates a region more or less extended, inside which circulation of information, merchants, and products is sufficiently stable and active to produce unified prices that take into account transportation costs. Such a region constitutes a unified space from the point of view of commercial transactions. It does not, however, have the same parameters for all products. At the end of the Republic and under the Principate the area around and including Rome, with its two ports, Ostia and, later, Portus, represented a unified market for bricks and tiles. The question is: what are the necessary and sufficient conditions to consider a market unified? How could we, for example, evaluate the wheat market in Rome? How far did it extend? A part of the wheat supplies arrived in Rome as a product of free trade. Another part, the African and Egyptian wheat, for example, supplied the capital as part of the taxes owed to the Empire. But, on the other hand, some wheat coming from Africa and Egypt was a product of free trade. So, should we then consider the African and Egyptian wheat as being part of Rome's wheat market? There is no easy answer; as for me, I would rather say no. In any case, the size and the location of these abstract markets varied according to the respective products and eras. [p. 173]

In addition, the word *market*, in its abstract sense, could be applied not only to merchandise, but to the entire economic life as, for example, when we speak of "market economy." But was there a "market economy" to speak of in antiquity? This question was posed repeatedly in the past, and most recently by P. Temin, who gives it an affirmative answer. What would be the definition and the inception point of such a "market economy"? According to R. Guesnerie, it is when "a substantial part of the economic activity is organized around institutions called markets, which play an important role in decentralized action, profits, and the adjustments of price play an essential role" (*L'Économie de marché*). According to P. Temin, a market economy exists when sufficient market transactions take place and when most resources are distributed based on prices that can be modified as a function of context. How many market transactions are needed to arrive at such an economy? P. Temin does not tell us.

Directly or indirectly, this question has been asked for a long time, vis-à-vis the Roman world. M.I. Rostovtzeff was convinced that, at certain points, the ancient economy was a market economy, but he never undertook to provide sufficient evidence for this argument, nor did he consider the concept of market. In his view, the mere abundance of economic activity was sufficient evidence. M.I. Finley, on the other hand, believed that the opposite was true. He even questioned the notion of competition and the demand and supply relationship. In *The Ancient Economy,* he argued that no abstract markets for nonmaterial goods or nonconsumable material goods existed in antiquity. He believed the same to be true for labor and real estate markets, and money or monetary markets. At the same time, he advocated the existence of consumable goods markets, that is, the areas in which these items would have been sold. Yet, he withheld the title of "market economy" from the ancient economy. [p. 174] According to E. Roll, he defined "market economy" as "an enormous conglomeration of interdependent markets" (*The Ancient Economy*, p. 22).

As soon as a product started or ceased to be sold well, the notion of competition enters the discussion, even though the term does not explain all the cycles of the ancient economy. This limitation was illustrated when we discussed fine ceramics. As we saw in chapter 3, section VII, informed by the excavation results on the *Cala Culip IV* shipwreck, J. Nieto insisted on the difference between principal and accompanying cargo. For example, if the sigillata vases from southern Gaul (La Graufesenque) were transported with amphorae or ingots, it was the latter that constituted the main freight: the tableware ceramics were there as a filler, to complete the cargo. In this case, the commercial success of the ceramics did not result from being in competition with the other products being transported, but simply because they accompanied the amphorae. J. Nieto emphasized that, under Vespasian, the dispersion of La Graufesenque ceramics declined abruptly while the sigillated African ceramics did not become popular till much later. So, there was no competition between these products for the same market: the African sigillata simply took over the commercial space abandoned by the sigillata from southern Gaul.

J. Nieto is not the only one to insist on the limitations associated with this concept of competition. C. Goudineau and A. Tchernia have also addressed this topic. The former noted that the grand Arezzo factories and their Lyon branch "closed their doors before the competition posed by the Ruteni workshops became a real danger." It follows then that, when the Ruteni sigillata conquered the markets of Gaul, the Germanies, then Spain and Italy, it was not as "a result of a ferocious battle, but simply because it was the only one available." Similarly, when the Tarraconaise wine from southern Gaul surpassed the Italian wine, we notice that there was a small time difference [p. 175] between the departure of the Italian product and the arrival of that from Tarraconaise. Finally, according to M.G. Fulford, the necessity of ceramic imports in the British province resulted from the fact that the local grain production was insufficient (as previously discussed, grains and ceramics were a matched pair of products). When Britain became self-sufficient in wheat production, it stopped importing not just the grain, but also the ceramic ware. It is believed that, in the fourth century, Britain had been so successful with its cereal productions that, instead of buying wheat as it had to do in the past, it actually supplied the Rhine army with the needed quantities. Maybe this move was necessary because of the decreasing production of the wheat fields in northern Gaul and Germany.

These examples are very convincing indeed, and it is quite advantageous to be careful of an improper and hurried use of the concept of competition. At the same time, however, I think it is impossible to eliminate it completely. It is impossible to deny that, in a marketplace, the buyers had, both in Rome and in Classical or Hellenistic Greece, a choice among several products, and that the producers and traders were thus competing with each other. Many of the urban areas used ceramic vases, terracotta lamps, and oil and wine amphorae produced in various places and sold by various traders. The most widely popular sigillata were not always available. Competition was present in most places, but not between the same kinds of ceramics (apart from the most widely distributed sigillata). The prices were calculated based on demand and supply, but demand and supply varied depending on each place. In addition, the more we learn about common ceramics, the more the existence of good quality, locally or regionally produced ceramics is validated, which could be placed at the top level of the ordinary kind of ceramics. The binary distinction between fine and common ceramics is thus not satisfactory, all the more so because not all the sigillata were of the same quality, as M. Picon showed, based on chemical tests. Besides, some sigillata workshops [p. 176] only sold their products on the local or provincial markets (as the Bram workshop did, in southern Gaul). Most commonly, at the beginning and the end of their production, most of the sigillata ateliers sold only at the regional level. It is necessary, of course, to react against a mechanical and short-sighted usage of the notion of competition. But we find the efforts to promote the idea of the absence of competition in the ancient economy unproductive and useless. We need to evaluate the situation case by case.

The presence of competition does not mean that the entire economy was subsumed to the market principle, nor that all goods, material or not, were the object of market transactions. P. Temin, whose beliefs fall at the extreme end of the "modernist" camp, believes that the Roman economy altogether was a market economy and had a unified money and labor market. Such ideas must be rejected: they are not supported by convincing arguments. The differences between products and regions were too striking for such a conclusion to be valid.

The case study of wheat and grain, which P. Temin uses, is instructive. Starting with six references on wheat prices, from regions geographically very distant (Palermo, Madrid, the Po valley, Antioch in Pisidia, Palestine, and Egypt), he strives to show that these prices were established based on the distance of their location from the city of Rome, because the wheat market is oriented toward Rome. It would be too easy to point out the striking disproportion between the scarcity of the available evidence and the categorical tone of his conclusions. It would be, however, a legitimate step inasmuch as his conclusions are both hasty and biased. If Rome was the final destination for wheat coming from various regions (northern Africa, Egypt), several sources such as Cicero's *On Grain*, the inscription from Antioch in Pisidia, and select passages from [p. 177] Dio Chrysostom's discourses show that the actual sales and distributions to the consumers were, in very many cases, carried out at a regional or local level. Both Cicero and Dio insisted on the fact that, in Asia Minor, the price of wheat varied from city to city, and was not Rome-dependent. On the other hand, as I have already mentioned, the wheat destined for Rome was divided in two categories: privately traded wheat and governmental wheat, which the State distributed to some of Rome's inhabitants.

To prove his case, P. Temin starts with the idea that the quantity of commercial wheat was by far the more important, but nothing proves this point. In addition to the grain consumed by the producers themselves, and which did not make it to the markets, there were other wheat "markets" that should be considered distinct from each other: the fiscal wheat (belonging to the imperial services and collected as taxes), commercial wheat destined for Rome (which interests P. Temin particularly), and the regional or local wheat markets. In this last category, the prices were thus established city by city, and province by province, as a function of supply and demand (and adjusted, if needed, by city magistrates or governors) at that particular locale or region. There was no such thing as a unified wheat market.

Another great example that supports the idea of the fragmented, abstract markets during the Roman period is that of the interest rate, which P. Temin also used to prove his theory of unified markets. I have examined this in detail in chapter 4. My conclusion for this claim is the same as it was for the wheat market: there was indeed a credit market, and M.I. Finley was wrong to deny the existence of such a market. It was, however, in no way a unified market. In the case of Rome and central Italy it was regional; in other locations it could be regional or local. We could not speak of a credit market on the scale of the whole Mediterranean region. [p. 178]

In the case of Classical Greece, R. Descat has emphasized several economic changes in the fifth and fourth centuries B.C.E.: relational changes between agriculture and markets; between agricultural and nonagricultural activities; the appearance of the *oikonomia attike*: ("economic phenomenon characterized by the double action of selling and buying"); increasing land sales. All of these constitute important changes and they point at the existence of markets that were developed but fragmented, and often existing in small spaces. According to A. Bresson's expression, Classical Greece, the Roman world at the end of the Republic, and the Empire were "economies with markets": economies functioning partially within the framework of abstract markets whose logic and modalities are important to understand. They were not, however, "market economies." We need to reject the idea that the Roman Empire had built "a global economic unit." Does this mean that Roman or Greek antiquity was more "archaic" than more recent periods, such as the end of the Middle Ages or early modern times? Not at all. Before we allow ourselves to be persuaded by such an archaism, we need to perform an in-depth comparison which, despite Karl Marx, Max Weber, and a few others, has not yet been done well.

II. Local and Regional Commerce

Many archaeological excavations, in various regions of the Roman Empire, allow us to be aware of the intensity of local or regional commerce, which has been neglected in favor of the long-distance trade routes. The latter were, obviously, more impressive because they required substantive transportation. The many discourses on exports and the globalization to which they gave rise are quite repetitive. Their authors have the impression that they are in line with current ideas and tastes, but such discourses fail to understand the basics of [p. 179] economic structures. One of the main tasks of the history of the ancient economy should be a more thorough study of local and regional economic phenomena. On one hand, such a study should inquire how the production and sale of the most widely distributed products came to be part of the respective urban or provincial contexts (as P. Ørsted and his team did for the city of Segermes, in Proconsular Africa; see chapter 2, section IX). On the other hand, an economic study should better emphasize the products distributed in smaller regions (a province, a part of a province, or even just a few cities) and inquire about their production and circulation. As P. Horden and N. Purcell show in *The Corrupting Sea*, the success of the Roman economy was possible because of these economic details and the important role that regional and local markets (in all senses of the word "market") played.

In the case of ancient ceramics, because of the exceptionally well-preserved evidence, it is very easy to study the patterns of local or regional production. I will mention here only two such examples from Narbonnaise Gaul.

The first example is that of Brune Orangée Biterroise (B.O.B.—brown-orange clay from Béziers), produced in the second and third centuries C.E., and consisting of a fine, sandy clay mixed with large amounts of mica. In 1998, S. Mauné concluded that it was produced by seven different workshops, close or relatively close to Béziers and distributed in a large part of western Narbonnaise, between Lunellois and Roussillon. It was produced in culinary forms (as a cooking pot with lid) and also in forms destined for table use (as a plate, for example). At the same time, the same ateliers manufactured construction materials (including bricks and tiles) and wine amphorae.

The second example is that of the pottery workshops in Aspiran (Hérault), where the sigillata were manufactured. These sites were equipped with eleven ovens, [p. 180] which functioned for an entire century—between the second decade of our era and the reign of Trajan—but not all at once. The majority of these ovens produced amphorae and common ceramics. During the reign of Tiberius, oven 6, for example, produced sigillata, but only for twenty years. It was of a smooth type resembling the La Graufesenque and influenced by its Italian counterparts. These Aspiran sigillata were only distributed in various regions of Hérault (Lattes, Murviel-les-Montpellier) and of Gard (Saint-Gilles du Gard), as well as in Narbonne and Orange.

The appearance and the ubiquity of these high-quality ceramics (which were often not sigillata) were signs of activity and prosperity especially when, in the same regions where they were produced, other products exported to distant lands were also found. All this information points us back to our theory of fragmented markets, whether they were local or regional. The sigillata surpass the limits of these markets, but they are never exclusive items: without exception, when they are offered in the local markets they are secondary merchandise. Focusing primarily on the sigillata gives the false impression that the entire ceramics market system was formed around them, and that it was on the scale of the entire Roman Empire or at least on the scale of half of the Mediterranean region. This, of course, was not the case.

III. The Traders

Based on certain literary texts, and primarily on the extant epigraphy, we know a lot about the men and women employed in the urban professions (almost always practiced by men, but women could be part of selected professions, too). The majority of them are known because of funerary inscriptions, sometimes accompanied by reliefs depicting the profession of the deceased (represented by tools and images of their trade). I should also mention the inscriptions [p. 181] marking professional associations (*collegia*). Accordingly, such individuals could be traders, financiers (moneychangers and deposit bankers), artisans, salaried or enslaved men and women working in different enterprises (see Migeotte, pp. 117–22, for trade skills in the Greek cities).

Based on the similarities in their social condition and the status of their trade, it is right to discuss the traders and the artisans at the same time. In fact, some artisans were also vendors of their own products. Yet, wholesale and retail were not always separate operations. The traders and the artisans clearly belonged to the same milieu: among them, there were slaves, freedmen, and free-born individuals (*ingenuus*). In Italy, at the end of the Republic and under the Principate, freedmen and slaves were the most numerous in these professions. Much later, and in some of the provinces, the *ingenui* constituted the greater numbers. Based on the information provided in literary texts (for example, Petronius' *Satyricon*) and funerary inscriptions, we know something about the marriages of some of these professional individuals, as well as about their friendships and social relations. In the case of freedmen, these relations were formed inside a group belonging to the same patron (the *familia*) or among freedmen. In the case of the *ingenui*, they were built up inside the professional circles of the various trades.

The patrons of some of these freedmen working as traders or artisans were notables in the cities where they worked, or in other cities. Some of them could even have senators or equites for patrons. Most of them, however, were the freedmen of other freedmen. It was quite common in these urban milieus for a freedman to have a slave he could trust, to whom he taught his occupation and then worked side by side with, the latter succeeding him later as the owner of the shop. [p. 182]

It is important to make a distinction between the number of business names and the number of their occurrences on the inscriptions. The number of known occupations is impressive. In Rome, at the end of the Republic and in the first two centuries of our era, 160 businesses are attested. Elsewhere, this number depended on the size of the city, but not without variation. Quite frequently, the number of businesses was higher in the most important ports. From the western cities, for which we have the most information, Rome was in first place, followed by Narbonne, Aquileia, Puteoli, and Capua. When it came to small businesses, the occupations were most varied in the Greek-speaking regions. As to the number of occurrences on inscriptions, this depended on epigraphical customs. Clearly, in some regions or cities it was not customary to indicate one's occupation on a funerary inscription. In others, the opposite was true.

As J.-M. Lassère remarked in his *Manuel d'Épigraphie romaine,* mentioning one's occupation was particularly interesting in the following cases: when it was very frequent in the inscriptions of a city; when it provided information on a skill less common in that area or pointed to an activity specific to that city or region (the leather industry in Pergamum, hemp crops raised for manufacturing ropes in a particular valley in Mysia); when the variation in technical terms allows us to pinpoint the functions of each occupation.

A hierarchy among these businessmen is clearly evidenced, as N. Tran shows, in inscriptions by professional *collegia.* It is also visible in the use of distinctions and municipal functions attributed to some men (for example, functions connected with the imperial cult, like those of the *augustales*, and those of the *seviri augustales*). The most important business was that of the traders, who were called *mercatores* at the end of the Republic, and then simultaneously *negotiatores* and *mercatores* under the Empire. In the western Mediterranean, these traders were the only ones from whose number emerged a [p. 183] few individuals who became *decuriones* or even municipal magistrates.

It is necessary make one or two remarks on the geographical origin of artisans and especially the traders. Two cases stand out. If the trader or the artisan was freeborn (an *ingenuus*), knowing his place of birth provides valuable information on the commercial and manufacturing importance of that region. The region that sold its products to exterior markets also had a tendency to export its traders, who played the role of correspondents who received shipments. In the second and the first centuries B.C.E. and then in the first century C.E., in regions outside Italy there were many freeborn Italians. This fact demonstrates Italian commercial influence during these periods. Conversely, beginning with the first century C.E., in the western Mediterranean and in Italy itself, we notice the increased presence of traders from provincial areas like the Iberian peninsula or Gaul. In the second century C.E. and in the following centuries, traders from the east, and for example from Syria-Palestine, started conducting business in the western Mediterranean. Until late antiquity, the *Syri negotiatores* were frequently mentioned in literary texts, which documents the commercial importance of the eastern provinces, and particularly Syria.

When the trader is a slave or a freedman, knowing his place of origin is not as helpful: while it is still important to know where the slave came from in order to understand better the sources of slaves, geographical origin is of less importance when it comes to his employment. The free-born Syrian who traveled to Italy for business preserved his relationships with his place of origin, and it is very likely that his commercial network included his place of birth. Conversely, a Syrian slave was in Italy because he had been bought by an Italian man or woman living in Italy. With a few exceptions, his activities were connected to those of his master and not those of [p. 184] his compatriots from his place of origin. A slave originally from Syria who is working in Gaul does not tell us much about the existing trade between these two regions, unless his master is also Syrian and has a business network with Syria. The same is true for freedmen.

They belonged to the province or region where they lived before they were freed, and even as freedmen, they remain geographically close to their previous masters. M. Christol nicely demonstrated how this worked in the case of slaves and freedmen living in Gaul.

Some traders (*negotiatores, mercatores*) were also ship owners (*navicularii*), using ships in their own commercial activities; the two occupations, though, are quite distinct. On the Dressel 20 oil amphorae it was the names of the traders and not those of the ship owners that were inscribed. The trading profession was mentioned in the funerary inscriptions—in the western Mediterranean this was a very rare occurrence for the ship owners. At the same time, this is almost never the case for the owners of private mines, or for those managing mines belonging to the Empire. This has to do with the fact that these manufacturers were not considered professional businessmen. They did, indeed, perform a specialized and technical activity, and gained money from doing it. Yet, they already belonged to the stratum of wealthy businessmen or even to that of the born-wealthy, even though they did not belong to the senate or the equestrian order, or the magistrates or decurions of their city. If the profession may end up on the funerary inscription, large financial affairs were never mentioned, and neither was their inheritance. The owner of a silver mine in Carthage, for example, would not indicate his occupation on his funerary monument.

A number of archaeologists, especially in Italy, think that even when a trader is mentioned, the name is but a placeholder for the [p. 185] producer and also, if he was a freedman, then he was a freedman of the producer, and was employed by the producer. In most cases it is impossible to prove such a theory, which leaves the door open to many interpretations. When it comes to senators and their possible association with commerce, the theory is very probably false. Several signs supporting this conclusion are found in chapter 1, section III, where I discussed the economic interests of the members of the elite: the reader is directed to that section for further details.

IV. Commercial Competition between Italy and the Provinces

In the case of the merchandise for which we have the most archaeological evidence, ceramic tableware and products transported in amphorae, we have noticed strong evolutions of the commercial patterns. At the end of the Republic and during the Augustan period, Italian products could be found not only in Italy but also in the provinces and sometimes even in regions beyond imperial borders. This is the case, for example, of the Dressel 1 wine amphora, used to transport wine from the Tyrrhenian coast of Italy, and manufactured for a century between 130 and 30 B.C.E. It is likewise the case of the black-glaze ceramic ware, also known as the Etrusco-Campanian. The tendency reversed entirely commencing with the end of the reign of Augustus and then under his successors. From that point on, there are more and more ceramics and amphorae from the provinces arriving in Italy while the same Italian products are sold less and less or not at all in the provinces. This particular situation is what has been called the "crisis of Italy." Whatever one thinks of the use of the word "crisis," there is in the phrase a historical phenomenon to discuss, and this section will explore it. [p. 186]

Generally influenced by Marxist thought, certain historians have considered this "crisis of Italy" as being connected with the crisis posed by the role slavery played in the economic life of the time. As we have seen in chapter 2, section IV, slavery played an important role in what we call "the slave villa," that is, a rural estate that Cato and Varro discuss in great detail in their works. It is a fact that, under the Principate, this type of exploitation was less used than at the end of the Republic, and that it is barely mentioned, if at all, during the second and third centuries C.E. Is it safe, therefore, to assume that the two crises are connected and the crisis of Italy overlaps with that of "slavery"? In my opinion, no. We should not extend such a claim over the entire social and economic life of the Roman Empire based on signs of depression in some of its sectors or regions. Even if Italy, and especially Tyrrhenian Italy, lost its influence during the Principate and economic activities diminished, a resulting crisis in Tyrrhenian Italy is not the equivalent of a crisis in the entire Empire. We have already discussed this topic in chapter 2. We will not revisit it here: the present section is dedicated to the commercial exchanges between Italy and the provinces, and not to a hypothetical crisis concerning the means of production.

Let's look at two examples of this strong evolution of trade patterns. First, we will take a look at fine tableware ceramics. Under the reign of Augustus, Italian sigillata was massively distributed outside Italy. Arretine was the best-known type, and it was primarily produced in Italy (Arezzo, Pisa, Puteoli), with additional production facilities in Gaul (Lyon). It could be found on all the Mediterranean shores (but mostly in the west), in various regions of Gaul, in alpine provinces on the right bank of the Danube, and even in southern Britain. From 15 C.E. onward, however, its diffusion was visibly reduced. It could [p. 187] no longer be found in Britain; in Gaul, it was only distributed on the Rhone–Saône–Rhine axis. And from 50 C.E. the "Tardo-Italic" ceramic type, which replaced the Arretine, was no longer found near the border of the Empire. Around 70–80 C.E., it was no longer sold in northern Africa, and instead, the A African red slip ware, manufactured in Proconsular Africa, started to appear in Italian markets. In the first part of the second century, the Tardo-Italic ceramic ware was no longer found in Italy and from this time on, for the duration of the Empire, all the fine tableware ceramics used in Italy were imported.

The second example to consider is that of wine. Overall, the number of Italian wine amphorae found in Rome and Ostia diminished strongly. They were 95% of the wine amphorae dating back to the middle of the first century C.E. and only 40% of the amphorae of the Flavian period. In the deposit of amphorae at Longarina, at Ostia, which dates from the beginning of our era, two thirds of the amphorae were produced in Italy. At the end of the first century C.E. and the start of the second, the situation was radically changed. Of course, even though some of the manufacturing facilities and vineyards were abandoned between the first and second centuries C.E., the Italian amphorae that replaced the Dressel 2–4 types could still be commonly found during the second and third centuries not only in Rome, but also at Augst, Lyon, Saint-Romain-en-Gal, Carthage, Corinth, etc. From this time on, they are more specialized than before in the grand crus of Campania. The production of grand *villae*, previously focused in Campania and Etruria, moved towards Rome, and the number of amphorae transported down the Tiber River became, not surprisingly, higher than that at Ostia.

From this time forward wine amphorae from Tarraconaise, Gaul, the Aegean Sea, and Asia Minor appeared in Rome. The wine amphorae from Asia Minor were obviously very popular during the Antonine period, since recent excavations discovered that one-third of the finds belonged to this amphora type. In the second century, the wine amphorae from southern Gaul found in Rome were as numerous as those from Italy. Since F. Laubenheimer has started studying the Gallic wine amphorae, [p. 188] the conclusions about wine commerce have changed considerably. We have learned that some Dressel 2–4 types of amphorae which, at their origin during the reign of Augustus, contained Italian wine, were then made in Gaul or in Spanish Tarraconaise and were used to transport the wine produced in these regions. On the other hand, between the middle of the first century C.E. and the reign of Marcus Aurelius, there was a very large output of Gallo-Roman wine amphorae, some produced in Narbonnaise and some in Lyonnaise. Columella himself wrote at one point: "We drink the wine of the Cyclades and of the Baetican and Gallo-Roman countryside" (*On Agriculture*, Book 1, *Praefatio*, 20).

The reader encountered similar remarks about oil commerce in chapter 2, section IX. Analogous comments could also be made about preserves and fish sauces and about oil lamps. In the last forty or fifty years, as our knowledge of various merchandise increases, the inversion of the trade patterns we talked about has become both clearer and more visible. In the case of wine, admittedly, as A. Tchernia correctly noticed, the diffusion of the barrel, which replaced the amphora during the second and third centuries C.E., makes our documentation more tenuous. In addition, we have to also pay attention to the containers holding jars (*dolia*). Moreover, the reversing of the trade patterns was not, chronologically speaking, identical for all products. Regardless, even taking this qualification into account, the principal pattern for the archaeologically best-known merchandise is clear.

Nonetheless, several questions remain. Should Italy be considered an independent economic unit even though its unity was only political, administrative, and fiscal (from the fiscal point of view, Italy was the only region of the Empire that was not a province, and for this reason was not subjected to the same taxation system as the provinces)? This objection is not very strong, since the central weight of Rome and its role as the heart of the Empire were such that the rest of Italy could not [p. 189] thrive when the capital was suffering. On the other hand, weren't certain regions of Italy, like the Adriatic coast, more prosperous than central and southern Tyrrhenian Italy between the first and third centuries C.E.? They were, in fact, and this argument carries more weight than the preceding.

In addition, could we say that these archaeologically best-known objects are representative for all the ancient commercial patterns between Italy and the provinces? Based on studies of the domestic budget in the Middle Ages and early modern times, the answer to this question is no. This is particularly true when we consider that, when it came to domestic budgets, more than 90% of the total amount was dedicated to food, lodging, and clothing. Even if wine and oil were part of the "alimentation" rubric, they did not constitute the most substantial part of the food category. Among the other important products, some were acquired by Rome from the provinces simply because of the former's supremacy over the latter. Such was the case with wheat, a part of which (used in grain distributions in Rome) came from tax levies. This was also the case for metals, including ore deposits, which for the most part were acquired by Rome or by the emperor as a result of conquests. We cannot say that such goods were produced by Italy or were imported by it. When it comes to textiles, even though Egyptian linen, wool, and various fabrics from Asia Minor and Syria-Palestine enjoyed an increasingly greater reputation starting with the first century C.E., a highly productive area developed in northern Italy, and to the north and south of the Po River, that provided similar items. However, this is not the place to analyze both agricultural productions and manufactured objects in greater detail, from the point of view of the growth of commercial routes. We could concede that, after a preliminary evaluation and despite the complexity of the question, we can see a clear reversal of commercial patterns between Italy and the provinces, between the reign of Augustus and the second century C.E. [p. 190]

So, it seems that we are witnessing a form of commercial competition between Italy and the provinces. How could we explain such a situation? This question has persisted ever since Rostovtzeff published his great synthetic work in 1926. It has given birth to four or five different answers, which are not entirely exclusive of each other.

The first one belongs to Rostovtzeff himself and focuses on the quality of the supply. This theory argues that the Italian manufacturers and agricultural elites were much less enterprising and lost their technical and commercial competence when the provinces progressed more rapidly. In this competition, Italy lost the game. This simple method of using basic, contemporary economic explanations to understand similar events in the past should not be excluded in all cases. But, in this precise case, it does not have the evidence necessary to support its claims: what do we really know about the commercial competence of the Italians, the Gallo-Romans, and the Africans in the first century C.E.? Certainly, in Ancient History, it is often impossible to demonstrate that a situation occurred as we assume it did. Nevertheless, it remains true that history is based on documentation and on proofs, and that the absence of such an element of proof is embarrassing.

The second response is focused on the other element of the commercial life, on the demand for products. If commercial routes have favored certain provinces over Italy, it is because they had a bigger demand for those products than Italy did. Two important categories of consumers were stationed in these provinces: one was the army (each legion, for example, constituted the kernel of an urban area), and the other was the elites. The enrichment of the elites created a cycle of cause and effect because it produced an increase in demand while providing supplementary financial opportunities (for investment in agriculture, or providing loans to artisans and traders). [p. 191]

The third response is based on an observation vis-à-vis conquest: A. Tchernia made it in regard to wine, but it could be extended to other products as well. After the conquest, many of the goods belonging to the provinces were confiscated by Rome (lands, mines) and tax levies were imposed. In addition, the conquest enabled the institution of specific exchange relationships, which were different from customary economic processes. Diodorus explains that the exchanges between the Italian traders (*emporoi*) and the Gallic peoples were very unfavorable to the latter, who had to pay the equivalent value of a slave in order to purchase an amphora of wine, whereas in Italy a slave was much more valuable than that. With the passing of time, as society moved farther from the era of conquest, this kind of unequal exchange could not be sustained and Italy ceased to derive such economic advantages. The decline of Italian wine exports, primarily to Gaul, was connected to the process of Romanization: the wine lost its status as a luxury item used in the conspicuous distributions that characterized the traditional Gallic society. On the other hand, the massive imports in Rome of wines produced in northern Italy and Spain can be explained by increased consumption of *vin ordinaire* in the capital. Vineyards from the Tyrrhenian coast could not provide sufficient quantities for the increasingly large population of Rome, especially when they produced mostly special vintage wines. A. Tchernia is convinced of the inequality of these exchanges but he refuses to attribute it to a competition that is economic in nature. In his eyes, other factors played important roles, the anthropological factor most of all.

The fourth and last answer was proposed by K. Hopkins and H.U. von Freyberg. In a way they, too, focused on results of the conquest, but they placed most importance on long-term tax levies instead of short-term consequences. Hopkins developed the so-called "taxes and trade" model. According to this model, during the entire duration of the Principate, [p. 192] depending on the fiscal conditions, the Roman-dominated territories could be divided into three large areas: the peripheral provinces, which paid taxes on the products of the land, but which received important subsidies from the State for the troops stationed there; the middle provinces, the oldest and the most Romanized, which paid the tax but housed no legions or auxiliary troops and thus received very few subsidies from the Empire; and finally, Italy, which did not pay this tax and received subsidies for various reasons, primarily because Rome was the seat of imperial power. The intermediate provinces, the least favored in this situation, had to sell products to pay this tax. This fiscal equilibrium, which lasted for almost three centuries, forced the inhabitants of these provinces to sell. The merchandise we just discussed and which replaced Italian products, was, in fact, produced in such provinces (Proconsular Africa, Baetica, Asia, Narbonnaise and, to a lesser degree, the other Gallic provinces).

H.U. von Freyberg has used the same model but in a modified form. He explained that the payment of taxes produced transfers of values from the provinces to

Italy, and consequently a rise in the Italian prices, so that the provincial merchandise became more affordable than that produced in Italy. Hopkins' model is more proactive: it explains why the inhabitants of the nonmilitary provinces were so motivated to produce and sell. Von Freyberg's is more mechanical: not only were these provinces eager to sell, but their commercial activities were implicitly met with success because of the resulting adjustment in prices.

These two schemas are very general and abstract, and it is easy to focus on the questions they raise: neither one [p. 193] should be considered as the perfect solution, as the miraculous model that explains everything. They imply that an important part of the taxes were collected in cash, and not in products, and that supplying the army was organized within the framework of free commerce. This is a theory that I share, and which was defended for example by L. Wierschowski, E. Lo Cascio, and A. Tchernia, but was opposed by J. Remesal Rodríguez. These models, however, rightfully point out the importance of the fiscal aspects of this commercial evolution and, because of this, they further the research. In the 1991 article titled "Mercato e mercati" (republished in the anthology *Patrimoines, échanges et prêts d'argent: l'économie romaine*), I emphasized the element of demand (the presence of the army and the elites, which stimulated both consumption and production in the provinces). Three years later, in another article, "L'Italie impériale et les provinces: Déséquilibre des échanges et flux monétaires" (article dedicated to H.U. von Freyberg's notions, and which was republished in the same anthology), I tried to show the importance of these theses. Now, I would conclude that this economic evolution is with difficulty questionable, even though it did not affect all products and even though all the regions of Italy did not experience it. I would also conclude that the fiscal factor evidenced by Hopkins and von Freyberg had, indeed, played an important role, but that it is not the only element that can explain the situation. The effects of conquest that A. Tchernia has identified have the same meaning as the fiscal factor. The evolution of demand has to be taken into account. This phenomenon of commercial competition is the result of several causes, the most important of which are closely connected with the consequences of conquest. [p. 194]

V. Commerce in the East

In the last decades, many studies focused on the economic relationships between the Roman world and the peoples living outside its borders, in Europe as well as in Asia and Africa. As it is impossible to address all these regions in the limited space of this volume, I will therefore limit myself to making a few remarks about what is called "the Oriental commerce," led by Syria-Palestine and Egypt.

The Greeks and the Romans bought from the eastern coasts of Africa, Arabia, and the countries of the Asiatic continent a certain number of exotic and expensive kinds of merchandise. This merchandise was expensive for Roman consumers, but not so for those residing near the sites of their production. Among these products were silk, produced by the Seres (who are generally considered as being Chinese, and lived in the central Asian oasis and in China proper); pearls and beryls; ivory; spices and aromatics from India, south Arabia, and neighboring African regions (pepper, cassia, cinnamon, incense, myrrh, nard).

A part of these products was transported by land. At the end of the Roman Republic, in southern Syria-Palestine, convoys of merchants and Nabatean caravans crossed the area from Arabia Felix to Petra, Gaza, and Rhinocolura. In Augustus' era, however, this southern land route detoured towards Egypt, from Myos Hormos to Coptos and Alexandria. Petra lost its commercial importance. The Nabateans, in the meantime, continued their trade, in the northern part of the Arabian peninsula, inside their kingdom.

More to the north, these products were transported by caravans that led to Syria-Palestine. Palmyra dominated commerce in this area beginning in the first century B.C.E. and under the Principate. Fascinated [p. 195] by caravan commerce, M.I. Rostovtzeff dedicated a book to it, titled *Caravan Cities*. M. Sartre noted, however, that only the city of Palmyra could be justifiably called a caravan city. Members of the camel-owning Palmyrene elite provided the means of transportation needed to cross the desert (that is, the camels, the guides, and the military escorts) and led the caravans. They provided security during the crossing all the way to the Euphrates and even beyond the limits of the Roman Empire. For their part, the Palmyrene merchants had a veritable network of stations, including some in Babylonia (Ctesiphon, Vologesias) and in the Persian Gulf (Spasinou Charax). We should note that this particular route could also include a segment on the river: a Palmyrene relief shows the image of a ship whose owner had traveled all the way to Scythia, that is, probably all the way to India. We infer that ships were used to travel down the Euphrates.

The most important period for the Palmyrene caravan inscriptions is the middle of the second century, between 130 and 161 C.E. It was the apogee of this type of commerce as later, in the third century, it seems to have lost its importance, perhaps because of the instability following the rise of the Sassanids in Persia, in 224 C.E.

Another group of these products from the east was transported by sea and ended up in Egypt. Commercial relationships between the Egypt of the Ptolemies and India started in the second part of the second century B.C.E. According to Strabo (2.5.12) they greatly developed under Augustus, after Egypt became a Roman province. Written toward the middle of the first century C.E., *The Tour of the Erythraean Sea* (*Periplus Maris Erythraei*) is a guide for merchants and sailors that describes the coasts of Arabia, Africa as far as Rhapta (Dar es-Salaam) and India: it is the only document of this type that we have. The ships returning from India docked in the Red Sea, at Myos Hormos or Berenike, and the merchandise they brought was redirected via the eastern desert routes of Egypt all the way to Coptos. Then, it descended [p. 196] the Nile, to Alexandria. The customs levy for its transportation was 25%, which was a particularly high tax rate as ancient rates went.

On two different occasions, Pliny the Elder provided specific numbers for these purchases in the Roman world. In one passage, he wrote that "not a year goes by that India does not get around fifty million sestertii from our Empire in return for merchandise sold here at a hundred times their price..." (*Natural History*, 6.26.101). In another passage, he talks about one hundred million sestertii that the Roman world paid each year to India, to the Seres, and the Arabian peninsula (*Natural History*, 12.41.84). These numbers are very likely taken from the customs ledgers and, for this reason, could be considered correct for his time. But are these numbers representing the difference between imports and exports, or just showing the imports, from which we should subtract exports? We know that, in exchange for these eastern products, the artisans and agricultural producers from Roman territories (and especially those from Syria) offered other products: glassware, textiles, ceramics (India was imitating types A and B of the eastern sigillata), metals, wines. Roman sales to the eastern peoples, however, did not reach the level of the imports, far from this. Pliny's texts have been much commented upon, yet they remain difficult to interpret.

More than six thousand denarii and around one thousand aurei (gold coins) have been found in India, to date. From among the eastern Indian ports mentioned in the *Periplus Maris Erythraei*, the most important ones seem to have been Barygaza and, a bit more to the south, Muziris. Excavations performed at Arikamedu (south of Pondicherry) on the eastern Indian coast, uncovered a relatively substantial quantity of Roman objects (fifty Arretine fragments and about six hundred amphora fragments). [p. 197]

From a financial point of view, the trade in the east was very important. A papyrus dating from the middle of the second century and published in 1958 (*SB* 18.13167) contains the end of a loan contract for a crossing between Alexandria and Muziris. We read that the cargo's value was estimated as being close to seven million sestertii. Only very wealthy individuals could provide such exorbitant sums of money. Some historians suggested that it could have been the emperor himself or members of his family who provided the money for this loan but, unfortunately, we do not have any proof that this was indeed the case.

After being very active in the first and second centuries C.E., this eastern commerce seems to have known a decline in the third century, prompted primarily by political and military events. Among these were the replacement of the Arsacid Persian dynasty with the Sassanids, relations between the Persian kingdom and its neighbors to the east, and the political instability in the regions situated to the south of Egypt. In the fourth century, strong tensions developed between Rome and the Persians, especially during the reign of Constantius II, while at the same time, its relationships with the Aksumite kingdom, to the south of Egypt, became more regular and less aggressive.

When Alaric the Goth besieged Rome in 408, he requested not only gold and silver, but also three thousand animal skins, four thousand silk tunics, and three thousand pounds of pepper (Zosimus, 5.41.6). This request, J.-P. Callu has noted, was symptomatic: "It showed that a part of the riches of the Empire consisted of foreign merchandise." [p. 198]

Texts

An Unequal Exchange: An Amphora for a Slave

The Gauls are exceedingly addicted to the use of wine and fill themselves with the wine which is brought into their country by merchants, drinking it unmixed, and since they partake of this drink without moderation by reason of their craving for it, when they are drunken they fall into a stupor or a state of madness. Consequently, many of the Italian traders, induced by the love of money which characterizes them, believe that the love of wine of these Gauls is a thing of great value. For they transport the wine on the navigable rivers by means of boats and through the level plain on wagons, and receive for it an incredible price; for in exchange for a jar of wine they receive a slave, getting a servant in return for the drink.

Diodorus Siculus, 5.26.3 (trans. C.H. Oldfather, Loeb Classical Library, 1952)

On this first century B.C.E. account, see A. Tchernia, *Le Vin de l'Italie romaine* (Rome: 1986): 91.

A Canal Project That Did Not Succeed

The heads of the army at the time were Pompeius Paulinus and Lucius Vetus. Not to keep the troops inactive, however, the former finished the embankment for checking the inundations of the Rhine, begun sixty-three years earlier by Drusus; while Vetus prepared to connect the Moselle and the Arar by running a canal between the two; so that goods shipped by sea and then up the Rhone and Arar could make their way by the canal, and subsequently by the Moselle, into the Rhine, and in due course into the ocean: a method which would remove the natural difficulties of the route and create a navigable highway between the shores of the West and North. [p. 199] The scheme was nullified by the jealousy of Aelius Gracilis, the governor of Belgica, who discouraged Vetus from introducing his legions into a province outside his competence and so courting popularity in Gaul, "a proceeding," he said, "which would awaken the misgivings of the emperor"—the usual veto upon honorable enterprise.

Tacitus, *Annals,* 13.53.2–4 (trans. John Jackson, Loeb Classical Library, 1969) [pp. 200, 201]

Chapter 6
Did Rome Have an Economic Policy?

Rome was a city-state which, at the end of the fourth century B.C.E. or toward the beginning of the third, had become a state with a vast territory. This new situation continued with the later conquests and the progressive extension of Roman citizenship, first in Italy, then outside of Italy. It had consequences for economic life and on the entire policy of the state. The following remarks pertain to the period after the institution of this situation (chapter 7 will discuss the period falling before). While first becoming a state with a vast territory, then an empire, Rome incorporated within its *imperium* other cities, whose autonomy was not inconsiderable. I have made brief remarks on the economic interventions of these cities in chapters 2 and 5; I will not mention them again here.

Did Rome have an economic policy? When it came to economic matters, did it have a "liberal" or an "interventionist" policy? To frame the problem in these terms would be wrong, since the ancient world did not have the same conception of economy as we do. They did not have the same conception of the State, either, or the same ideas when it came to the ways the State could intervene in what we now call the economy.

Despite the existence of the Greek word *oikonomia,* the notion of economy, as we understand it today, was unknown in both Greece and Rome. Regardless, the Ancients had a very clear idea that a certain number of activities were necessary to ensure the maintenance and reproduction of human life. This is exactly what Cicero writes at the beginning of the second book of [p. 202] his *Treatise on Duties.* He lists the things that contribute to the conservation of life, that is, minerals, flora, fauna, and also people. In fact, without the work (*manus*), the knowledge (*ars*), and the management (*administratio*) of men, there could be no treatment for sickness, no navigation, no agriculture, no harvests or grain stockpiles. It was based on such formulas that inhabitants of the ancient world designated what we call economy. They did not, however, write treatises or studies of these activities, thinking of them as a whole. Some wrote treatises about land management (we call these texts agronomic). Merchants, too, had texts written specifically for them in antiquity (like *The Tour of the Erythraean Sea*). Questions that we consider economic were raised in such treatises: they were mentioned and discussed in legal texts or in moral and philosophical treatises as well. But no Greek or Roman ever composed a *Treatise of Political Economy* the likes of those written in the eighteenth century in Europe by Richard Cantillon (*Essai sur la nature du commerce en général [Essay on the Nature of Trade in General]*) and Adam Smith (*An Inquiry into the Nature and Causes of the Wealth of Nations*).

Another element to take into account is that, for both the Greeks and the Romans, professional activity, daily life, and various ways to earn money belonged to the private sphere. In Rome, the periodic census, which under the Republic fulfilled political, military, and fiscal roles, was a way to inventory the results of the private activities of the citizens. It was not meant as a method of building up private estates, or to intervene in their management. The city categorized its citizens based on the goods they had acquired, but it did not extend help in their acquisition. [p. 203]

To speak of "liberalism" or "economic interventionism" in this situation is anachronistic, because such terms suggest voluntary interventions in an economic activity perceived as a global system. The Greeks and the Romans did not imagine such a system existed, and did not intend to intervene in the creation and the management of private properties. On this situation J.-M. Carrié has remarked: "Imperial legislation did not concern itself with encouraging or discouraging private economic activities. It clearly considered that it had nothing to say on this subject."

Despite this, the opposite theory is not entirely unjustified, since ancient cities, kingdoms, and empires were often forced to take what we would consider "economic" measures. If we take into account such actions, we could have the illusion that some economic policies were in place. This situation explains why this question is much debated. Anyway, despite much progress in the economic sciences, the economic measures that our present-day governments are taking are, in some cases, nothing but a mish-mash of interventions more or less coherent, which often result from the action of pressure groups, and are sometimes even internally contradictory. We need to acknowledge that, in antiquity, such measures were never thought of as being part of a system. In our times, even the most empirical or worst ministers with economic responsibilities strive to show that their actions are coherent and have the power to influence the economic system as a whole. Such an ambition did not exist in antiquity.

It remains a fact that the Roman civic powers intervened in areas that, according to our present beliefs, are part of the economic system. I am going to discuss the directions of these interventions in the following four successive points. The first concerns the economic interventions resulting from the needs and the imperatives of the city and the Empire, as public power. The second and third focus [p. 204] on what the city and the Empire owed their citizens: on one hand, the means to pursue their chosen activities and to move freely, on the other hand, basic supplies. Finally, we will take up agricultural problems and other things pertaining to agriculture, because these questions held a separate place in ancient thought. One of the reasons they did not conceive of economic life as a global system is precisely because, for them, agriculture and related questions occupied a different place from commerce, manufacturing, and banking. So, even if the city, and then the Roman Empire, did not have an economic policy per se, it did have an agrarian policy in place.

I. Measures Addressing Economic Needs of the Roman State

As a political power, the city, and then the Empire, had fiscal and defense policies in place and, through them, intervened in economic matters, but without having economic objectives per se. The defense policy was responsible for engendering powerful economic and social transformations. When a legion was stationed for a longer period of time in an area, a city formed around it: five or six thousand men, with women and children and the producers and merchants needed to ensure the survival of this population. Some regions, and particularly the frontiers along the Rhine and the Danube, housed more legions and auxiliary troops, while others retained fewer, or none at all. In the first and second centuries C.E., on the other hand, the manufacturing centers responsible for the production of circulating goods (agricultural products and manufactured objects) seemed to have been situated in regions without any troops. In his "taxes and trade" model, K. Hopkins explained this situation by [p. 205] the influence of taxation on agricultural production (as I explained in some detail in chapter 1, section VII, and in chapter 5, section IV, so I will not revisit it here).

The Vindolanda tablets, found in northern Britain, provide information on supplying the army. They confirm that this provisioning process influenced the agricultural organization of large territories and was the starting point of trade, too, both inside the Empire and outside its borders.

The question arises in the same terms when it concerns the exploitation of the public patrimony, and, in particular, the mines. Even if the city of Rome and the various cities of the Empire did not hold a monopoly over mines—and even if there always existed privately owned mines—the city of Rome did manage to own extensive mining sites in light of its need for metals for the manufacturing of arms and coinage. For this reason, the silver-bearing lead mines from the Iberian peninsula, those from Cartagena and Sierra Morena, or the gold mines from northwest Spain and later, those from Dacia, were the property of the city of Rome or the emperor himself. The manner in which the state exploited these mines had social and economic consequences. If they were under direct management, as was the case for those in northwest Spain, the mines did not contribute as much to the economic and social prosperity of the region. If the management was entrusted to large business entities, like the famous publican societies, as was the case for the mines in Italy and in southern Gaul during the Republic, mining operations and primary metallurgy took place within the framework of these specialized organizations and the resulting profits returned, first of all, to Italians who were also Roman citizens. In other cases, the Empire granted smaller concessions, within the province itself, and free men who were not Roman citizens had the right to exploit them. The local elites, in this case, profited most from these kinds of mining and metallurgical activities [p. 206] and the region in question prospered as well. This is one of the reasons explaining the growth of the province of Baetica, in southern Spain, and of a part of the Danubian provinces.

Similar remarks could be made concerning the fiscal policy of the Empire. When it came to collecting taxes, the city, then the Empire, had the same three choices: large concessions to particular, specialized associations; smaller ones; or direct management. I believe that these governmental interests of the public powers had strong economic consequences, even though, officially, the State did not decide its actions because of economic reasons.

II. Public Order and the Citizens' Freedom of Action

Even when core functions or political interests were not involved, the State had the right and the duty to exercise control over private activities, whether they were of an economic nature or not. This means that the State had to maintain law and order. According to Aristotle, each individual tends to look out for personal, private interests. These interests can overlap within certain limits, but when opportunities for enrichment are unlimited, the interests become antagonistic. The city then has to intervene, discipline private actions gone astray, and correct the resulting injustices. The same reasoning applies to the city of Rome and then to the entire Roman Empire. This is what P. Veyne called a disciplinary design of the State [*une conception disciplinaire de l'État*]: do not intervene in private affairs, but regulate and discipline them.

It is not difficult to find examples of such disciplinary measures. I am thinking, among other things, of the quality control exercised on the manufactured and sold objects, or the control the censors exercised over the patrimony of the elite (senators and equites). Let's confine ourselves to one example, which concerns a [p. 207] decision made by the Emperor Augustus. Certain convicts belonging to the elite were required to leave Italy and live outside its borders, which prevented them from engaging in the social and economic activities in which they were previously involved. According to Dio Cassius (56.27), Augustus noticed that, while abroad, some of them enjoyed luxurious lifestyles and used their situation to acquire even greater wealth, so he forbade them from owning more than twenty slaves and more than one ship carrying ten thousand amphorae, and he reduced the amount of actual cash they could have in their possession. It was one way he tried to prevent them from participating in big commercial transactions and to limit them to smaller commercial endeavors. It would be absurd to assume that these Augustan measures were founded upon a grander economic or even social project. It was just one way to uphold the law and preserve the exiles' experience as a punishment instead of allowing them to pursue unlimited opportunities for enrichment. On the other hand, this measure confirms what we already gathered from other documents, namely that when freed for one reason or another from his "profession" as a citizen or as a notable, the ancient *homo politicus* found himself in a position to throw himself into economic enterprises.

Meanwhile, the Roman state had to act as the caretaker of all its people. It could not afford to leave its citizens without protection. At the same time, there were others who deserved and needed its support, including, as they took part in the Empire, the free men and women from the conquered regions, the allied Italians before the Social War, and the *peregrini* in the provinces. It was the state's duty to ensure that each group and individual was taken care of according to rank and in a way compatible with the laws and needs of the city and its public powers. If the Roman state did not, itself, develop commerce, it was its duty to protect those who did, i.e., the merchants, who came under the state's authority.

This duty was particularly important when it concerned Roman citizens. In the last of the *Verrine Orations* (*On Punishments, De Suppliciis*), Cicero proclaimed that Roman citizenship [p. 208] protected its bearers to the ends of the known world. It served to assure the safe passage of ordinary men who did not have the means to find guarantors. In the same text, Cicero adds: "How many wars, and of what importance, do you think that our ancestors fought because Roman citizens were injured, ship owners were detained, and merchants were despoiled?" (2 *Verr.* 5.149, 166–67). In the speech *On the Imperium of Cn. Pompey* (*De Imperio Cnaei Pompei*, 11 and 19) he says: "Our ancestors often engaged in wars because of insults brought upon our merchants and our ship owners" (the use of the possessive "our" implies that these merchants and ship owners were Roman citizens). It is not sure that these interventions were as frequent as Cicero would have us believe. On the other hand, sometimes, these grand principles could not prevent those living in the provinces from receiving the worst possible treatment at the hands of their governors. It was also true that they justified interventions based on patron-client relationships: for example, if a merchant were connected with equites or senators, and if at the same time that he increased his wealth he also added to their already remarkable fortunes, then he would very likely have a better chances of being protected by Roman authorities. But it was important that the official policy be as described, and that it was practiced, even though it did not always succeed.

Let's look at an example that illustrates this doctrine. In his speech *On the Imperium of Cn. Pompey*, dating from 67 B.C.E., Cicero writes about a particular situation that took place that year in the Aegean Sea and in Asia Minor. The King of Pontus, Mithridates, threatened the Roman province of Asia. This threat had an impact on revenues (that is, taxation) the state derived from that province, but also on the affairs of several social groups that had vested interests in Asia: the *publicani* who collected the taxes for the State, the Italian businessmen who lived in that province, and all those who lived in Italy but had interests in that province. The provincials themselves were feeling the consequences as well. Cicero [p. 209] also evokes their complaints and their hardships. Cicero considers commerce and exchanges through the actions of the merchants and businessmen, and through tax levies such as customs duties. He writes that if the threat became very clear, "the transport of merchandise [would be] suspended," *mercatorum navigatio conquiescit*, and customs duties would not be collected (*On the Imperium of Cn. Pompey*, 15 and 32). There is no remark on the decline in trade as such and its role in economic depression and impoverishment.

The guarantee that the city and the Empire granted their citizens was connected to the idea of freedom of circulation. There was a direct relationship between the freedom of circulation, the exercise of private activities, and care for the food supply. Caesar explained that in the Gallic Wars, for example, the Alps passage, present-day Valais, was very dangerous for the merchants (*mercatores*), and they had to pay very high customs and toll rates to the peoples living in that region: the Nantuatae, the Veragri, and the Seduni. He deployed a legion to the area, which was victorious and got the locals to strike a deal: Caesar claimed that he did so in order to "open the route" (*The Gallic War*, 3.1.2). He did not take this action with the intent to promote commerce, but in order to impose Roman rule, assure freedom of circulation, and protect the life and interests of the merchants.

To the circulation of people and goods we now turn to that of coinage. Even though we do not have any treatises on money dating from the Republic or the Principate, the measures taken during monetary or financial crises and debt crises show that the public powers were anxious to remedy problems in monetary flow. Regardless of what certain numismatists claim, the authorities probably did not have the power to limit or increase the volume of coinage production according to changing needs. They were not in a situation to do so, since they had no way to introduce more money into circulation except by means of [p. 210] increasing public spending. However, as the signs of crisis became visible they were anxious, at least at the end of the Republic and during the Principate, to find solutions and, in some cases, to find them quickly. Several options were available: increase the rate at which coins were struck; offer free loans, debt refinancing, and even partial debt forgiveness (Rome never abolished debts completely). These financial or monetary crises weren't considered to be connected to economic ones. Until the beginning of the debt crisis that led, in 63–62 B.C.E., to the Catilinarian Conspiracy, or that of 33 C.E., nothing appeared to indicate that these financial problems went hand in hand with a decline in agricultural production. The currency flow was blocked because of the accumulation of debts. The authorities tried to reestablish monetary flow to its precrisis condition, but no measures were taken to remedy a possible production crisis, which is not mentioned, anyway, in contemporary texts. This behavior on the part of the authorities is surprising, as it implies the presence of a rather refined and abstract understanding of monetary phenomena, but contrasts sharply with the absence of a proper "economic" (in the actual sense of the word) reflection.

III. Supply

The food supply was a constant preoccupation of the ancient city. It was the main way for the ancient city to guarantee the existence of its population, and it was closely related to the idea of free circulation. Ancient Greeks and Romans often placed commerce and supply in the same category as travel and transportation. It is not a coincidence that the word *commeatus* means both to come and to go, the possibility and the ability to move, the convoy, the caravan, and the supplies. In his discourse *On the Imperium of Cn. Pompey*, Cicero speaks [p. 211] of the situation in Italy before Pompey was victorious over the pirates in 67 B.C.E. Several times he repeats the noun *commeatus* and the verb *commeare*, to express at the same time travel and supply. He writes, for example:

> Once, we were not content to extend our protection only to Italy, we were able to guarantee the security of all our allies, to the most distant borders, merely by the prestige of our Empire. While Delos, so far from us, in the Aegean Sea, visited by navigators from all parts of the world, carrying their merchandise and cargoes [*commeare*], filled with riches, although small and without protective walls had nothing to fear, [most recently] it is not only our provinces, the coasts of Italy, and our ports that are now inaccessible to us [because of pirates], but the *Via Appia*, as well. (*On the Imperium of Cn. Pompey*, 55)

We find in this passage all the things mentioned before: the desire to guarantee, based on rank, the best possible conditions for the life and the activities of citizens and the whole population of the Roman Empire, the concern with freedom of circulation, and the need for an appropriate food supply.

The same topics can be found in one of the letters that Pliny the Younger wrote to Trajan while he was a governor of the province of Bithynia, between 111 and 113 C.E. (*Letters*, 10.41, 10.42). The letter concerned Lake Sunonensis, which was situated in the territory of the city of Nicomedia and which flowed out into the Black Sea (the Euxine Sea) through the Sangarius River. Pliny was suggesting to the Emperor that the lake should be connected to the Sea of Marmara, via a man-made canal. This way, numerous products (marble, agricultural products, wood for heating and construction) could be transported via the waterway to Nicomedia, to the urban center of the city. Traditionally, the merchandise had to be transported on the roads between the lake and the city, an operation that required much effort and was both labor-intensive and costly.

In the letter, Pliny presents this project as an achievement adding more glory to the reign of [p. 212] the Emperor, his addressee. Trajan actually responded favorably to this proposition but recommended that the governor proceed with caution. Pliny added that the excavation of this canal would be beneficial for all the citizens of Nicomedia. It is certain that the merchants would find great value in it, as it allowed them to bring their wares to the city market on a shorter route, but Pliny does not go into more specific details. The economic utility of the project was estimated in relation to the increased merchandise quantities that could be transported on it. Yet, the main objective of the project was not presented as having to do with the further development of commerce.

When it comes to supply, the best known institution in Rome was clearly the management of the *annona*, which made possible—starting with the Gracchi and lasting until the end of the Empire—the distribution of wheat to the population of Rome, first at a discounted price, then for free. Most of this wheat came from various provinces, from Sardinia, Sicily, and Africa at the end of the Republic, then, during the Empire, from Egypt as well. It stemmed from taxes, but as we saw in the *Verrines*, the Roman state was buying additional wheat as well. The administration of the *annona* and the distribution of free wheat in the city of Rome constituted only a part of the food-related worries of the city and then of the Empire. Even before the second century B.C.E. the city used to secure its wheat supply; as early as the archaic period, if the harvests were poor, we hear about wheat being procured from outside its territory.

One specific trait of the Roman Empire is the overlapping of imperial structures with local ones (those of each city). This duplication of public authorities meant that every city was ruled simultaneously by the local magistrates and the imperial power (that is to say, in the provinces the power of the governor); the consequence of this situation is particularly visible when it comes to the food supply. An inscription at Antioch in Pisidia, in Asia Minor, is illustrative of this. It concerns the 93 C.E. edict of the legate [p. 213] Lucius Antistius Rusticus (governor of the provinces of Cappadocia and Galatia). The previous winter had been very harsh, it was obvious that the wheat harvests would be poor, and the prices had started to rise, even before the harvest. The magistrates and the city council of Antioch could not keep up with these problems, and were clearly afraid of hoarding, which would have inflated prices even more (on the topic of hoarding, please see chapter 2, section VIII, dedicated to grains). The magistrates and the council appealed to the governor of the province for help. So that the populace had a chance to buy wheat (as stated in the edict), the governor required that the inhabitants of the city declare the quantities of wheat they already had. He set the date for the grain's sale on 1 August, which was a whole month after the harvest, so that he would have sufficient time to process their declarations. Then, he established a maximum price, about double the price from the preceding fall. Before that winter, the running price was eight or nine *asses* per bushel (equal to two sesterces or a bit more). Lucius Antistius Rusticus had fixed the maximum price at a denarius, that is, four sestertii or 16 *asses* (*AE* 1925, 126b).

IV. Agrarian Problems

Land ownership and agriculture were considered a separate matter in the ancient world. Not only were they considered more noble ways of producing revenue than other occupations, they were also an integral part of citizenship. According to Roman legend, Romulus granted each head of family a piece of land two *iugera* in size as private property. Aside from these small parcels, as I have already mentioned, citizens had the right to use public lands that belonged to the city, and thus to everybody. [p. 214] These traditions explain many of the social conflicts that later marked the Roman Republic. With each conquest, the area of the Roman public land (the *ager publicus*) in each city increased because it was customary for Rome to confiscate part of the conquered lands and attach them to its public territory. In general, the Senate was interested not to have the *ager publicus* diminish in size since part of it was lent out to private individuals in return for rents. It is very likely that the members of the elite profited enormously from these concessions, since the rents the lessees paid for them were rather low. The plebeians, on the other hand, usually insisted that a part of the public lands should be parceled into small lots and distributed to poor citizens. The lots could be used to found colonies, that is, cities officially created by Rome, provided with a rural territory, and populated with Roman or Latin citizens. For more information on this subject the reader is asked to consult chapter 2, section II.

Despite what some historians might say, during the Republican period, when the members of the senatorial elite were the only ones to hold power, the social content of political debates was often quite clear. Karl Marx remarked that we cannot understand the history of the Roman Republic if we do not pay attention to the predominant role of the agrarian question. But the divergent forces that often placed the plebeians in opposition with the elite and the Senate did not only have social implications, but economic ones as well. Indeed, the exploitation of large areas leased by the city was very likely to contribute to the commercialization of agricultural products and to help better supply the city of Rome with products such as meat, for example. Even though he criticized the increase in the size of domains and patrimonies, Pliny the Elder noted that their existence tended to lower the prices of agricultural products. He wrote that, in the third century B.C.E., [p. 215] the prices of oil, wine, flour, and meat were at their lowest, and that, however, this situation could not be explained by the existence of very large domains since, during this period, Licinius Stolo's law forbade possession of areas larger than five hundred *iugera*, that is to say 125 hectares (*Natural History*, 18.4.17).

The social structure of the colonies, on the other hand, being very egalitarian, favored an economic life consisting of modest local exchanges, but at the same time it contributed to the reproduction of a peasant class, with small or modestly sized properties, which formed the majority of the infantry corps in the Roman army. This is another case in which the political and social debates had obvious economic consequences that the Roman magistrates could not have ignored.

If the symbolic value of agriculture and livestock continued to be very important, and the economic importance of these two activities remained stable, the ancient tradition of the peasant and soldier declined severely during the last centuries of the Republic. From the beginning of the second century B.C.E. until the end of the Republic, the key elements of the Roman agrarian system, which I just described, were swept away by the profound transformations taking place within the city. The public lands of Rome, the *ager publicus*, tended to disappear after the agrarian laws of the first century B.C.E.; the members of the elite ceased to occupy them and settled on being mere large property owners; colonization changed its character and became a means of settling the veteran professional soldiers; and, the increase of the areas of large properties tended to increase the gap in wealth between the elites and the rest of the population.

With the advent of the Empire, the main features of the agrarian policy changed yet again and, in some cases, marked the return to traditional foundations. As a practice, colonization continued and the process always favored the veterans. But the various cities of the Empire possessed estate lands that they lent out to private individuals or offered for [p. 216] common use, in the same way that the ancient Roman *ager publicus* used to be employed. The lands of the State were reconstituted in the form of imperial properties, and some scholars have noted that the distribution of lots to *coloni*, that is to tenants paying rents to the owner, was another way to perpetuate if not smallholdership, then, at least, small productions.

In addition, I noted that the cadaster practices (which I discussed in chapter 2, section III), also show how the public Roman powers, both during the Republican period and under the Empire, were interested in land ownership.

What I have previously said about circulation, and monetary circulation in particular, and what I have just said about agrarian problems, allows us to grasp some of the characteristics of Roman policy vis-à-vis the phenomena we call economic. In addition to safeguarding the citizens and the whole population of the Empire, the main concerns turn toward freedom of movement and the maintenance of social and statutory equilibriums. On one hand, it was necessary to guard against the destruction of these equilibriums and, to the degree that it was possible, tend to the needs of various groups. On the other hand, it was important that daily life, professional activities, and commercial transactions were carried out as regularly as possible, and that merchandise and those who traded it were able to circulate as freely as possible. In other words, what was important and necessary was that the social connections were stable and the "economic" activities were mobile. The latter were very important to the state, especially when it came to issues of taxation, their satisfactory progress, and those who engaged in it. We do not see, in antiquity, the kind of opposition between social and economic logic that is so common and visible in our day. The reason for this situation is that, in antiquity, the economic phenomena were apprehended through the lens of political and social logic, as well as the logic of social and statutory categories. [p. 217]

Chapter 7
Remarks on the Evolution of the Roman Economy

Roman history textbooks often divide the twelve centuries that separate the foundation of the city of Rome (according to ancient authors, in the middle of the eighth century B.C.E.) from the end of the western Roman Empire (476 C.E.) in four or five big phases. They are: the archaic period (between the eighth and the fourth century B.C.E.); the first centuries of the Roman conquest (between the fourth and the second centuries B.C.E.); the end of the Republic up to the rise of Augustus (31 B.C.E.); the Principate (up to 235 C.E.); late antiquity. In this book I could have used this periodization, although it is essentially political and military and not economic or social. This is what W. Scheidel, I. Morris, and R. Saller, the editors of the recent *Cambridge Economic History of the Greco-Roman World*, did in their volume. For the Roman world, they distinguished the following phases: the archaic period and the first centuries of the Republic (until 133 B.C.E.); the end of the Republic, from the Gracchi to Augustus; the beginning of the Empire, and finally, the third century, the transition towards late antiquity, which has not been discussed in their work.

Writing a book as short as this one does not require adherence to the same strict rules as those imposed on the editors of a tome nearing nine hundred pages, like theirs. But beyond that, does this primarily military and political periodization have a meaning in economic matters? For example, does the transition from Republic to the reign of Augustus have a major impact on the economy? It is not at all certain. [p. 218]

Moreover, I think that, at least during a large part of its history, the city of Rome enjoyed some constants: a chronological approach could easily neglect some of these constants while repeating others too often. For these reasons, I have decided not to use such an approach, or to dedicate an entire chapter to the archaic period in the history of Rome, nor to the final centuries of the Empire in the west.

In drawing up the chapters on the various sectors of the economic life (chapters 2 to 5), and even the first chapter, dealing with historiography and some of the big questions addressing fundamental structures, we have seen that the various periods in the history of Rome did not have the same economic and social relevance, or to me, at least, they did not seem to do so. I was constantly led to provide details, and even very chronological ones, on the period of conquests, between the third century B.C.E. and Augustus' death (14 C.E.) and on the most stable centuries (the first and the second century C.E.). On the other hand, I am cognizant that I cannot make the same comments for late antiquity and the Principate. I notice, however, that the phenomena of the third and fourth centuries C.E. seem a continuation of preceding events (it is true that they were different continuations, but only up to a point). When it came to the archaic period, on the contrary, it seemed to me that this particular time exhibited clear specificity and needed to be treated separately. Aside from mentioning a few specific cases, like the *heredium* of two *iugera* that Romulus distributed to his citizens (see chapter 2, section II), I did not need to talk about the archaic period when discussing the rest of the economic history of Rome.

Consequently, based on these observations, I have instead chosen to use a synchronic approach, on economic sectors (see chapters 2 to 5), add a chapter dedicated to "economic policy" (chapter 6), [p. 219] and conclude with this chapter 7, dedicated to the main developments. So, in this chapter I will first deal with the archaic period, about which I have said scarcely anything elsewhere, and then with late antiquity, to which I sometimes alluded when I talked about this or that aspect of production, commerce, and financial activities.

The centuries of conquest (from the fourth century to the first century B.C.E.) are probably the most studied (both through the ancient texts and archaeological excavations), but the connection between the conquests and the economic transformations in Rome and Italy remains difficult to articulate. This connection is obvious, it can be described, yet it is very difficult to explain. I have discussed it in chapter 2 and justifiably so, as the agrarian problem plays a central role in these conquests and their consequent effects. It is difficult to say more here. One of the most important characteristics of this period (and especially of the fourth, third, and second centuries B.C.E.) is the driving force that wars and military policy were in it—a military policy very different from what it became under the reign of Augustus. In the Republican period, the city was constantly in arms, the city was constantly at war—and all its other activities were more or less arranged in connection with the war. What changed radically between those three centuries of the Republic and the Empire is the military policy. The first century B.C.E. was a transition period. Formerly, the city was always at war. But starting with the second part of Augustus' reign, it practiced an imperial policy of defending existing territory. Even though under Claudius and then under Trajan there were new conquests, the main concern was to wage war as little as possible and, with that as a goal, develop an efficient defensive system. [p. 220]

I. Archaic Rome

I refer to the four centuries that separate the founding of the city (traditionally believed to be 753 B.C.E.) from the middle of the fourth century B.C.E. as the "archaic period." Even though I have explained in the introduction that economic history cannot be separated from its social and political counterparts, for lack of space, this book has to limit itself to focusing on economic matters, and even on certain aspects of the economy. For this reason, the problematic events surrounding the founding of Rome cannot be addressed here (on this subject see the works of A. Grandazzi and T.J. Cornell).

The archaic period at Rome is not politically, socially, economically, or technically homogeneous. Three distinct and successive periods can be discerned. First, there are two centuries of progressive evolution: the eighth and the seventh. Then there is the first peak of Rome's expansion, in the sixth century B.C.E. or what is commonly referred to as "the grand Rome of the Tarquins." A century of decline followed, marked by numerous external wars and deep internal crises, the fifth century and the beginning of the fourth. We could say this period of decline ends around the third quarter of the fourth century when, as a result of political and military regional events, Rome took a hegemonic role in central Italy that then prompted radical changes in its social and economic sectors. The first bronze and silver Roman coins seem to date from the end of the fourth century. However, long before this time, the so-called *aes signatum*, bronze (copper and tin) ingots mixed with lead and weighing between 1.5 and 1.6 kg, were being circulated in Roman territory and used as coinage. There was another type of bronze blocks (mixed with iron), of Etruscan origin, called *ramo secco*, which was also in circulation at this time. The Greek cities in southern Italy produced their own silver coins. Thus, it is incorrect to assume that the Roman city did not use [p. 221] "coinage" (in a generally economic sense) before the minting of round coins.

The population of the city of Rome increased very much between the eighth and the seventh centuries, as known necropolises show. The urban population increased, and likewise the presence of an active urban center exercised an influence on the demography of the rural territories, as often happens. C. Ampolo estimated, in the fourth century, a density of 40 inhabitants per km^2. For the sixth century, the ancient authors mention record population numbers: 80,000 for the reign of Servius Tullius (Livy, 1.44.2), and 130,000 immediately after the revolution that deposed the Tarquins (Dionysius of Halicarnassus, 5.20). These numbers suggest very high population densities and most historians do not consider these estimations correct. They are useful though, as they show that in antiquity people believed that the Roman population greatly increased between the eighth and the sixth centuries and even during the course of the latter.

It is difficult to understand and even to describe the economic life of the city of Rome at this time without also paying close attention to Magna Grecia and the Etruscan domain, both of which were, from an economic point of view, much more important than Rome and Latium. During the first half of the sixth century all the wine drunk in Marseille was of Etrurian origin and Etruscan iron also played a very important role in trade.

When it comes to the material life and the economy of archaic Rome, writers of that time produced two parallel traditions, sometimes partly contradictory. Some, including Varro (*On Agriculture*, 2.1), insisted on the pastoral vocation of the ancient Romans; others, like Pliny the Elder (*Natural History*, 18.2–3), insisted that it was agriculture that played an important role in the early history of Rome. Both these theories have been defended in the modern period. Even though B. G. Niebuhr, T. Mommsen, and M. Weber have all three insisted on the [p. 222] agrarian character of archaic Rome, the theory based on the idea that Rome started as a community of shepherds or was founded on livestock practices became very popular during the first half of the twentieth century. A. Piganiol is the one who developed it and supported with the most conviction.

This thesis, however, should be abandoned. During the last decades, some archaeological and palaeobotanical studies (on the site of Sant' Omobono and in the necropolis of the forum) finally answered it. During the eighth and seventh centuries the territory of Rome was cultivated with grains and legumes like beans and peas. Certainly, these kinds of finds do not exclude the possibility that the Romans raised animals and ate meat (in small quantities, as the diet was based on grains and legumes). From this time period, and probably even before, we find in Rome and Latium the remains of bovines, and especially swine, sheep, and goats, alongside agricultural products and complementary to them. Within the framework of subsistence agriculture, certain forms of animal husbandry were indispensable, as the animals' manure was used during the fallow period, and the oxen provided the animal energy that was necessary for plowing. So, this was not a society of animal breeders, nor one leading a pastoral life. The archaic calendar and fragments of the Law of the Twelve Tables (middle of the fifth century B.C.E.) confirm this conclusion. The idea of a society of animal breeders is a product of myth: in the ancient world, it stemmed from a theory of the genres of life, which had been developed by Greek geographer Dicaearchus. Concerning transhumance, it partially depended on political and legal factors, especially when the animals were transported across long distances. It is certain that transhumance was practiced in Italy during subsequent periods as several remaining documents prove, but we should not generalize and assume that it had always existed. [p. 223]

For a long time, Rome's agriculture in part or in whole was one of subsistence. This theory is supported by certain literary sources and palaeoenvironmental (analysis of vegetative remains) finds. The remains of grains were almost always mixed with those of legumes (beans, in particular). It was not the case of alternating cultures but rather of associated cultures, and the two types of flour (of grains and legumes) were likely mixed.

During the archaic period, several types of grains were cultivated in central Italy: spelt in the more humid zones, barley in the more arid zones, and almost everywhere hard or durum wheat "from the husked grains," and especially the starchier type (*far*). During the first centuries of the Republican period, this "husked" wheat was considered inferior and was replaced with the "nude" or "soft" type, less hard, more tender. Until the third century C.E. the soft shell wheat was called *triticum*, a word from the same root as the verb *terere*, to thresh the wheat. In fact, it is almost impossible to thresh the *far*, whose kernels were stored whole in granaries: only soft-shell wheat can be threshed. The term *frumentum*, on the other hand, could be applied to all the species of wheat, and even to barley. For a long time, from these types of grains, the Latins made a sort of porridge more or less solid, called *puls*. Even during Plautus' time (the end of the third century and the beginning of the second B.C.E.), the Greeks called the Romans "*puls* eaters" (Plautus, *Mostellaria*, 828, and *Poenulus*, 54). Later, the Romans converted to a bread diet. The Roman countryside, however, was not very fertile. The lands situated in present day Frascati—for example those in Tivoli and in Lavinium—were considered of poor quality (Varro, *On Agriculture*, 1.9.5): in these areas, grain crops were not very successful. In fact, when it comes to this topic, we should take these judgments on the fertility of the soil with caution, since the authors who made them sometimes contradict each other. In any case, in the archaic period, and particularly in the fifth century, Rome [p. 224] did receive wheat from the Etruscans, the Volsci, the Greeks at Cumae and those from Syracuse.

The animal most commonly bred was the pig (and this remained true for later periods), followed by the sheep, raised primarily for its wool. Bovines were necessary for the exploitation of the land, but beef was very rarely eaten. The horse was important in wars and was considered a symbol of distinction.

The beginning of viticulture in Rome and in Latium dates very likely from the end of the eighth century B.C.E. and the first half of the seventh. The soils of this region were propitious for this type of crop, which required changes in the way agricultural exploitation was conducted. It required a more stable and enduring ownership of the land and very likely coincides with the ascent of the aristocratic elite. Two methods of cultivating vines coexisted: the Etruscan method, where high vines were paired with trees, and the Greek method, where low vines were supported by posts.

Because of the powerful Greek influence, growing olive trees was common in Etruria and is attested in the area starting with the middle of the seventh century. It is quite possible that this crop reached Rome only in the first part of the sixth century, as indicated by the excavations at Sant'Omobono.

Toward the third quarter of the eighth century, potters and bronze artisans could be found in different cities of Latium. Beside handmade ceramics, the wheel—probably the influence of the Greeks—was also being used starting in the eighth century. It became quite common in the seventh century and, from this period on, the ceramic forms are much more diversified. The occasional (but probably not permanent) presence of Greek merchants dates from the eighth century. We know that bronze, and also iron and silver, were being used during this time: these metals were used to manufacture the weapons found in the tombs of men, and also the objects for personal adornment that can be found in the tombs of women. There were also some unisex adornments [p. 225] used by both men and women (bronze and silver fibulae), bronze tools (axes), and bronze ware. Similar adornment objects were found in different sites, but this does not mean, however, that they were produced in the same location. When it comes to tools, we could safely assume that they had a larger circulation, as early as the eighth and seventh centuries.

The city of Rome has a very good location: it is situated on the route that follows the valley of the Tiber River, and close to a place where the river could be easily crossed; thus its siting is very propitious for commercial transactions in this period and later. Moreover, the mouth of the river was a key location for the salt trade. During periods of military success (the sixth century, for example), booty contributed to the city's prosperity.

As we know, Polybius reported three successive treaties that were signed between Rome and Carthage. The first one dates from 507 B.C.E., a little after the fall of the Tarquins (Polybius, 3.22). There was much debate around the exact date of this treaty, which T. Mommsen suggested should be moved one hundred and fifty years later. Now, there is a greater inclination, however, to think it quite possible that Rome and Carthage signed such a treaty at the end of the sixth century. Based on what Polybius says, at this time Rome already controlled the Tyrrhenian coast to the south of the city up to Tarracina, that is, up to one hundred kilometers away from the city. Although he does not mention this particular treaty, Livy writes that Tarquin the Proud had extended his sphere of influence all the way to Circei (Livy, 1.56). We could assume that the two authors had the same idea about Roman expansion at the end of the era of the Tarquins and this fact attests to Polybius' correct dating of these particular events.

The critical period of the fifth century, however, slowed down the progress of urban, artisanal, and commercial life in the area. The radical decrease in the quantity and the quality of military loot was certainly one of the most important causes of this situation. This century was no longer one of progress for the cities on [p. 226] the Etruscan coast, as the slowdown in the construction of temples shows. On the other hand, the interior cities, like Volsinii (Orvieto) and Clusium, were quite prosperous.

In Rome, the fifth century was marked by crippling food shortages, which explain, in part, the social and political crises pitting the plebs against the Senate, and particularly the Plebeian Secession of 492 (Dionysius of Halicarnassus, 7.1.1–2). The situation was so dire that, in 440–39, the starving poor threw themselves in the Tiber to show their despair (Livy, 4.12.11). Later, however, the agrarian situation improved considerably. When, at the beginning of the fourth century, Rome conquered Veii, the rural landscape of the Etruscan city had changed drastically: this conquest furthered its development. Even though in 393 the plebeians received lots of seven *iugera* from the Veian territories, henceforth the lots are not any more modest than in the archaic period, as the 367 B.C.E. *lex Licinia* shows. Bearing on the occupation of the lands belonging to the city (*ager publicus*) by individuals, it set a limit of 500 *iugera* (that is 125 hectares) per family head (Varro, *On Agriculture*, 1.2.9). True, the same Romans were not concerned in both cases: those who received land from Veii were the poor, while those who benefitted from the privatization of the *ager publicus* were members of the elite. Nevertheless, the figure of 125 hectares could be looked at as a sign that, from that time on, from an agrarian point of view, times had changed. This fact, however, could not prevent other serious crises (debt problems, land disputes, and fights between the plebeians and the patricians) from transpiring during the fourth century.

II. The Third and Fourth Centuries C.E.

The evolution of the Roman economy in the third and the fourth centuries C.E. presents us with sensitive topics, and is itself the subject of notable debates. For a long time, in the economic realm as well as [p. 227] in others, these debates centered around the concepts of "crisis" and "decline." Should we, or should we not, talk of a "crisis of the third century"? Should we, or should we not, consider the fourth century as one of decline compared to the preceding centuries? The two questions are not related. We could focus on the crises occurring in the third century (especially in the second half) and not consider the fourth as one of obvious decline.

In any case, the word "decline" should be banned because it is vague and highly ideological, and also because it involves nonquantifiable aspects of human life, such as the domain of motivations and values. Yet, as A. Giardina rightfully noted, the word "prosperity" is as ideological, and as vague and difficult to define, as the word "decline." There are, in economic history, quantifiable observations, based on which we can draw pertinent conclusions for phenomena occurring in recent times. For example, if we notice a decline of the gross domestic product (GDP), we speak of depression. If the rise of the GDP is merely reduced (without depression even being hinted at), we speak of recession. Unfortunately, for antiquity, the available data are insufficient to produce concrete results, even though some (like R.W. Goldsmith) have tried, with inconclusive results. Our task then is to focus on quantifiable elements: Did the area of cultivated lands increase or decrease? How did the harvests and crops perform, the numbers of livestock, the volumes of goods manufactured and sold? While looking to answer such questions, we have to remember, however, that we cannot really quantify any of these economic elements. As Y. Modéran noted, for antiquity it is less difficult to "analyze the structures of the production than to measure the production itself."

For about twenty-five years, a good part of the scholarship concerning these two centuries (the third as well as the fourth) has been of a polemical nature, and in general has attempted to "rehabilitate" these centuries from all points of view, especially from the economic point of view. It is sometimes difficult [p. 228] to discern between pleadings (some of them quite eloquent) and substantial analyses. In addition, this scholarship reveals the presence of two concerns, both of them legitimate, if partially contradictory: on one hand, showing evidence of the particularities of late antiquity, on the other, showing that the period has been faithful to the institutions and practices of the preceding period. This is, indeed, a contradictory task. if the third and the fourth centuries are so evidently similar to the first and the second, how could we then consider them as a distinctive period of time?

In the synthesis that concludes the *Cambridge Economic History of the Greco-Roman World,* A. Giardina rightfully notes that it is, indeed, necessary to make a distinction between the third and fourth centuries C.E. He writes that the third century was one of the most dramatic periods of the entire history of Rome, that it was one of "crisis." According to him, it started at the beginning of Marcus Aurelius' reign (161), marked by plagues and military difficulties, and ended with the advent of Diocletian (284). So, while not yet late antiquity, the period marked the transition towards it. Conversely, by the fourth century, we enter late antiquity, a particular period of time that does not constitute a time of decline, when compared to the Principate. A. Giardina criticizes those who tend to deny the reality of the crisis (by comparing various aspects of society and the economy one by one to show that the crisis was exaggerated and the portrait of the Empire it painted was too somber; or, by starting with an apocalyptic vision of the idea of crisis, so as to show that the third century was not similar to such a vision). But he also criticizes those who try to present this particular century as the beginning of an inexorable decline that continued well into the Middle Ages. Within the framework of this double-sided argument—to which I subscribe—we need to assume that the end of the third and the beginning of the fourth centuries were marked by an economic boost.

Yet, this manner of presenting the problem does not solve all our difficulties! As always, one of the most pressing troubles resides in the indispensable historical critique of all existing documents. Let's look at [p. 229] two examples. The first comes from a passage of the *Panegyrics* by an anonymous rhetor who, in 312 C.E., was charged by the city of Autun with thanking Constantine for tax relief in favor of this city. According to this rhetor—whose text appears at the end of the chapter (*Latin Panegyrics* VIII.3–5)—"all that had formerly been a fair ground has been buried under the marshes or invaded by weeds." Such a clearly rhetorical passage, typical of the literary genre of panegyric, cannot be given much importance. Yet, should it be entirely dismissed? Isn't it the case that, despite its "literary" status, this passage provides us with indirect testimony of the situations and the preoccupations of its time?

The other example is borrowed from Egypt, where the documentation is more abundant than anywhere else. R. Bagnall had so much material available that he can actually compare the tax documents of several villages in Fayum (the Arsinoite nome) dating from the second century to other documents from the same villages dating from the beginning of the fourth century. At Karanis, between the second century and the years 308–309, the number of taxpayers had decreased by 90% and the total amount of the tax on wheat had decreased by 95%; at Theadelphia, between 167 and 312, the total amount of this tax decreased by 99% and the number of taxpayers by 96%! And yet, even this spectacular and extreme change in Fayum did not convince him that the whole of Egypt was going through an agricultural depression. Bagnall is correct: things are not that simple. It is also necessary to take into calculation the rate of taxation and its growth, the manner in which it was calculated, the maintenance of the irrigation system, the productivity of the lands. On the other hand, the lands of abandoned villages were no longer irrigated. They remained very dry during the ensuing centuries, so that more papyri from such places were preserved.

If we speak of crisis, should we have it start as soon as the reign of Marcus Aurelius? It is debatable. In any case, it seems undeniable that the events of the third century had negative effects [p. 230] on the economic life of the Empire, even when foreign attacks and the plague did not affect all provinces and cities equally. Even though Britain and Proconsular Africa did not experience the foreign invasions of the third century, the latter experienced the plague that, at the beginning of the 250s, after striking Egypt, seems to have been particularly deadly in the region of Carthage. Moesia and Thrace were greatly affected by the invasions in 250–51 and 267–69; Lower Pannonia was harassed by the Sarmatians and the Vandals, and then later decimated by the plague. Gaul suffered heavy losses in 260 and in 275–76. Northern Italy was invaded in 260 and 270–71, and it also went through a series of usurpations and resulting civil wars: the siege of Aquileia by Maximinus Thrax (238), and the battle of Verona between Philip the Arab and Decius (249). Syria was pillaged by Sapor, the king of the Persians, in 253 and 260. When considering epidemics, that of Marcus Aurelius' reign and that from the third century, the human destruction thus caused has been calculated to be at least 10% of the population according to J.-M. Carrié's estimation, at least 20% according to A. Giardina, and 25% to 30% according to other scholars in the field. D. Rathbone has estimated that in Egypt, at the end of the second century, 20% to 33% of the population had disappeared. In the Roman Empire as a whole, it is impossible not to conclude that there was a fall-off in production and trade between 250 and 280.

We also need to take into account the weight of the taxation system and the evasion of the peasants; the decrease of euergetic activity (even if the epigraphic habit may have changed, so that the generosity of the notables, while still practiced, was more rarely invoked in honorific and funerary inscriptions); the decrease in the area of cultivated lands (even though some of them were tended to again, later); the paralysis of banking and financial activity, due to a very high rate of inflation (until the middle of the fourth century), etc. Faced with this crisis situation, the state, whose actions there is no space for here, tried to increase its resources and, it seems, to do it [p. 231] without imposing too much on the interests of the elite. One of the methods used by the emperors to achieve these goals was the extension of the public estate. Another was monetary intervention, which resulted in the depreciation of currency.

When it comes to economic activities of the fourth century, there are two more ideas that need to be abandoned in addition to the idea of decline. First, that old idea—so dear to M.I. Rostovtzeff—of a "state socialism," which had erased all personal liberties. In all sectors, or in almost all, private activities continued. Second, we must reject the idea that the fourth century already represents a transition towards the Middle Ages, and that the *coloni* were already the serfs attached to the land.

One of the central problems, and one that sparks intense debates, is that of the *coloni*. The *colonus* was the tenant, the inhabitant of a piece of land that did not belong to him but that he was entrusted to cultivate. This type of agrarian situation had been around for centuries. As several legal texts (and especially a constitution from 332, the *Theodosian Code* 5.17.1) show, however, measures taken by the public powers starting in the first decades of the fourth century had drastically changed its arrangement and had attached the *colonus* to the land. A constitution from the end of that century pertaining to Thrace says, for example, that "it considers [the *coloni*] as enslaved to the land where they were born, that they did not have the liberty to move where they wanted or to change their domicile" (*Justinian Code*, 11.52.1). How can we interpret these measures? There are two main possible explanations. The first, suggested by J.-M. Carrié and D. Vera, and which I also approve, considers them as tax measures, resulting from the reforms set in motion by Diocletian: the taxpayer is contained in his geographical residence and in the occupation he had previously practiced. This penalty was imposed on the *coloni*, but not only on them: it was also applied, in one way or another, to *curiales*, ship owners, soldiers, etc. The second explanation, [p. 232] on the other hand, sees the *colonus* of late antiquity as a real social and economic status, between slavery and freedom, created by the public powers. To the interdiction to leave their place of work and move somewhere else, several others were later added: the interdiction to sue their master, to marry at their own will, and to sell their possessions, whence comes the frequently defended idea that these measures, which were tax-related at the beginning, had become primarily social towards the end of the century.

If these measures do not touch upon the relationship between the *colonus* and the landowner, or between the *colonus* and the big farmer (the *conductor*), and if these relationships are not the subject of imperial constitutions, it is very likely because they are relevant as much to custom as they are to the law: because the state was primarily interested in the fiscal dimension of the situation, the immobility of the *colonus* constituted the principal condition in the stability of the fiscal system. In many cases, the colonate measures were probably favorable to the owners, but this does not mean that they were intended to be so, in a premeditated fashion.

Besides, the economic and social situations of the *coloni* were not the same everywhere. We need to make a distinction between the imperial lands and private domains, and also among the regions themselves. For example, in Syria and Palestine, the available documentation (texts from the *Talmud,* archaeological evidence from villages) suggests conditions rather favorable for the *colonus*, even after he was forbidden to leave the lands he was entrusted to cultivate. The short-term contract, agreed upon orally and highly valued by local customs, was predominant in Palestine and Egypt, but not in Gaul or in Spain. From this point of view too, then, we should not envision the Empire as a homogeneous unit. On the other hand, neither social suffering nor economic progress was directly connected [p. 233] to such measures regarding the status of *coloni*, and the latter were not even connected to each other. As D. Vera has mentioned, several of Augustine's texts describe the social suffering of the African *coloni*, while most historians constantly insist on the excellent economic situation of this province in the fourth and at the beginning of the fifth century: one situation does not exclude the other.

When it comes to slaves, it is not clear whether, throughout the Empire, their numbers decreased between the first and the fourth centuries C.E. In Egypt during the Principate there were not many slaves, and a large number of them did not even work in agriculture. For the first and second centuries, R. Bagnall estimates their number at around 13% in the cities and 9% or 10% in the villages. The situation does not seem to change in the third and the fourth centuries. Some of these slaves worked as domestics, or as trusted confidants, "managers" assisting their masters with the management of their respective businesses (stewards, cashiers, etc.). However, the most humble and only slightly wealthier owners, with few resources, often had a slave or two as agricultural workers. During the Principate, paid work was a rather seasonal affair, while slaves were employed to work the land on a more permanent basis.

What about the slavery by teams which defined "farm slavery" and which some also called "plantation slavery"? It is no longer mentioned in the third and fourth centuries, in any of the regions of the Empire, and it seems to have completely disappeared, or nearly so. It is no coincidence that the treatise of Palladius (which dates more likely from the fifth and not the fourth century) never took place in the "slave villa" of centuries past. Slaves continued to work in agriculture but, in the fourth century, they were either slave tenants (*servi quasi coloni*), or farm laborers. As slave tenants, they received from their masters a piece of land that they cultivated in the same manner that the free men, the *coloni*, did. Such slave settlers existed under the Principate, but their numbers, it seems, were small; [p. 234] by the fourth century, however, the great majority of the slaves working in agriculture were very probably slave tenants.

Based on recent scholarship, the decrease in the area of cultivated lands in the fourth century (compared to that of the first or the second century) was much less drastic than previously thought. Very likely, we cannot speak of a generalized decrease in the entire Empire: the situation changed from region to region. Proconsular Africa was, without doubt, the best-managed region. The archaeological excavations in the Kasserine and Segermes regions show an increase in the number of agricultural sites exploited between the third and the fifth century. The sale figures for wine, oil, cured meats, and fish sauces produced in Africa are impressive. B. Hitchner's and D.J. Mattingly's studies have established how important the African oil production was. Egypt, Cyrenaica, and Asia Minor also seem to have experienced a good economic situation in the fourth century.

In the European part of the Empire, the situation was less bright. In 1991, T. Lewit questioned the decrease in the area of cultivated lands and production. She based her research on the buildings in the rural villages excavated in Gaul, Britain, on the Iberian peninsula, and in Italy. But the dating is not always accurate, in fact far from it, and we do not know whether the area of the domains was proportional to that of the buildings. Consequently, her conclusions, which are very clear-cut, should be taken with a grain of salt. According to other sources, the situation in Italy and in Spain differed from one region to the next: in Italy, while the occupation of the land diminished in Etruria, the same did not happen in Cisalpine Gaul. In the west, the end of the third and the fourth centuries are characterized by the presence of gigantic rural farms (Piazza Armerina in Sicily, Montmaurin in the Pyrenees, Sao Cucufate and Foz de Lumbier in Portugal). Their presence, however, does not by itself imply the prosperity [p. 235] of the entire region. At the same time, survey and excavation campaigns in northern Gaul have shown a more dense occupation of the land than previously thought (see P. Van Ossel's book on this subject). In conclusion, the most popular theory at the present time is that we need to reject the idea of an agricultural depression in the fourth century.

In the European regions of the Empire, the large occupation of lands in the course of the fourth century was very likely favored by the arrival of barbarians whom

Rome installed inside the imperial borders. Most often they could be found in the western provinces, and were quite common near the borders, but some of them could also be found in northern Italy, for instance near the Po.

Were the grand landowners less numerous than in the first and second centuries? We don't know for sure. Were they richer than those living during the Principate? Did they possess more lands than their counterparts under the Principate? Even though their properties continued to be dispersed throughout the Empire the same way, or even more so than they were during the Principate, I think that the answers to these questions are affirmative, although they are not unanimously accepted. The annual revenue numbers were impressive as was the luxury of the rural estates. Such numbers, it is true, were reported particularly in the west: the revenues of the members of the elite in the east seem to have been more modest. The best evidence we have regarding small- and medium-sized landowners comes from Egypt, Syria, and Asia Minor.

The tendency to accumulate lands, more or less continued from the Republican period, had obvious effects. We should not forget, however, that there were other sources of revenues of a nonagricultural nature as, for example, those from real estate rents. An interesting example is that of Vestina, a woman of the senatorial order, who, around 400 C.E., drew half of her revenues from her rented building in Rome. To these great estates belonging to private individuals we need to add two others: that of [p. 236] the emperor, which continued to grow over time (thanks to inheritance and confiscations), and that of the Church, or rather churches (since the diverse Christian communities were autonomous when it came to properties). During the fourth century, the churches acquired a great expanse of lands, thanks to the donations of the faithful and, most of all, to those of the emperor.

There were debates on the lifestyle of the rich owners: did more of them live in the countryside than did their predecessors in the previous centuries? Were they more interested or less in the productivity of their lands and the work of their dependents? Had they become more "rural" in the western part of the Empire while remaining more "urban," more "civic," in the eastern part? It is difficult to answer these questions with any degree of certainty.

On the other hand, it is practically certain that the disappearance of slavery by teams benefitted small rather than big farms, and indirect over direct management. Direct exploitation, which we discussed in chapter 2 apropos the slave villa, contributed to the direct benefits of the owner and those under his orders, even though he did not work the land himself; an owner typically had a slave manager conducting daily business in his stead. During the third and the fourth centuries this method lost much of its importance. There were large estates, but they were divided in small lots: some were rented out to *coloni*, while most were assigned to big farmers, the *conductores*. The latter gave a fixed sum to the owner, and received royalties from the *coloni* (royalties also seem to have been fixed in this era, even when paid in kind). Or, when there were no *conductores,* the owner's managers acted as the immediate contacts for the *coloni.*

The importance of indirect management helps explain the fact that the annual global revenue of such-and-such an owner began to be mentioned in the records of the time (this [p. 237] was not the case beforehand: at the beginning of the Empire it was the value of the owner's estate that was measured, not his annual revenue).

Did this evolution make the owners behave more like "annuitants" with an annual income and less like "entrepreneurs"? It is certain that the two strategies (that of the renter and that of the entrepreneur), which existed already at the beginning of the Empire, continued to exist in the fourth century. But which one dominated, and were they not antagonistic? Based on L. Cracco Ruggini's work, D. Vera produced solid findings and persuasive conclusions on this topic. Vera showed that, because of the great quantities of food he received in kind (from the *coloni,* from the lands exploited in direct management), the owner could influence the prices used in agricultural markets. According to Vera, he was an annuitant because the biggest part of his estate provided him with a fixed income, in silver. Yet, because he influenced market prices through the sale of his products, and was thus involved in commerce, a part of these strategies also qualified him as an entrepreneur. He became an agent in the commercial sector, not because he sold his products (sales and commerce should not be confused: see the beginning of chapter 5), but because through selling them he could influence the prices used by the intermediaries involved in the exchange transactions.

Concerning manufacturing and commerce, given the way in which the fourth century was previously considered, recent studies have focused primarily on three main points: the nature and the extent of the control exercised by the state on these agents and their professional associations; the growth of private enterprises, the growth of the volume of production and that of commerce (were they decreasing or not?). On this third point, what I have said about agricultural production also goes for manufacturing, and the regions that sold the most are those I mentioned already, e.g., Africa, whose [p. 238] red slip ware, marble, and oil lamps could be found in great quantities in many regions of the Empire.

For the textile sector, the synthesis presented by J.-M. Carrié in the publication of the 2003 symposium of the Association of Late Antiquity, in Lyon, captures very well the continuity, the changes, and the innovations, over a long period of time from the beginning of the Roman Empire to the Middle Ages. It is a clear and stimulating way of presenting the western and eastern regions of the Mediterranean, by referring to both preceding and following centuries. For many manufacturing sectors we have yet to produce such detailed studies chronicling their development over a long period. On one hand, it is apparent that the two decisive innovations (the loom; the dissociation between fabric production and the manufacturing of the garment, and the production of fabric "by yardage") date from the Middle Ages, not antiquity. On the other hand, several less important innovations that had previously been attributed to late antiquity have been recently proven to date from the Principate. This is, for example, the case of certain developments in the weaving business: the fabrication of shaped and weft-faced fabric, the invention of the vertical weaving technique using two horizontal bars, the diffusion of colored dyes and colored fabrics, and that of mixed gold and purple fabrics. Certainly late antiquity did not constitute a period of decline for textiles, and J.-M. Carrié was correct when he talked about its vitality instead. The most important developments, however, happened either before or after this period. In the long and slow forward movement of that sector, late antiquity definitely played an important role in this sense, but it was mostly fueled by the momentum of the Principate's achievements.

With respect to the control of the state, imperial factories had been created beginning with Diocletian's era, and certain artisans, grouped in associations called *collegia,* were officially tied to their occupations in a manner similar to that of peasants tied to the land. [p. 239] Despite this fact, there is a tendency today to think that the control of the state was not as important as previously thought, since the Empire was mostly interested in its own fiscal advantages and the satisfaction of its own priorities. If the Empire exercised direct control over the artisans grouped in collegia, this happened because it wanted to ensure that the obligatory financial services were fulfilled as expected. Those who were thus surveilled were otherwise able to engage, in addition to these official services, in private projects that were either not subject to this control or to a lesser degree of control. In addition, such a situation had inherent advantages for the workers of these associations as they received, in return for accepting control by the state, benefits from the public powers. What this proves is that the state had far more difficulty keeping up with services it depended upon.

The evolution of commerce is connected to that of the cities. As before, the cities constituted economic units. Was the elite of the landowners less happy to live in the cities than before? There is no convincing evidence in this sense, and the cities continued to be dominated by this elite. There is no evidence that many of the artisans and traders left the cities to work in the villages or in rural estates. Starting with the reign of Constantine a new tax was imposed, the *collatio lustralis,* and nothing suggests that the amount of this tax had diminished considerably during the fourth century. Do archaeological excavations indicate a reduction in the area of the cities? For the eastern Mediterranean and northern Africa the answer is no, but this is not the case for the European part of the Empire. The ceramics finds show that the exchanges continued to be very intense. In fact, besides the largest cities (Rome, Constantinople, Alexandria, Carthage, Antioch, and Ephesus), many other cities needed outside supplies, and not only in times of [p. 240] poor harvests. How about the municipal elites, the curiales? Didn't their lot have consequences on the state of the cities, and particularly on the towns? We see that it is very difficult to come up with a diagnosis on the fourth century C.E. especially in the western part of the Empire, which fell apart during the fifth century.

Texts

Development of the Roman Lifestyle in the Last Centuries of the Republic

But in more recent times, when most nations had already been subjugated in war and there was a long period of peace, the ancient practices gave way at Rome to pernicious tendencies. After the cessation of warfare the young men turned to a soft and undisciplined manner of life, and their wealth served as purveyor to their desires.... Of wines, any that gave but moderate pleasure to the palate were rejected, while Falernian, Chian, and all that rival these in flavor were consumed without stint, as were the fish and other choice foods... A jar of wine, for example, sold for a hundred drachmas, a jar of Pontic smoked fish for four hundred drachmas...

Diodorus Siculus, 37.3.1–4 (Loeb Classical Library, trans. by F.R. Walton, 1967)

On this passage see A. Tchernia, *Le Vin de l'Italie romaine* (Rome: 1986): 63–64.

A Rhetor Speaks of the Sad State of the Territory of the Aedui

For we have, as I have said, both the number of persons that was recorded, and the amount of land, but both are rendered worthless owing to the inactivity of men and the treachery of the earth. For where are we going to find a field or a farmer comparable to those of the Remi, [p. 241]the Nervii, or even of our closest neighbors the Tricasses, whose returns match their labor? Although one would fairly pardon the cultivators themselves, whom it irks to labor without profit, if a field which that meets its expenses is abandoned out of necessity, especially when you consider the poverty of the country folk, for whom there was no possibility either of draining water off their land or cutting back the woods, reeling under their debts as they were. Thus whatever was once tolerably fertile land has now either degenerated into swamps or been choked with brambles. Indeed even that famous district, the Arebrignian, is spoken about with empty envy, for cultivation of the vine is conspicuous in only one place; for the rest of it, by contrast, is impassable because of forests and rocks, the dens of untroubled wild beasts. That plain, moreover, which lies under it and extends as far as the Saône was indeed once a delightful spot as I hear, when uninterrupted cultivation throughout the properties of individual proprietors carried away the overflow from springs in open channels. Now, however, that their courses have been blocked because of desolation, whatever had been very fertile because it was low-lying has been converted into marshes with deep holes.

Latin Panegyrics, 5.6.1–5 (trans. C.E.V. Nixon and B.S. Rodgers (Berkeley, CA, 1995), based on text by R.A.B. Mynors) [pp. 242, 243]

Conclusion

We have discussed separately, and over a long period of time (seven or eight centuries), the four large sectors of economy: agriculture and livestock; manufacturing; financial life; commerce. Within these big categories, particularly in those dealing with production (agriculture, livestock and fishing, manufacture), we have also identified and discussed several subcategories. Thus, in agriculture, we discussed primarily grains and arboriculture; in manufacturing, primarily textiles, glass, mines and metallurgy, stone quarries and construction materials, bricks and tiles, oil lamps, and ceramics.

If we consider the totality of these parallel histories and the conclusions they engendered, we are left with two main conclusions. On the one hand, production and marketing conditions varied from one product to the other and we have discussed them on several occasions, for example, at the beginning of chapter 5. At the same time, on the other hand, their overall evolution is almost always identical. After the archaic period, there was a phase of very rapid progress between the third and first centuries B.C.E. It cannot be denied that trading had greatly increased at this time, and that more and more quantities were sold and shipped to increasingly more distant locations. This is true for wheat, even though a part of it passed through the tax system. It is true for the tree crops; it is also true for ceramics. And so on…

In general, it is much more difficult quantitatively to evaluate production than commerce. But, during Roman antiquity, the progression of commerce was associated with a major transformation [p. 244] in agriculture, which we see clearly from ancient texts and from excavated or surveyed building remains in the countryside: the dissemination of the villa. It spread first in Italy where it was, most of the time, a "slave villa" (described in chapter 2, section IV), then in the western provinces. Under the Empire, in the provinces, the nature of the labor force is mostly unknown. This fact, however, does not prevent the visible presence of the villa phenomenon, which constitutes the most evident sign of "economic Romanization." This revolution in the way lands were exploited—which Cato's treatise, written during the second quarter of the second century B.C.E., has come to symbolize—was in a direct relationship with the progress of trade. One cannot exist without the other. They symbolize the move to an agriculture centered on the commercialization of certain products, which were never monocultures, but were widely predominant in the villas where they were cultivated. *Mutatis mutandis*, we could describe their evolution as being similar to that of ceramics or glassmaking (starting with the invention of blown glass). In addition, to these transformations in commerce and production we can add several other phenomena exhibiting analogous development patterns, such as the growth of monetary emissions and financial transactions.

This rapid progression of exchanges and production does not seem to have suffered the often very troubled fate of internal Roman politics. The civil wars of the first century certainly caused great damages, and I have talked briefly about the crises of payments and debt they produced. They were not sufficient, however, to reverse this strong trend directed toward the top. With the exception of the Hannibalic War (218–201 B.C.E.), whose effects were felt very strongly, external wars did not affect it much. It is true that, from 201 B.C.E. until the death of Augustus (14 C.E.), external wars [p. 245] were almost always successful, and their victorious outcomes meant more booty, lands, and slaves.

Later, starting with the second half of the first century B.C.E. (the time of Caesar's dictatorship and the reign of Augustus), this rhythm changes. From then on, the focus moved from progressing to maintaining the status quo. It is important that, in modern scholarship, one of the main questions regarding the third and the fourth centuries C.E. and even sometimes apropos the first and the second centuries, is that of economic decline. Was there a decline, was there a dip, were things going as well as before? The mere fact that we are asking this question means that the incredible progress of the second and first centuries B.C.E. was no longer a reality. A different phase has started, roughly together with the imperial regime that we call the Principate. This was not a period of decline per se. However, even though certain provinces continued to profit from the previous economic impetus (in some of them, the dissemination of the villas, for example, dated from the imperial period, and the success of African products continued to grow until the beginning of the fifth century), this was not a period of progress for the Roman Empire as a whole. This economic change is not the consequence of the political change from Republic to Empire, and it is not its cause, either. The two transformations, political and economic, were roughly contemporaries of each other, but neither one of them was the cause or the result of the other. The reader must note that political temporality is not the same as economic temporality. And while we know the precise date of establishment of the imperial regime, economic change is more progressive—it is impossible to date it to one or two years prior, especially since the chronology of economic change varies according to the provinces. [p. 246]

If we are to conclude, as we did in chapter 7, that there was no economic regression until the beginning of the fifth century C.E., we have to accept the idea that, various adjustments considered (new balances of power between Italy and the provinces, and among provinces themselves), the economic life of the Empire was, *grosso modo*, the same over four centuries. Technological progress has certainly taken place, especially in the countryside and in manufacturing activities, and I talked about the water mill and briefly mentioned certain innovations in the textile field. On the other hand, slavery by teams had gradually disappeared. These innovations, however, did not produce great upheavals, and did not disturb the mindset of the inhabitants of the ancient world. Or, we do not see them reflected in the ancient texts.

Only after the fragmentation of the western Empire did things change. At this particular moment, it is very clear that things took a turn for the worse, at least in the western Mediterranean. This conclusion well demonstrates the impressive economic solidity achieved under Roman domination in this area. It also showed how very dependent this situation was on the existence of the Empire. It did not depend on the hazards of internal politics or the nature of the political regime, but rather it was dependent on the existence of the Empire as a powerful controlling force over the entire Mediterranean area and over certain parts of Western Europe. One can discuss the consequences of the wars of Marcus Aurelius or even those of the plague, but it is irrefutable that, when the western Empire fell apart in the fifth century, many things changed, as a result, in the western Mediterranean. The amplitude of the Roman imperial economy, which could seem similar to more modern examples, is what separates it from them. To use Braudelian terms, we could say that the conclusions we derived from our studies show the Roman world to have been not an economy-world, but an empire-world. Even if the emperor [p. 247] did not actively pursue an economic policy (as we saw in chapter 6), the Roman economy was not completely independent of the political domain, and when the latter experienced an upheaval (in the western part of the Empire), the former could not continue on its previous path, at the same level, which had lasted for centuries.

I have discussed the Bücher-Meyer controversy at length. I will complete my conclusions by making a few additional remarks. M.I. Finley had the habit of criticizing the "butterfly collectors." In this category he included the historians and archaeologists who accumulated much detailed data but did not use it to ask any general questions. Instead of such a practice he proposes a "problem-history," starting with questions that have been, *a priori*, deemed important, and that the historians should then attempt to answer with the help of existing documentation. In one sense, he was correct, and it is rather difficult to defend those he metaphorically called "butterfly collectors." He was, however, only partially correct. The available documentation for antiquity is not only rare, but it also varies greatly from one field to another, from one question to another, from one region to another. And this scarcity changes with time. Not only does the quantity of available evidence increase markedly (due primarily to new archaeological finds), but it does so selectively. Not all the fields of history experienced this augmentation in evidence, and neither did the economic sectors. What was the practice of land leases during the Roman Empire? What percentage of the agricultural surplus was given to the *colonus*? In light of the available documentation, the answers to these questions could be of a juridical nature and we could study the exact procedures, but it is impossible to sketch their concrete evolution and practices. Was the gross domestic product of the Empire inferior or superior to that of medieval Italy or France? [p. 248] This is another very important question, to which, unfortunately, in the absence of supporting documentation, we cannot find a satisfactory answer. R. Goldsmith has tried to measure the gross domestic product of several ancient economies: did he arrive at a credible conclusion? Could we trust his findings? The answer is no.

While we acknowledge the merits of the problem-history, we also note that it is necessary to start with the available documentation and use it to the extent that it allows. To press the evidence against the grain, if I dare say, is not productive. This does not mean, however, that the study of quantities and model elaboration should be excluded practices. The studies of the last thirty or forty years illustrate very well what brilliant results (whether they are quantitative or even theoretical models) could be achieved based on the available documentation. The evidence is scarce, but it is productive if we pay attention to its inherent logic and do not insist on manipulating this evidence into supporting something it cannot support. D. Rathbone's book on the archive of Heroninos is an excellent example of what can be achieved when the documentation is chosen well and the scholar gives careful thought as to how to use it. D. Rathbone did not start with a problem, but with a dossier upon which inquiries were formed. It was a good method. One can challenge his conclusions or, at least, some of his conclusions, and I have done so. But his book remains a great accomplishment nevertheless. The same is true for A. Tchernia's book on wine. What was it inspired by? By the shapes of the amphorae and the places where they were found. What could be more similar to a butterfly collection than this research on the shapes of amphorae? And yet, the content of the book shows just how many essential historical problems this research touched upon. It addresses several concrete economic practices, from the relationships between the Roman conquest and the history of viticulture, to the economic behavior of the elites and the traders, to the history of [p. 249] food, to the evolution of cultural Gallic habits, and thus to the process of Romanization itself.

The above laudatory passages do not seek to confer hyperbolic praise on the authors of these two books, but they do point at how, in my opinion, historical research should be performed. It is possible to mention several other such examples. They all show how important it is to make the most out of the existing documentation. A model is only instructive if it is based on an in-depth evaluation and analysis of the available evidence and its characteristics.

In several areas of economic history at Rome, the efforts of the last thirty or forty years show at the same time the growth in the available documentation and the results that it can allow (or doesn't allow). One of these domains is the history of technology. I have tried to give it a relatively important place in this small volume because I believe that it holds the answers to many larger questions, despite some necessary detours (though one need not fear detours). For example, it has led us to the big questions addressed in several sectors discussed in chapter 3: the mines and metallurgy sector, that of glass, and that of textiles. It has also led us to do the same when certain aspects of the agricultural sector (see chapter 2, sections VIII and IX) and financial life are under consideration.

If in the recommended bibliography, besides D. Rathbone's book, I have added a relatively consistent set of articles and books on the economic life of the Roman Egypt, it is because I believe that these sources have helped us—and will continue to do so in the years to come—to find answers to questions that could not be solved in other regions of the Empire.

We have talked in great detail about more or less recent research projects. How can we situate them in dialogue with the Bücher-Meyer controversy? I do not think that is desirable to pretend that [p. 250] this controversy does not exist, or to stand apart from its debates. By choosing to do so one is, in one manner or another, still taking a stand. For this reason, then, I have tried to situate this book at the very center of the controversy (this was the purpose of chapter 1). What are the results that this attitude produces?

First of all, it guides the idea that we cannot accept the same conclusions for all the themes of the controversy. The debate over the consumer city is badly conceived and should be abandoned. Instead, the debate on the patrimonial interests of the elite should take a more central role, since it sheds light on the mentalities, the strategies, and the economic behaviors of those vested in these operations. This debate is central to understanding the Roman economic system. In all preindustrial historical societies, there always existed such socio-political elites deriving power from land ownership, even though their relationships with politics and economy were not the same in all cases. An in-depth comparative study is necessary. M. Weber has started such a project, but it is possible to develop it even further, especially since historical knowledge has grown since the time he conducted his research. So, this project should be revisited again. The market debate presumes concrete and precise research of every production sector and every region, in every time period. I have advanced a few preliminary conclusions on these subjects, but further intensive research projects on these topics are absolutely necessary in the near future.

A different idea: it is indispensable to abandon this controversy, but several recent books and articles on the topic have clearly demonstrated that we are far from doing so. To outgrow this debate we first need to take into account its problems, and reflect on strategies we could deploy to avoid falling into the fallacious approach that engendered the controversy in the first place. What this means is to start not with one question, but with a set of questions, and pay close attention to the manner in which these questions are related to each other and how they create a type of system. To avoid repeating the same questions and the same patterns, it is necessary [p. 251] to find some support outside the controversy. At the center of the controversy is the teleological vision of the history of Western Europe from antiquity to the present time. This teleological approach functions by using the most recent historical periods as the measuring stick for more remote historical periods, that is, to compare the ancient economy with the medieval one, or with the early modern one, in Western Europe and, by extension, in North America. Where could we situate the Greco-Roman period in relation to these time periods? A comparative approach to this question could be one way to bypass the controversy, but on condition that the comparisons would not be made between ancient Rome and sixteenth-, seventeenth-, or eighteenth-century England or France, as we have done and as others continue to do. In one sense, it is of little importance if we decide that the Roman economy resembles that at the end of the Middle Ages or at the beginning of the eighteenth century. In either case, such studies will not only perpetuate the controversy but reinforce it.

To outgrow this controversy it is necessary to compare Greco-Roman antiquity to preindustrial economies from outside the perimeter of Western European history, for example, to the civilizations of the Far East. Or, we can try to engage the help of other disciplines beyond their summary aid provided so far, which could enable us to formulate new concepts and develop new approaches that will allow us to free ourselves from the style of thought transmitted to us by K. Bücher, E. Meyer, J. Hasebroek, M.I. Rostovtzeff, and a few others.

Texts Discussed

Chapter 1

Plutarch, *Crassus,* 2.1–7
Livy 21.63.3–4

Chapter 2

Strabo 12.6.1
Pliny the Younger, *Letters,* 8.2

Chapter 3

CIL III, tablet no. 10, p. 948
CIL XV.21
CIL XV.90b
CIL XV.160

Chapter 4

CIL IV.3340.6
Hippolytus of Rome, *Refutation of All Heresies,* 9.12

Chapter 5

Diodorus Siculus 5.26.3
Tacitus, *Annals,* 13.53.2–4

Chapter 7

Diodorus Siculus 37.3.1–4
Latin Panegyrics 5.6.1–5

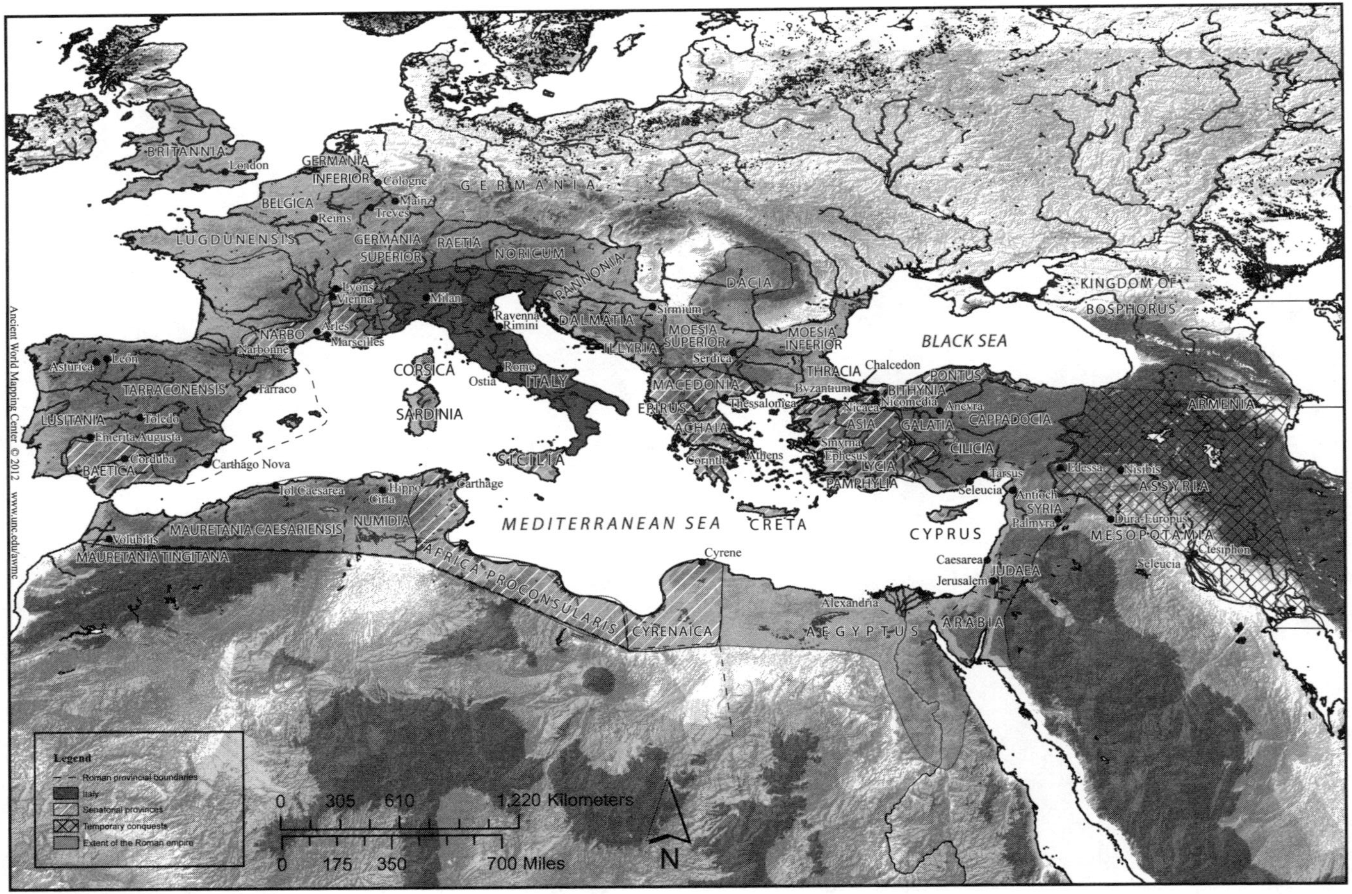

Ancient World Mapping Center © 2012 www.unc.edu/awmc
BRITANNIA
London
GERMANIA INFERIOR
Cologne
G E R M A N I A
BELGICA
Mainz
Treves
Reims
LUGDUNENSIS
GERMANIA SUPERIOR
RAETIA
NORICUM
PANNONIA
DACIA
KINGDOM OF BOSPHORUS
Lyons
Vienna
Milan
Ravenna
Rimini
Sirmium
DALMATIA
MOESIA SUPERIOR
MOESIA INFERIOR
BLACK SEA
NARBO
Arles
Marseilles
Narbonne
Asturica
León
TARRACONENSIS
Tarraco
CORSICA
Rome
Ostia
ITALY
ILLYRIA
Serdica
MACEDONIA
THRACIA
Chalcedon
Byzantium
BITHYNIA
PONTUS
Nicaea
Nicomedia
Ancyra
ARMENIA
LUSITANIA
Toledo
SARDINIA
EPIRUS
Thessalonica
ACHAIA
ASIA
GALATIA
CAPPADOCIA
Emerita Augusta
Corduba
BAETICA
Carthago Nova
SICILIA
Corinth
Athens
Smyrna
Ephesus
LYCIA
CILICIA
PAMPHYLIA
Tarsus
Seleucia
Antioch
Edessa
Nisibis
ASSYRIA
Iol Caesarea
Hippo
Cirta
Carthage
SYRIA
Palmyra
Dura-Europus
NUMIDIA
MAURETANIA CAESARIENSIS
MEDITERRANEAN SEA
CRETA
CYPRUS
MESOPOTAMIA
Ctesiphon
Seleucia
Volubilis
MAURETANIA TINGITANA
AFRICA PROCONSULARIS
Cyrene
Caesarea
Jerusalem
JUDAEA
Alexandria
CYRENAICA
A E G Y P T U S
ARABIA
Legend
Roman provincial boundaries
Italy
Senatorial provinces
Temporary conquests
Extent of the Roman empire
0 305 610 1,220 Kilometers
0 175 350 700 Miles
N

0 130 260 Kilometers
0 90 180 Miles
N
CISALPINE GAUL
VENETIA
Aquileia
HISTRIA
Milan
Ticinus
Adda
Cremona
Placentia
Po
LIGURIA
AEMELIA
Bononia
Rimini
ADRIATIC SEA
Luca
Pisa
Arno
Metaurus
Arretium
ETRURIA
PICENUM
Lake Trasimene
Perugia
Castrum Novum
Hatria
Spoleto
Narnia
UMBRIA
Cosa
Tiber
CORSICA
Carsioli
Alba Fucens
SAMNIUM
Rome
LATIUM
Ostia
Ardea
Sora
Fregellae
Aesernia
Luceria
CAMPANIA
Cales
APULIA
Circeii
Beneventum
Capua
PONTIAE
Venusia
Brindisi
Pompeii
MESSAPIA
Puteoli
Naples
LUCANIA
SARDINIA
TYRRHENIAN SEA
Paestum
Copia
IONIAN SEA
BRUTTIUM
Vibo Valentia
SICILIA
Ancient World Mapping Center © 2012 www.unc.edu/awmc

Bibliography

General Works

Austin, M.M. and P. Vidal-Naquet. *Economic and Social History of Ancient Greece, An Introduction.* London, 1977.

Bresson, A. *La Cité marchande.* Bordeaux, 2000.

—. *L'Économie de la Grèce des cités, fin sixième–premier siècle av. J.-C.* 2 vols. Paris, 2007–8.

De Martino, F. *Storia economica di Roma antica.* 2 vols. Florence, 1979.

Duncan Jones, R. *The Economy of the Roman Empire: Quantitative Studies.* Cambridge, 1974. 2nd ed., 1982.

Finley, M.I. *The Ancient Economy.* Berkeley, CA, 1973. Translated into French as *L'Économie antique.* Paris, 1975.

Frank, T., ed. *An Economic Survey of Ancient Rome.* 5 vols. Baltimore, 1933–40.

Giardina, A., ed. *Società romana e Impero tardoantico.* 4 vols. Rome-Bari, 1986.

— and A. Schiavone, eds. *Società romana e produzione schiavistica.* 3 vols. Rome-Bari, 1981.

Lassère, J.-M. *Manuel d'Épigraphie romaine.* 2 vols. Paris, 2005.

Migeotte, L. *L'Économie des cités grecques de l'archaïsme au Haut-Empire romain.* 2nd ed. Paris, 2007. Translated by Janet Lloyd as *The Economy of the Greek cities: From the Archaic Period to the Early Roman Empire.* Berkeley, CA, 2009.

Rostovtzeff, M.I. *The Social and Economic History of the Hellenistic World.* Oxford, 1941. Translated as *Histoire économique et sociale du monde hellénistique.* Paris, 1989.

—. *The Social and Economic History of the Roman Empire.* 2nd ed. Oxford, 1957. Translated as *Histoire économique et sociale de l'Empire romain.* Paris, 1988.

Scheidel, W., I. Morris, and R. Saller, eds. *The Cambridge Economic History of the Greco-Roman World.* Cambridge, 2008.

— and S. von Reden, eds. *The Ancient Economy.* Edinburgh, 2002.

Schiavone, A. *L'Histoire brisée.* French translation. Paris, 2003.

—, ed. *Storia di Roma.* 4 vols., 7 parts. Turin, 1988–93.

Other Books and Articles

Alcock, S.E. *Graecia Capta: The Landscapes of Roman Greece.* Cambridge, 1993.

Amouretti, M.-C. "L'attelage dans l'Antiquité, le prestige d'une erreur scientifique." *Annales, Économies, Sociétés, Civilisations* 46 (1991): 219–32.

Ampolo, C. "Rome archaïque: une société pastorale?" In *Pastoral Economies in Classical Antiquity,* ed. C.R. Whittaker, 120–33. Cambridge, 1988.

—. "Su alcuni Mutamenti sociali nel Lazio tra l'VIII e il V secolo." *Dialoghi di Archeologia* 4–5 (1970–71): 37–68.
— and A.M. Bietti Sestieri, eds. "La Formazione della citta nel Lazio." *Dialoghi di Archeologia*[2] 2 (1980).
Andreau, J. *Banking and Business in the Roman World.* Cambridge, 1999.
—. *La Vie financière dans le monde romain, les Manieurs d'argent de métier (IVe siècle av. J.-C.-IIIe siècle apr. J.-C.).* Rome, 1987.
—. *Les Affaires de Monsieur Jucundus.* Rome, 1974.
—. "L'Italie impériale et les provinces: Déséquilibre des échanges et flux monétaires." In *L'Italie d'Auguste à Dioclétien,* 175–203. Rome, 1994.
—. "Mercati e mercato." In *Storia di Roma,* II.2, *L'Impero mediterraneo, I principi e il mondo,* ed. A. Schiavone, 367–85. Turin, 1991.
—. *Patrimoines, échanges et prêts d'argent: L'économie romaine.* Rome, 1997.
—. "Remarques sur les intérêts patrimoniaux de l'élite romaine." *Cahiers du Centre Gustave Glotz* 16 (2005): 57–77.
— and W. Berelowitch, eds. *Michel Ivanovitch Rostovtzeff.* Bari, 2008.
—, P. Briant, and R. Descat, eds. *Economie antique: les échanges dans l'antiquité: le rôle de l'État.* Saint-Bertrand-de-Comminges, 1994.
— and V. Chankowski, eds. *Vocabulaire et expression de l'économie dans le monde antique.* Bordeaux, 2007.
— and R. Descat. *Esclave en Grèce et à Rome.* Paris, 2006.
— and R. Étienne. "Vingt ans de recherches sur l'archaïsme et la modernité des sociétés antiques." *Revue des Études anciennes* 86 (1984): 55–83.
Aubert, J.-J. *Business Managers in Ancient Rome: A Social and Economic Study of Institores, 200 B.C.-A.D. 250.* Leiden, 1994.
Bagnall, R.S. *Egypt in Late Antiquity.* Princeton, 1993.
—. *Later Roman Egypt: Society, Religion, Economy and Administration.* Aldershot, 2003.
— and B.W. Frier. *The Demography of Roman Egypt.* Cambridge, 1994.
Bang, P.F. *The Roman Bazaar: A Comparative Study of Trade and Markets in a Tributary Empire.* Cambridge, 2008.
Bats, M. *Vaisselle et alimentation à Olbia de Provence (v. 350-v. 50 av. J.-C.): Modèles culturels et catégories céramiques.* Paris, 1988.
Bémont, C. and J.-P. Jacob, eds. *La Terre sigillée gallo-romaine, Lieux de production du Haut-Empire: implantation, produits, relations.* Paris, 1986.
Bernard, H., M.-P. Jézégou, and E. Nantet. "L'Épave Ouest-Embiez 1, Var: Cargaison, mobilier, fonction commerciale du navire." *Revue archéologique de Narbonnaise* 40 (2007): 199–223.
Billeter, G. *Geschichte des Zinsfusses im griechisch-römischen Altertum bis auf Justinian.* Leipzig, 1898.
Bloch, M. "Avènement et conquête du moulin à eau." *Annales d'Histoire économique et sociale* 7 (1935): 538–63. Republished as M. Bloch, *Mélanges historiques,* 800–21. Paris, 1983.
Blume, F., C. Lachmann, and A. Rudorff. *Die Schriften der römischen Feldmesser.* 2 vols. Berlin, 1848–52.

Bogaert, R. *Banques et banquiers dans les cités grecques.* Leiden, 1968.
—. *Trapezitica Aegyptiaca, Recueil de recherches sur la banque en Égypte gréco-romaine.* Florence, 1994.
Bonsangue, M.L. "Aspects économiques et sociaux du monde du travail à Narbonne, d'après la documentation épigraphique (Ier siècle av. J.-C.-Ier siècle apr. J.-C.)." *Cahiers du Centre Gustave Glotz* 13 (2002): 201–32.
Borgard, P. "À propos des teintureries de Pompéi: l'exemple de l'*officina infectoria* V, 1, 4." In *Les Artisans dans la ville antique,* ed. J.-C. Béal and J.-C. Goyon, 55–67. Lyon, 2002.
—, J.-P. Brunet, and M. Picon, eds. *L'Alun de Méditerranée, Actes du colloque de Naples et Lipari (4–8 juin 2003).* Naples, 2006.
Bouet, A., ed. "Aquam in altum exprimere." *Les Machines élévatrices d'eau dans l'Antiquité.* Bordeaux, 2005.
Bowman, A.K. *Life and Letters on the Roman Frontier: Vindolanda and Its People.* London, 1994.
—. *The Vindolanda Writing-Tablets, Vol. III: Tabulae Vindolandenses.* London, 2003.
— and J.D. Thomas. *Vindolanda: The Latin Writing-Tablets.* Gloucester, 1984.
Braudel, F. *Civilisation and capitalism, 15th-18th century.* 3 vols. London, 1981–84. Translated by Siân Reynolds. *Civilisation matérielle et capitalisme.* Paris, 1967.
Brenot, C., X. Loriot, and D. Nony. *Aspects d'histoire économique et monétaire, de Marc Aurèle à Constantin.* Paris, 1999.
Bresson, A. "Les Accords romano-carthaginois." In *La Mobilité des personnes en Méditerranée de l'Antiquité à l'époque moderne. Procédures de contrôle et documents d'identification,* ed. Cl. Moatti, 649–76. Rome, 2004.
Briant, P. "Villages et communautés villageoises d'Asie achéménide et hellénistique." *Journal of the Social and Economic History of the Orient* 18 (1975): 165–88.
Bruhns, H. "De W. Sombart à M. Weber et à M.I. Finley: la typologie de la ville antique et la question de la ville de consummation." In *L'origine des richesses dépensées dans la ville antique,* ed. P. Leveau, 254–73. Aix-en-Provence, 1985.
Brun, J.-P. *Archéologie du vin et de l'huile en Gaule romaine.* Paris, 2005.
—. "Une Parfumerie romaine sur le forum de Paestum." *Mélanges de l'École Française de Rome. Antiquité* 110 (1998): 419–72.
—. "The Production of Perfumes in Antiquity." *AJA* 104 (2000): 277–308.
— and J.-L. Fiches, eds. *Énergie hydraulique et machines élévatrices d'eau durant l'Antiquité.* Naples, 2007.
Brunet, J.-P. and F. Laubenheimer, eds. "La Viticulture en Gaule." *Gallia* 58 (2001): 1–260.
Brunt, P.A. *Italian Manpower, 225 B.C.-A.D. 14.* Oxford, 1971.
Burnett, A.M. *Coinage in the Roman World.* London, 1987.
Callu, J.-P. "Problèmes monétaires du IVe siècle (311–395)." In *Conflits et transformations au IVe siècle,* Colloque de la F.I.E.C., 103–26. Bordeaux, 1970. Bonn, 1978.
Capogrossi Colognesi, L. "Dalla *Villa* al *saltus*: continuità e trasformazioni." In *Du Latifundium au latifondo, Un héritage de Rome, une création médiéval ou moderne?,* 191–211. Bordeaux-Paris, 1995.

—. *Persistenza e innovazione nelle strutture territoriali dell'Italia* romana, *L'Ambiguità di una interpretazione storiografica e dei suoi modelli.* Rome, 2002.
Carandini, A., ed. *Settefinestre, una villa schiavistica nell'Etruria romana.* 3 vols. Modena, 1985.
Carrié, J.-M. "Le 'colonat du Bas-empire': un mythe historiographique?" *Opus* 1 (1982) (2): 351–70.
—. "'Colonato del Basso-Impero': la resistenza del mito." In *Terre, proprietari e contadini dell'impero romano,* ed. E. Lo Cascio, 75–150. Rome, 1997.
—. "Les Échanges commerciaux de l'État antique tardif." In *Les échanges dans l'antiquité: le rôle de l'État,* ed. J. Andreau, P. Briant, and R. Descat, 175–207. Saint-Bertrand-de-Comminges, 1994.
—, ed. "Tissus et vêtements dans l'Antiquité tardive." Actes du Colloque de l'Association pour l'Antiquité tardive. *Antiquité tardive* 12 (2004): 9–252. See especially J.-M. Carrié, "Vitalité de l'industrie textile à la fin de l'Antiquité: considérations économiques et technologiques," 13–43.
— and A. Rousselle. *L'Empire romain en mutation des Sévères à Constantin (192–337).* Paris, 1999. See especially chapter 8, "Économie globale, économies régionales," 513–61.
Casson, L. "The Role of the State in Rome's Grain Trade." In *The Seaborne Commerce of Ancient Rome: Studies in Archaeology and History,* ed. J.H. D'Arms and E.C. Kopff, 21–33. Rome, 1980.
Centre national de la recherche scientifique. *Du latifundium au latifondo: Un héritage de Rome, une création médiéval ou moderne?* Bordeaux-Paris, 1995.
Chouquer, G. "Les Transformations récentes de la centuriation. Une autre lecture de l'arpentage romain." *Annales Histoire, Sciences Sociales,* 63 (2008): 847–74.
— and F. Favory. *L'arpentage romain: histoire des textes, droit, techniques.* Paris, 2001.
Christol, M. "Marchands gaulois et grand commerce de l'huile de Bétique dans l'Occident romain. Quelques données provenant des amphores." In *Vivre, produire et échanger: reflets méditerranéens,* Mélanges offerts à Bernard Liou, ed. L. Rivet and M. Sciallano, 325–34. Montagnac, 2002.
—. "Remarques sur les naviculaires d'Arles." *Latomus* 30 (1971): 643–63.
— and T. Drew Bear. "Documents latins de Phrygie." *Tyche* 1 (1986): 41–87.
Coarelli, F. "Fregellae, Arpinum, Aquinum: *lana* e *fullonicae* nel Lazio meridionale." In *Les Élites municipales de l'Italie péninsulaire des Gracques à Néron,* ed. M. Cebeillac-Gervasoni, 199–205. Naples and Rome, 1996.
—. "I Sanniti a Fregellae." In *La Romanisation du Samnium aux IIe et I[e] siècles av. J.-C.,* 177–85. Actes du Colloque de Naples, 1988. Naples, 1991.
Cohen, E.E. *Athenian Economy and Society, A Banking Perspective.* Princeton, 1992.
Cornell, T.J. *The Beginnings of Rome: Italy and Rome from the Bronze Age to the Punic Wars: 1000–264 B.C.* London-New York, 1995.
Crawford, M.H. *Coinage and Money under the Roman Republic, Italy and the Mediterranean Economy.* London, 1985.
—. "Money and Exchange in the Roman World." *JRS* 60 (1970): 40–48.

Criniti, N. *La Tabula alimentaria di Veleia.* Parma, 1991.
Crouzet, F. "Angleterre et France au XVIIIe siècle. Essai d'analyse comparée de deux croissances économiques." *Annales, Économies, Sociétés, Civilisations* 21 (1966): 254–91. Republished in F. Crouzet, *De la Supériorité de l'Angleterre sur la France,* 22–49. Paris, 1985.
—. *Capital Formation in the Industrial Revolution.* London, 1972.
"La Culture maritime dans l'Antiquité, III." Joint publication, *Mélanges de l'École Française de Rome. Antiquité* 112 (2000): 7–171.
D'Arms, J.H. *Commerce and Social Standing in Ancient Rome.* Cambridge, MA, 1981.
Debord, P. "Populations rurales de l'Anatolie gréco-romaine." *Atti del CERDAC* 8 (1976–77): 43–69.
De Ligt, L. "Demand, Supply, Distribution: The Roman Peasantry between Town and Countryside." In *Münstersche Beiträge zur antiken Handelsgeschichte* 9.2 (1990): 24–56 and 10.1 (1991): 33–77.
—. *Fairs and Markets in the Roman Empire.* Amsterdam, 1993.
De Romanis, F. *Cassia, cinnamomo, ossidiana, Uomini e merci tra Oceano Indiano e Mediterraneo.* Rome, 1996.
— and A. Tchernia, eds. *Crossings, Early Mediterranean Contacts with India.* New Delhi, 1997.
De Ruyt, C. *Macellum, marché alimentaire des Romains.* Louvain-la-Neuve, 1983.
Desbat, A. "La Sigillée claire B de la vallée du Rhône: état de la recherche." In *Céramiques hellénistiques et romaines,* ed. P. Lévêque and J.-P. Morel, 2.267–77. Besançon-Paris, 1987.
Descat, R. "L'Économie antique et la cité grecque, un modèle en question." *Annales Histoire, Sciences Sociales* 50 (1995): 961–89.
Domergue, C. *La Mine antique d'Aljustrel (Portugal) et les tables de bronze de Vipasca.* Bordeaux-Paris, 1983.
—. "L'État romain et le commerce des métaux à la fin de la République et sous le Haut-Empire." In *Les échanges dans l'antiquité: le rôle de l'État,* ed. J. Andreau, P. Briant, and R. Descat, 99–113. Saint-Bertrand-de-Comminges, 1994.
—. *Les mines antiques, la Production des métaux aux époques grecque et romaine.* Paris, 2008.
—. *Les mines de la péninsule Ibérique dans l'Antiquité romaine.* Rome, 1990.
—. "Production et commerce des métaux dans le monde romain: l'exemple des métaux hispaniques d'apres l'épigraphie des lingots." In *Epigrafia della produzione e della distribuzione, Actes de la VIIe Rencontre franco-italienne sur l'épigraphie du monde romain, 1992,* 61–91. Rome, 1994.
— and G. Hérail. *Mines d'or romaines d'Espagne: le district de la Valduerna (Léon), Étude géomorphologique et archéologique.* Toulouse, 1978.
Dubois, C. *Étude sur l'administration et l'exploitation des carrières.* Paris, 1908.
Duncan Jones, R. "The Impact of the Antonine Plague." *JRA* 9 (1996): 108–36.
Enciclopedia dell'arte antica classica e orientale. Atlante delle forme ceramiche: ceramica fine romana nel bacino mediterraneo. 2 vols. Rome, 1981–85.
Étienne, R. and F. Mayet. *Salaisons et sauces de poissons hispaniques.* Bordeaux-Paris, 2002.

Feinstein, C.H. and S. Pollard. *Studies in Capital Formation in the United Kingdom, 1750–1820.* Oxford, 1988.
Ferdière, A. *Les campagnes en Gaule romaine.* 2 vols. Paris, 1988.
Finley, M.I. "Technical Innovation and Economic Progress." *Economic Historic Journal* 18 (1965): 29–45.
Fischer, T. *Der Ölbaum, Seine geographische Verbreitung, seine wirtschaftliche und kulturhistorische Bedeutung.* Leipzig, 1904.
Foy, D. and M.-D. Nenna. *Échanges et commerce du verre dans le monde antique. Actes du Colloque de l'Association Française pour l'Archéologie du Verre. Aix et Marseille, 7–9 juin 2001.* Montagnac, 2003.
Von Freyberg, H.U. *Kapitalverkehr und Handel im römischen Kaiserreich (27 v. Chr.-235 n. Chr.).* Freiburg im Breisgau, 1989.
Früchtl, A. *Die Geldgeschäfte bei Cicero.* Erlangen, 1912.
Gabba, E. and M. Pasquinucci. *Strutture agrarie e allevamento transumante nell'Italia romana (III-I sec. a.C.).* Pisa, 1979.
Garnsey, P. *Famine and Food Supply in the Graeco-Roman World: Responses to Risk and Crisis.* Cambridge, 1988.
—. *Non-Slave Labour in the Graeco-Roman World.* Cambridge, 1980.
—. "Trade, Industry and the Urban Economy." In *The Cambridge Ancient History,* vol. XIII, 2nd ed., ed. A. Cameron and P. Garnsey, 312–37. Cambridge, 1998.
—, K. Hopkins, and C.R. Whittaker, eds. *Trade in the Ancient Economy.* London, 1983.
— and R. Saller. *The Roman Empire, Economy, Society and Culture.* London, 1987. On "models," see pp. 43–51.
— and C.R. Whittaker. "Rural Life in the Later Roman Empire." In *The Cambridge Ancient History,* vol. XIII, 2nd ed., ed. A. Cameron and P. Garnsey, 277–311. Cambridge, 1998.
Genty, P.-Y. and J.-L. Fiches. "L'Atelier de potiers gallo-romains d'Aspiran (Hérault), Synthèse des travaux de 1971 à 1978." *Figlina* 3 (1978): 71–92.
Giardina, A. "Aristocrazia terriera e piccola mercatura, Sui rapporti fra potere politico e formazione dei prezzi nel tardo Impero romano." *Quaderni Urbinati* 36 (1981): 123–46.
—."The Transition to Late Antiquity." In *The Cambridge Economic History of the Greco-Roman World,* ed. W. Scheidel, I. Morris, and R. Saller, 743–68. Cambridge, 2007.
Godelier, M. *Rationalité et irrationalité en économie.* 2 vols. Paris, 1971.
Goldsmith, R.W. "An Estimate of the Size and Structure of the National Product of the Early Roman Empire." *Studies in Income and Wealth,* Series 30.3 (1984): 263–88.
—. *Premodern Financial Systems: A Comparative Historical Study.* Cambridge, 1987.
Goudineau, C. "La Céramique arétine." In *Céramiques hellénistiques et romaines.* 1 (1980): 123–38.
—. *La Céramique arétine lisse.* Rome, 1968.
—. "Les Villes de la paix romaine." In *Histoire de la France urbaine,* ed. G. Duby. I: *La Ville antique,* 233–398. Paris, 1980.
Grandazzi, A. *The Foundation of Rome: Myth and History.* Ithaca and London, 1997.
—. *Les Origines de Rome.* Paris, 2003.

Grenier, J.-Y. *L'Économie d'Ancien Régime.* Paris, 1996.

Guesnerie, R. *L'Économie de marché.* Paris, 1996.

Harris, W.V. "A Revisionist View of Roman Money." *JRS* 96 (2006): 1–24.

—. "Roman Terracotta Lamps: The Organization of an Industry." *JRS* 70 (1980): 126–45.

—, ed. *The Monetary Systems of the Greeks and Romans.* Oxford, 2008.

Hasebroek, J. *Trade and Politics in Ancient Greece.* Chicago, 1978. Originally published as *Staat und Handel im alten Griechenland.* Tübingen, 1928.

Hayes, J.W. *Late Roman Pottery.* London, 1973.

—. *A Supplement to Late Roman Pottery.* London, 1980.

Helen, T. *Organization of Roman Brick Production in the First and Second Centuries A.D., An Interpretation of Roman Brick Stamps.* Helsinki, 1975.

Hesnard, A. *L'Épave romaine 'Grand Ribaud' D (Hyères, Var). Archaeonautica VIII.* Paris, 1988.

Hopkins, K. "Taxes and Trade in the Roman Empire." *JRS* 70 (1980): 101–25.

Horden, P. and N. Purcell. *The Corrupting Sea: A Study of Mediterranean History.* Oxford, 2000.

Howgego, C. "The Supply and Use of Money in the Roman World, 200 B.C. to A.D. 300." *JRS* 82 (1992): 1–31.

L'Huile d'olive en Méditerranée: histoire, anthropologie, économie de l'Antiquité à nos jours. Actes de la table ronde d'Aix-Marseille, novembre 1983. Aix-en-Provence, 1985.

Inglebert, H., ed. *Histoire de la civilisation romaine.* Paris, 2005.

Ioannatou, M. *Affaires d'argent dans la correspondance de Cicéron: L'aristocratie sénatoriale face à ses dettes.* Paris, 2006.

Jacques, F. "L'urbanisme en Italie et en Afrique romaines." *JRA* 2 (1989): 238–44.

Jongman, W. *The Economy and Society of Pompeii.* Amsterdam, 1988. 2nd ed. 1991.

Kaplan, S.L. *Provisioning Paris: Merchants and Millers in the Grain and Flour Trade during the Eighteenth Century.* Ithaca and London, 1984.

Kehoe, D.P. *The Economics of Agriculture on Roman Imperial Estates in North Africa.* Göttingen, 1988.

King, A.C. "Diet in the Roman World: A Regional Intersite Comparison of the Animal Bones." *JRA* 12 (1999): 168–202.

Kolendo, J. *L'Agricoltura nell'Italia romana, Tecniche agrarie e progresso economico dalla tarda Repubblica al Principato.* Italian translation. Rome, 1980.

Kron, G. "Archeozoological Evidence for the Productivity of Roman Livestock Farming. *Münstersche Beiträge zur Antiken Handelsgeschichte,* 21.2 (2002): 53–73.

Labarre, G. and M.-T. Le Dinahet. "Les Métiers du textile en Asie Mineure de l'époque hellénistique à l'époque impériale." In *Aspects de l'artisanat du textile dans le monde méditerranéen (Egypte, Grèce, Monde romain),* 49–116. Lyon-Paris, 1996.

Lamboglia, N. "Nuove osservazioni sulla 'terra sigillata Chiara'." *Revue d'Etudes Ligures* 24 (1958): 257–330, 29 (1963): 145–212.

Laubenheimer, F. *La Production des amphores en Gaule Narbonnaise.* Besançon-Paris, 1985.

—, ed. *Les Amphores en Gaule: production et circulation.* 2 vols. Besançon-Paris, 1993–98.

Le Goff, J. *Marchands et banquiers du Moyen Âge.* 9th ed. Paris, 2001.
Lepelley, C. *Les Cités de l'Afrique romaine au Bas-Empire.* 2 vols. Paris, 1979–81.
Le Roux, P. *Romains d'Espagne: Cités et politique dans les provinces (IIe siècle av. J.-C.–IIIe siècle apr. J.-C.).* Paris, 1995.
Lerouxel, F. "Les Femmes sur le marché du crédit en Egypte romaine (30 av. J.-C.–284 apr. J.-C.)." *Cahiers du Centre de Recherches Historiques* 37 (April 2006): 121–36.
Leveau, P. *Caesarea de Maurétanie, une ville romaine et ses campagnes.* Rome, 1984.
—. "Les Moulins de Barbegal, 1986–2006." In *Énergie hydraulique et machines élévatrices d'eau durant l'Antiquité,* ed. J.-P. Brun and J.-L. Fiches, 185–99. Naples, 2007.
—. "The Western Provinces." In *The Cambridge Economic History of the Greco-Roman World,* ed. W. Scheidel, I. Morris, and R. Saller, 651–70. Cambridge, 2007.
—, P. Sillières, and J.-P. Vallat. *Campagnes de la Méditerranée romaine, Occident.* Paris, 1993.
Lewit, T. *Agricultural Production in the Roman Economy, A.D. 200–400.* Oxford, 1991.
Liou, B. and A. Tchernia, "L'Interprétation des inscriptions sur les amphores Dressel 20." In *L'Epigrafia della produzione e della distribuzione,* 133–56. Rome, 1994.
Lo Cascio, E. "La dinamica della popolazione in Italia da Augusto al III° secolo." In *L'Italie d'Auguste à Dioclétien,* 91–125. Rome, 1994.
—. "L'Approvigionamento dell'esercito romano: mercato libero o 'commercio amministrato'?" In *The Impact of the Roman Army (200 B.C.–A.D. 476): Economic, Social, Political, Religious and Cultural Aspects,* ed. L. De Blois and E. Lo Cascio, 195–206. Leiden-Boston, 2007.
—. "The size of the Roman population: Beloch and the meaning of the Augustan census figures." *JRS* 84 (1994): 23–40.
—, ed. *Credito e moneta nel mondo romano.* Bari, 2003.
—, ed. *Mercati permanenti e mercati periodici nel mondo romano.* Bari, 2000.
Łoś, A. "Les Affaires commerciales des notables municipaux." *Antiquitas* 28 (2005): 81–109.
Macqueron, J. *Contractus scripturae, Contrats et quittances dans la pratique romaine.* Camerino, 1982.
Marcone, A. *Storia dell'agricoltura romana: Dal mondo arcaico all'età imperiale.* Rome, 1997.
Mattingly, D.J. "Oil for Export? A Comparison of Libyan, Spanish, and Tunisian Olive Oil Production in the Roman Empire." *JRA* 1 (1988): 33–56.
Mauné, S. *Les Campagnes de la cité de Béziers dans l'Antiquité (partie nord-orientale), IIe siècle av. J.-C.–VIe siècle apr. J.-C.* Montagnac, 1998.
Mayet, F. "Les Céramiques à parois fines: état de la question." In *Céramiques hellénistiques et romaines,* 201–29. Paris, 1980.
—. *Les Céramiques sigillées hispaniques.* 2 vols. Bordeaux-Paris,1984.
Meillassoux, C. "Essai d'interprétation du phénomène économique dans les sociétés traditionnelles d'auto-subsistance." *Cahiers d'Études Africaines* 1 (1960): 38–67.
Migeotte, L. *The Economy of the Greek Cities: From the Archaic Period to the Early Roman Empire.* Berkeley, CA, 2009. Originally published in French as *L'Économie des Cités Grecques.* 2nd French ed. 2007.
Millett, P. *Lending and Borrowing in Ancient Athens.* Cambridge, 1991.

Minaud, G. *La Comptabilité à Rome: Essai d'histoire économique sur la pensée comptable commerciale et privée dans le monde antique romain.* Lausanne, 2005.
Mitchell, S. *Anatolia, Land, Men and Gods in Asia Minor.* 2 vols. Oxford, 1993.
—. "Olive cultivation in the Economy of the Roman Asia Minor." In *Patterns in the Economy of Roman Asia Minor,* ed. S. Mitchell and C. Katsari, 83–113. Swansea, 2005.
Modéran, Y. *L'Empire romain tardif, 235–395 apr. J.-C.* 2nd ed. Paris, 2006.
Morel, J.-P. *Céramique campanienne: Les Formes.* 2 vols. Rome, 1981.
—. "La ceramica e il vetro." In *Pompei 79,* ed. F. Zevi, 241–64. Naples, 1979.
—. "La Céramique campanienne: acquis et problèmes." In *Céramiques hellénistiques et romaines,* 85–122. Besançon-Paris, 1980.
Morley, N. *Trade in Classical Antiquity.* Cambridge, 2007.
Nenna, M.-D. *La Route du verre: Ateliers primaires et secondaires du second millénaire av. J.-C. au Moyen Âge.* Lyon, 2000.
Nicolet, C. *Rendre à César: Économie et société dans la Rome antique.* Paris, 1988.
—. *Rome et la conquête du monde méditerranéen.* Vol. 1, *Les Structures de l'Italie romaine.* 10th ed. Paris, 2001.
—. *The World of the Citizen in Republican Rome.* London, 1980; Berkeley, CA, 1988.
—, R. Ilbert, and J.-C. Depaule, eds. *Mégapoles méditerranéennes: géographie urbaine rétrospective.* Actes du colloque de Rome (8–11 mai 1996). Paris-Rome, 2000.
Nieto, J. "Cargamento principal y cargamento secundario." *Cahiers d'Histoire* 33 (1988): 379–95.
—. "El Pecio Culip IV: observaciones sobre la organización de los talleres de *terra sigillata* de La Graufesenque." *Archaeonautica* 6 (1986): 81–115.
Oleson, J.P. *Greek and Roman Mechanical Water-lifting Devices: The History of a Technology. Phoenix* Suppl. 16, 1984.
Ørsted, P., J. Carlsen, L. Ladjimi Sebai, and H. Ben Hassen, eds. *Africa Proconsularis III.* Copenhagen, 2000.
De Pachtère, F.-G. *La table hypothécaire de Veleia: étude sur la propriété foncière dans l'Apennin de Plaisance.* Paris, 1920.
Panella, C. and A. Tchernia. "Produits agricoles transportés en amphores: l'huile et surtout le vin." In *L'Italie d'Auguste à Dioclétien,* 145–65. Rome, 1994.
Parker, A.J. "Il Relitto romano delle colonne à Camarina." *Sicilia archeologica* 30 (1976): 25–29.
Pavolini, C. "Le Lucerne nell'Italia romana." In *Società romana e produzione schiavistica,* ed. A. Giardina and A. Schiavone, 2.139–84. Bari, 1981.
—. "Le Lucerne romane fra il III sec. A.C. e il III sec. D.C." In *Céramiques hellénistiques et romaines,* ed. P. Lévêque and J.-P. Morel, 2.139–60. Besançon-Paris, 1987.
Peacock, D.P.S. and V.A. Maxfield. *Mons Claudianus: Survey and Excavation, 1987–1993. Volume I, Topography and Quarries.* Le Caire, 1997.
— and D.F. Williams. *Amphorae and the Roman Economy: An Introductory Guide.* London, 1986.
Picon, M. *Introduction à l'étude technique des céramiques sigillées de Lezoux.* Dijon, 1973.
Pleket, H.W. "Greek Epigraphy and Comparative Ancient History: Two Case-Studies." *Epigraphica Anatolica* 12 (1988): 25–38.

—. "Models and Inscriptions: Exports of Textiles in the Roman Empire." *Epigraphica Anatolica* 30 (1998): 117–28.

—. "Wirtschaft des Imperium Romanum." In *Handbuch der Europaïschen Wirtschafts- und Sozialgeschichte,* ed. W. Fischer and others, 1.25–160. Klett-Cotta, 1990.

Poux, M. *L'Esprit du vin.* Montagnac, 2004.

Procaccini, P. "Ancora a proposito dell' 'industria' delle lucerne nell'Impero romano, Note in margine ad un recente studio di storia economica." In *Scritti sul mondo antico in memoria di Fulvio Grosso,* ed. L. Gasperini, 507–21. Rome, 1981.

Pucci, G. "La Ceramica italica (terra sigillata)." In *Società romana e produzione schiavistica,* ed. A. Giardina and A. Schiavone, 2.99–121. Bari, 1981.

—. "Le Officine ceramiche tardo-italiche." In *Céramiques hellénistiques et romaines,* 135–57. Paris, 1980.

Raepsaet, G. "Attelages antiques dans le nord de la Gaule. Les systèmes de traction par équidés." *Trierer Zeitschrift* 45 (1982): 215–73.

— and C. Bommelaere, eds. *Brancards et transport attelé entre Seine et Rhin de l'Antiquité au Moyen Âge.* Treignes, 1995.

— and M.-T. Raepsaet-Charlier. "Aspects de l'organisation du commerce de la céramique sigillée dans le nord de la Gaule au IIe siècle de notre ère." *Münstersche Beiträge zur Antiken Handelsgeschichte* 6.2 (1987): 1–29 (1, *Les données matérielles*),and 7.2 (1988): 45–69 (2, *Négociants et transporteurs, La géographie des activités commerciales*).

Rathbone, D. *Economic Rationalism and Rural Society in Third-Century A.D.: Egypt, The Heroninos Archive and the Appianus Estate.* Cambridge, 1991.

Remesal Rodriguez, J. *La Annona militaris y la exportacion de aceite betico a Germania.* Madrid, 1986.

Rickman, G. "The Grain Trade under the Roman Empire." In *The Seaborne Commerce of Ancient Rome: Studies in Archaeology and History,* ed. J.H. D'Arms and E.C. Kopff, 261–75. Rome, 1980.

Roman, Y. and J. Dalaison, eds. *L'Économie antique, une économie de marché?* Lyon-Paris, 2008.

Roth, U. "Cicero, a Legal Dispute, and a *Terminus ante quem* for the Large Scale Exploitation of Female Slaves in Roman Italy." *Index* 36 (2008): 575–83.

Rowlandson, J. *Landowners and Tenants in Roman Egypt: The Social Relations of Agriculture in the Oxyrhynchite Nome.* Oxford, 1996.

Sartre, M. *D'Alexandre à Zénobie, Histoire du Levant antique, IVe siècle av. J.-C.–IIIe siècle apr. J.-C.* 2nd ed. Paris, 2003.

—. *The Middle East under Rome.* Cambridge, MA, 2005.

Scheidel, W. "The slave population of Roman Italy, speculations and constraints." *Topoi* 9 (1999): 129–44.

Schiavone, A., ed. *Storia di Roma,* III.1, *L'Età tardoantica, Crisi e trasformazioni.* Turin, 1993. See the articles by J. Kolendo, L. Cracco Ruggini, and J.-P. Callu, 425–524.

Shatzman, I. *Senatorial Wealth and Roman Politics.* Brussels, 1975.

Spruytte, J. *Études expérimentales sur l'attelage: Contribution à l'histoire du cheval.* Paris, 1977.

Steinby, E.M. *Indici complementari ai bolli doliari urbani (CIL XV, 1).* Rome, 1987.

Steinby, M. "I Senatori e l'industria laterizia urbana." In *Epigrafia e ordine senatorio,* 1.227–37. Rome, 1982.

Sternini, M. *La fenice di sabbia: storia e tecnologia del vetro antico.* Bari, 1995.

Suolahti, J., ed. *Lateres Signati Ostienses.* 2 vols. Rome, 1978.

Tchernia, A. "La Crise de l'Italie impériale et la concurrence des provinces." *Cahiers du Centre de Recherches Historiques* 37 (avril 2006): 137–56.

—. "Italian Wine in Gaul at the End of the Republic." In *Trade in the Ancient Economy,* ed. P. Garnsey, K. Hopkins, and C.R. Whittaker, 87–104. London, 1983.

—. "Moussons et monnaies: les voies du commerce entre le monde gréco-romain et l'Inde." *Annales Histoire, Sciences Sociales* 50 (1995): 991–1009.

— and J.-P. Brun. *Le Vin romain antique.* Grenoble, 1999.

Temin, P. "The Economy of the Early Roman Empire." *Journal of Economic Perspectives* 20 (2006).

—. "Financial Intermediation in the Early Roman Empire." *Journal of Economic History* 64 (2004): 705–33.

—. "A Market Economy in the Early Roman Empire." *JRS* 91 (2001): 169–81.

— and D. Rathbone. "Financial intermediation in First-Century A.D. Rome and Eighteenth Century England. In K. Verboven, K. Vandorpe, and V. Chankowski, eds. *Pistoi dia tène Technèn: Bankers, Loans, and Archives in the Ancient World.* Leuven, 2008, 371–419.

Tortorella, S. "La Ceramica africana: un riesame della problematica." In *Céramiques hellénistiques et romaines,* ed. P. Lévêque and J. P. Morel, 2.279–326. Besançon-Paris, 1988.

—. "La Ceramica fine da mensa africana dal IV al VII sec. d. C." In *Società romana e impero tardoantico,* ed. A. Giardina, 3.211–25. Rome-Bari, 1986.

Tran, N. *Les membres des associations romaines: le rang social des "collegiati" en Italie et en Gaules sous le Haut-Empire.* Rome, 2006.

Van Andringa, W., ed. "Sacrifices, marché de la viande et pratiques alimentaires dans les cités du monde romain." *Food and History* 5 (2007).

Van Minnen, P. "Urban craftsmen in Roman Egypt." *Münstersche Beiträge zur Antiken Handelsgeschichte* 6.1 (1987): 31–88.

—."The Volume of the Oxyrhynchite Textile Trade." *Münstersche Beiträge zur Antiken Handelsgeschichte* 5.2 (1986): 88–95.

Van Ossel, P. *Établissements ruraux de l'Antiquité tardive dans le nord de la Gaule.* Paris, 1992.

Vera, D. "I Silenzi di Palladio e l'Italia: osservazioni sull'ultimo agronomo romano." *Antiquité tardive* 7 (1999): 283–97.

—. "La Legislazione sul colonato tardoantico: *cui prodest?,*" *Rivista Storica dell'Antichità* 35 (2005): 327–43.

—. "Strutture agrarie e strutture patrimoniali nella tarda Antichità: l'aristocrazia romana fra agricoltura e commercio." *Opus* 2 (1983): 489–533.

Verboven, K. *The Economy of Friends: Economic Aspects of Amicitia and Patronage in the Late Republic.* Brussels, 2002.
—, K. Vandorpe, and V. Chankowski, eds. *Pistoi dia tèn technèn: Bankers, Loans, and Archives in the Ancient World, Studies in Honour of Raymond Bogaert.* Leuven, 2008. See especially articles by F. Lerouxel, "La Banque privée romaine et le marché du crédit dans les tablettes de Murecine et les papyrus d'Egypte romaine," 169–97; K. Verboven, "*Faeneratores, Negotiatores* and Financial Intermediation in the Roman World (Late Republic and Early Empire)," 201–10; P. Temin and D. Rathbone, "Financial Intermediation in First-Century A.D. Rome and Eighteenth-Century England," 371–419.
Verley, P. *La Révolution industrielle.* Paris, 1985.
—. "La Révolution industrielle anglaise: une révision." *Annales, Économies, Sociétés, Civilisations* 46 (1991): 735–55.
Veyne, P. *La Société romaine.* Paris, 1991.
—. "La Table des *Ligures Baebiani* et l'institution alimentaire de Trajan." *Mélanges d'Archéologie et d'Histoire (École Française de Rome)* 69 (1957): 81–135, 70 (1958): 177–241.
—. "Rome devant la prétendue fuite de l'or: mercantilisme ou politique disciplinaire?" *Annales Économies, Sociétés, Civilisations* 34 (1979): 211–44.
Virlouvet, C. *Tessera frumentaria: les procédures de distribution du blé public à Rome à la fin de la République et au début de l'Empire.* Rome, 1995.
Weber, M. *The Agrarian Sociology of Ancient Civilizations.* Originally published as *Agrarverhältnisse im Altertum,* 1909. Atlantic Highlands, NJ, 1976; London, 1998.
Whittaker, C.R. "Do theories of the ancient city matter?" In *Urban society in Roman Italy,* ed. T.J. Cornell and H.K. Lomas, 1–20. London, 1993. Republished as Chap. 9 in C.R. Whittaker, *Land, city and trade in the Roman Empire.* Aldershot, 1993.
—. *Land, city and trade in the Roman Empire.* Aldershot, 1993.
—, ed. *Pastoral Economies in Classical Antiquity.* Cambridge, 1988.
Wierschowski, L. *Heer und Wirtschaft: das römische Heer der Prinzipatszeit als Wirtschaftsfaktor.* Bonn, 1984.
Wilson, A. "Timgad and Textile production." In *Economies beyond agriculture in the classical world,* D.J. Mattingly and J. Salmon, eds., 271–96. London-New York, 2001.
—. "Urban Production in the Roman World: The View from North Africa." *PBSR* 70 (2002): 231–73.
Wörrle, M. "Polis et chôra à Oinoanda de Cibyratide, Perplexités d'interprétation devant un document nouveau." In *Sociétés urbaines, sociétés rurales dans l'Asie Mineure et la Syrie hellénistiques et romaines,* ed. E. Frezouls, 115–16. Strasbourg, 1987.
—. *Stadt und Fest in kaiserzeitlichen Kleinasien.* Munich, 1988.
Young, G.K. *Rome's Eastern Trade: International Commerce and Imperial Policy, 31 B.C.-A.D. 305.* London, 2001.
Zaccagnini, C., ed. *Mercanti e politica nel mondo antico.* Rome, 2003.

Index

The Economy of the Roman World

Designed and typeset in Ann Arbor, Michigan
www.michiganclassicalpress.com
Maps provided by the Old World Mapping Center,
University of North Carolina – Chapel Hill
Printed and bound by Edwards Brothers Malloy, Inc., Ann Arbor, Michigan
www.edwardsbrothersmalloy.com
Composed in Bodoni and Minion Pro

✧ ✧ ✧